2021

2021

A Year Inverse

Douglas Palermo

2021
A YEAR INVERSE

iUniverse books may be ordered through booksellers or by contacting:

iUniverse
1663 Liberty Drive
Bloomington, IN 47403
www.iuniverse.com
844-349-9409

ISBN: 978-1-6632-3718-7 (sc)
ISBN: 978-1-6632-3717-0 (e)

Library of Congress Control Number: 2022904900

Print information available on the last page.

iUniverse rev. date: 03/18/2022

December 31st

This is my last statement as a writer.

This book. This piece. This sentence.

This is my last statement as a writer.

I'm not saying it'll be the last thing I publish. And I will always be writing something. But as a vehicle for personal self-exploration and artistic expression..

This is my last statement as a writer.

Through all my lifetimes I have developed and perfected my voice. I have explored and practiced all genres and styles. And I have pushed the limits and redefined the craft in ways no others have done in the past. Because I have nothing more to prove or accomplish..

This is my last statement as a writer.

In order to achieve what I have as an artist, I had to open myself up to all the hidden sickness in the universe. I had to explore the darkest aspects of my personality. And I had to fully experience danger, chaos, and insanity. Because my soul has no more uncharted territories and I rather enjoy the pleasures of safer harbors..

This is my last statement as a writer.

The highest expression of any form of art is worship. If you can sing, sing for God. If you can play the trombone, play the trombone for God. If you can paint, teach, build, or dance, do it all for God. Not for yourself. Not even for others. Just for God. That's why..

This is my last statement as a writer.

Lord Heavenly Father, thank you for giving me the gift of writing and allowing me to develop and use it for so many years. Thank you Holy Spirit for giving me the words to help inspire, entertain, and instruct so many people. And thank you Jesus for guiding me to not use my talents for self-serving or destructive purposes, but only to elevate and enlighten. Please continue to guide and protect me in all ways and allow me to spend eternity walking humbly by your side and serving you in any way you will. I love you, God. I'm sorry, God. Please forgive me, God. Thank you, God. All praise be to the Father, Son, and Holy Spirit. Amen.

That was my first statement as a soul who writes.

December 30th

Dear Good People at WFMU,

Please graciously accept these two copies of my most recent book, 2021: A Year Inverse. I am sending you two copies instead of one to show you just how eager I am to share it with you all. Three would be creepy and excessive, like I'm trying to push it on you or something. But in all honesty, I just wanted you to have them because 2021 was my first full year of having WFMU as my primary 24/7 source of music, culture, and entertainment. And I plan on continuing that until either you or me are taken off the air. So WFMU was playing in the background while I wrote nearly every word of this book. It's the hickory smoke infused in this juicy slab of beef. Almost every piece has some form of allusion to WFMU, either explicitly or very thinly veiled. I would have to create a multi-page addendum to truly catalogue all of them. So I challenge you to try to find them yourselves. Some will be easy to spot, some I may even have trouble recognizing anymore. Start with 10/3/21. That's the most obvious one. Besides this one. Obviously.

But seriously. WFMU is the greatest place in the Universe, and you are all the best personalities on the planet. Sometimes I'm afraid that my heart isn't big enough to contain all the love that I have for you guys. And that is saying a lot because I have a big fucking heart. So big that this was the only time in this book that I felt it was necessary to curse, and I put no shackles on my writing during any part of this project. There's no seven second delay when I write.

I have surrendered my soul to Jesus Christ, but WFMU has a large portion of my consciousness. And I have complete trust that you will continue to take me to the most amazing places and show me the most glorious things.

When I came home today there was a postcard in my mailbox from Clay Pigeon. It made me very happy.

Thank your for making me happy, Clay Pigeon. Thank you for making me happy, WFMU. Thank you for making me happy dear reader, whoever you are.

Thank you. Thank you. Thank you.

With the deepest love,

Douglas Palermo
(Listener #259843)

December 29th

Kinda like Nas flipping through his book of rhymes, sometimes you have to go through an old notebook to see what pearls of wisdom were left behind by past versions of yourself. So let's see if some old Doug's can teach us some new tricks.

Beware of the poison pawn.. don't just take everything handed to you.

Teach your students anyway you can, and when all else fails, use words.

Know yourself. Accept yourself. Become the creator.

It's when people start taking about caduceus coils that I start to lose interest.

When everybody does better, everybody does better.

I am not a good person. I just live in an overwhelmingly good and loving Universe, and I have allowed myself to be shaped and guided according to its will.

We have a right to our labor, but not to the fruits of our labor.

Every human being we save is one last zombie we have to fight.

You are your life's only variable.

No soul is indigenous to the Earth.

A heart can't break.. only a mind can.

When you ask why too much you are why-ning.

Plan with your left brain, teach with your right.

Life is a collection of the games people play and the stories we tell each other.

Paranoia is an over-active imagination flirting with the ego.

And to leave you with the immortal words of my grandfather, Peter Bernard McCue:

Just do your best, that's bad enough.

December 28th

Sun Ra is the patron saint of this book. His influence can be found on every page. He too was a poet. He too was from worlds far beyond this one. May he bless me as I begin to learn the craft of music.

When the light began, I was just a child. I didn't know who I was or what this place is. I only knew the trees, the forest, the river, all the turtles, and the frogs. Born in water, destined for land. Born of flesh, destined for spirit. Quite a big hop.

A fetus oscillating through the wavelengths of the Universal mind. Down in the middle of Little Italy, Daphne and Delia diddling with the dials of musical harmony. Sisters with transistors saying piss off to the misters who missed her. Your story will be told. Your credit is overdue. Like Rakim, it will be paid in full.

We are in the long rally. So flip your caps and break out the monkeys. We're bringing 2002 back. When the juiced-up giants were felled by the angels in the outfield. Stop placing your bets, the outcome has already been determined. The good guys won, because the fix was in.

What a mess. This excess of success is such a test. Without proper rest, I'm not at my best. Writing letters like Paul, 'cause I can't do any less.

Break out the anemometer. The winds of change are blowing the trees bare. There's work to be done and fun to be had. So rake it up and jump in the pile.

We ain't gonna be back here for a while.

It's time to throw in the towel.

This page was brought to you by DJ Scott McDowell.

December 27th

So that was certainly a trip. I left for work Wednesday morning at 6:30 and I just got home now. And I never stopped working the entire time.

Now I'm just sitting here numb. My head is either spinning way too fast, or not at all. I can't even tell anymore. Empty or overflowing. Who knows?

Whether I have nothing to give you or way too much, it ends up feeling the same. All I do is just pick up the pen and write about what's on the surface. Because I'm either already on the floor, or things are way too dense to go any deeper.

So let's see what's on the surface.

My brother just texted me. We are arranging a time this week to meet up so we can put together a treadmill for our mom. It looks like it will be Thursday morning.

I like the sound of my text alert. It's bamboo. But I get upset when I hear other people with the same tone. It should be exclusively mine.

I'm drinking a kombucha right now because I'm better than you. It's got lavender, chamomile, damiana, rose, and jasmine green tea in it. I had to look up what damiana is. It's a shrub. But don't ask me the difference between normal green tea and jasmine green tea. I guess the obvious answer is that jasmine green tea has jasmine in it. But what's jasmine? I don't feel like looking it up.

Techtonic is over so I can turn back up the volume and enjoy the Arbitrarium. And no knock to Techtonic, that was my bridge to WFMU as I was escaping the podcast quagmire. I just can't write while listening to a talk show. Especially in this mental state.

Mark Hurst is fighting the good fight. But it's a fight in a war that I'm not marching in anymore. So more power to him.

And come 2022, I will not be writing anymore. At least not for you.

So enjoy it while it lasts.

December 26th

So I made it around 360 days before making my first serious blunder of this whole operation. Made a trip up to Connecticut with my mom to start clearing out my aunt's house and I forgot to bring my Moleskine. And to make matters worse, there is not a single piece of paper in my room at the Hampton Inn in Rocky Hill.

What kind of hotel doesn't at least put a notepad next to the phone or on a desk or something? Never saw that before. There isn't even a Bible in here. Could have used that in a pinch if I needed, but whatever. Whatta ya gonna do? As my brother and Tony Soprano like to say. Whatta ya gonna do?

Well this is what I'm doing. I may have forgotten my notebook, but I never forget to bring a book. That habit is too deeply embedded to fail. And I also have a pretty solid habit of using index cards as bookmarks. You never know how something you read may spark the muses and make you need to jot some words down. I am a writer, you know.

So that's what I'm doing now. Writing these words down on a blank, yellow index card that was previously in page 63 of I Am Thyron by Craig Campobasso. Interesting book so far, by the way. Little weird, some clunky writing, but definitely interesting. The Lucifer Rebellion fascinates me, so I had to get the whole trilogy when I heard about it.

But anyway, my main concern is judging how long to make this. Usually I just ramble on for about a page and a half and know that'll translate to a page typed in Word. I don't know what the exchange rate is for small index cards, though. I guess we'll just have to stop now and find out.

So this may be a little short, a little long, or just right. We shall see. But regardless of what happens, good or bad.. whatta ya gonna do?

Seriously people. At the end of the day. When all is said and done.

What are you going to do?

December 25th

Merry Christmas!

I'm not going to pretend that Jesus was actually born on December 25th. But today is the day we have set aside to remember and celebrate Jesus's birth and reflect on his life. So let's do that.

He lived a perfect, sinless life. That's pretty impressive.

Human beings did not have access to eternity until Jesus came and conquered death. We owe him a lot for that.

I am fully convinced that had Jesus come before him, Buddha would have become a Christian. Instead of sitting under a tree to find his answers, he could have just read the Gospels.

Every little annoying aspect of being a human being was experienced by Jesus. In addition to all the pain, heartache, and despair. And he did it all while still being God. He had the power to stop it anytime he wanted. But he didn't. He wanted to experience everything we experience. He took it all in and he took it all on. That is love.

I like how Jesus gave his friends cool nicknames like "The Rock" and "The Sons of Thunder". He definitely had a flare for the theatric. And a rich sense of humor. I would have loved to try to make Jesus laugh. Maybe someday I'll be able to have that opportunity. Face to face, I mean. I'm sure I already make him laugh all the time with my constant sin and folly.

And he forgives us. Plain and simple, Jesus forgives. No matter how low or dark we go, he is always waiting for each of us with open arms. He will never give up on you. All you have to do is take that first step towards him, and BAM! His kingdom es su kingdom. How great is that?

Jesus Christ is my Lord and Savior. I don't think I have to say any more than that. He is my Lord and Savior.

Merry Christmas!

December 24th

I woke up to a blanket of snow. A day early, but we'll take it. The treetops resemble a bowl of Frosted Mini Wheats.

I'm sitting on the couch. Numb. Home from the toughest battle of my life. I emerged victorious. But I can't get the sound of gunfire out of my head. And the war is still waging on. So there will be no medal pinned to my chest anytime soon. And I wouldn't want one, anyway.

I just want to smooth out all the wrinkles in my mind. Slowly. Through the force of gravity. Pulling me towards the event horizon of God's love.

As I sit here. With my muses trapped in molasses. The ethers are thick today. Probably for the best.

Wesley Willis, Sun Ra, and Daniel Johnston. Three kings bringing gifts heralding the coming of our Lord. With Jim the Poet holding the shepherd's staff.

I wonder if any of them had mornings like this. Sitting on the couch. Numb. On Christmas Eve. Pondering and perseverating. After being pushed from the precipice of your past. Facing the freefall of eternity.

Did they have to go through this chamber? Did they have to solve this puzzle? Before they located the star that guides them. In this world and beyond.

While a girl wheels her suitcase into the middle of Times Square. Sets it down. And takes a picture of the future.

Will she find her star? Will I? Will any of us?

So much hope. Yet so much uncertainty.

Twas the morning before Christmas.

December 23rd

I've come to appreciate the waiting room experience. It's one of the rare instances in life where you're expected to do nothing else except to sit down quietly. Normally when I sit down quietly there is a part of me thinking of all the other, more productive ways of spending my time. But in a waiting room I have no other choice but to just sit down and be quiet. I like that.

So that's where I am right now. In a waiting room. At Towne Toyota in Ledgewood. My Tacoma is due for its 15,000-mile service. I hope it doesn't take too long, but I really wouldn't mind too much if it did. I like it here. Plenty of workspaces, couches, comfy chairs, vending machines, and a TV that is never turned on. Good place to catch up on some work or do a little reading. But I still don't know where the bathroom is yet. That's key.

I like the artwork in this place, too. Very Mark Rothko-esque. I find comfort in their colors and simplicity. Thinking about the abstract can be painful. Looking at it hanging on a wall is a balm.

It's a relatively quiet afternoon here. I was expecting more with the holidays coming up. I bet this past weekend was a madhouse. Probably why I couldn't get an appointment. But today there's just four other souls here with me.

The old guy in front of me teaching himself Python. The lady with the bright orange hair. An Asian man who just found out he needs to replace all four of his brake pads. And some random dude just sitting, staring out into space.

Two of them have masks on, two of them do not. I'll let you guess which ones do and which ones don't.

I don't, though. It's not required, and there's plenty of space. And this was never my pandemic, anyway. Just another thing I have to wait out. Like I'm doing right now.

In this waiting room.

December 22nd

I-22, quack quack, ducks on the pond. But I'm getting ahead of myself. That's tomorrow's game.

Today's just kind of an extra day. Not anything special about it. Just a square on a calendar that we all have to get through in order to get to the next one. And the one after that. And the one after that.

On and on and on we go. When it will stop, nobody knows. Like a thief in the night. The tipping point will reach us all. Infinite waters. Be prepared to dive deep.

As I rest atop the board. Weary from the long climb up the ladder. Admiring the still, crystal blue pool below me. It's not the fall that's causing me to hesitate. It's not knowing how to swim once I hit the surface.

I guess that's why they call it a leap of faith. And any good leap of faith is preceded by a long series of hops of humility.

So you better start humbling yourself, fool. This ain't about you.

It's about something so much bigger and complex and important and completely out of your control and comprehension.

Your puzzle piece is big. But the picture in your head is so incomplete it's laughable.

So stop trying to figure it out and focus on what's in front of you. Today was good, but we've been here before.

Break the cycle.

Take the leap.

You'll learn to swim on the way down.

December 21st

Ladies and gentlemen, the world is in flames.

Ok, maybe not the whole world, but parts of it. Like Route 287 is in flames. Whatever road this dude is on in Warsaw, Indiana doesn't seem to be on fire in any way, though.

Ladies and gentlemen, Route 287 is in flames.

Ok, maybe not the whole Route 287, but parts of it. Like Route 287 South is in flames. And not all of Route 287 South. I think things are fine in Bound Brook. But specifically Route 287 South in Wanaque. Definitely a lot of fire there.

Ladies and gentlemen, Route 287 South in Wanaque is in flames.

Ok, maybe not the whole of Route 287 South in Wanaque, but parts of it. According to Clay's traffic report on the radio, only the right lane is closed. There's a tractor trailer fire. You're looking at maybe 25–30-minute delays. Sucks to be stuck in that.

Ladies and gentlemen, a tractor trailer in the right lane of Route 287 South in Wanaque is in flames.

Ok, maybe not the whole tractor trailer, but parts of it. I drove past it this morning on the way to work. Luckily, I was going north. I saw the thick black smoke in the air about three miles before I saw the fire. The cab was completely engulfed, but the trailer was untouched. Humans may have been hurt, but commerce was spared, if only delayed.

Ladies and Gentlemen, the cab of a tractor trailer in the right lane of Route 287 South in Wanaque is in flames.

But I bet they put it out by now.

Nothing lasts forever.

December 20th

The wheels are coming off. I held it together for a while, but the wheels are definitely coming off. Probably for the best, though. Where we're going, we don't need any wheels.

Just roots and wings as always. Roots and wings.

And my wings have always been sound. I just don't always have the space to fully spread them, let alone fly. Too many beings threatened by the sight of them unfurled. Afraid they would lose all hold of me if they let me use them. And they're right. They would. But they're also wrong. Because they never had hold of me to begin with.

So if you want me in your life, you better let me soar. And then I'll decide if you're worth landing for. Because as long as I remain grounded. You are all suspects.

As specious as my roots used to be until I dug deeper. Beyond the façade of family and friends. And their emotional mercantilism. Expecting you to exist only for them and their needs. And calling it ego and arrogance for wanting more.

I am excavating those weeds. So I can be connected to and nourished by my true core. Family bonded by spirit, not blood. Friends connected by enrichment, not experience. Roots.

The road is endless. But where we are going, we don't need any roads.

Back to a future that once belonged to us before it was robbed.

Stolen by those not ready to make the leap.

As their wails are muffled by the widening gap between your world and theirs.

We are all leaving or left.

Behind.

December 19th

It wasn't rock bottom. Or a wake-up call. Or some great epiphany. It was you stuck in the middle of a muddy crossroads. Frozen by your habits and addictions. Unable to fight or flee.

So you wallow. A pathetic state.

Chip taught you what to do if you ever got caught in quicksand. You are denser than the quicksand. Lie back and float on the quicksand. Float on the quicksand. Paddle to safety.

And the dense vortex of reality is just a phone call away. A phone call you now have to make. In order to lift the weekend's anchor. Good luck with that.

It really wasn't as bad as I thought. I maintained proper boundaries and distance. Deflecting all blows without needing to go on the defensive. As I continue to float atop the quicksand. Further from safety. But no longer stuck.

Fittingly, I have one more level, eight stages, to finish before I complete the book of Mark. It should be a nice haul. All in a day's work. Tell me something good.

I'm washed up, refreshed, and ready to go. Just waiting for the signal. But I know this is a day that I will not have much control over. So why should right now be any different?

But once again. It really wasn't as bad as I thought. I maintained proper boundaries and distance. And was happy to be of use. Even if it was more my truck than me. At least now it's over. And I got a peek behind the curtain of a life I want no part of. Like returning to the scene of a crime. An innocent bystander. Ready to take the stand. And flip the script.

What we started.

Has no choice but to finish.

So you might as well let us guide it.

And make this thing work.

December 18th

Through the strength, grace, guidance, protection, love, and light of my Lord and Savior Jesus Christ I must make this the end of hello thoughts. And if you haven't figured out what hello thoughts are by now, may the Lord help you. Because it's two-thirty in the morning and there is no comfort in the bloody shadows. But some in the blackened one. As he lurks in the snowy memories of our past. Nearly a lifetime ago since I last picked up the pen and the haze is upon me. This is where I will be for a while. So I better get used to it. At least I'll have my music. But I may need a shower. Or I may just feel the grime all day long. Down in the swamps with Lynyrd Skynyrd. I have finished the necessary work of the day. At 1:50pm. Not bad. But I have no drive to do anything above or beyond. This is a day of vegetative self-care. A luxury few can afford, but we all desperately need. I'm fading fast. I don't know if it's the weed. Or the egg foo young. Or the rain. Or the clinical depression. But I'm at a low point. Struggling to make it through the long haul. Like a teamster. Coming like Whitney. The greatest love of all. I remember where I was when I first heard Smooth on the radio. I was crossing Durban driving on Brooklyn Mountain Road. I think I was in the Reliant, but I may have been in the Tempo. I'm pretty sure it was the Reliant, though. But as soon as I heard the guitar I knew it was something different. The angels got him on the radio. I remember my Uncle Sal was friends with Whitney Houston's father. They grew up together in Newark. They would always talk to each other on the phone around the holidays. "What's this I hear in the news about your kid?" I would hear my Uncle Sal ask him. I can't believe it isn't 5pm yet. I did oh so much and oh so little today. As least I got my laundry done. My mother raised me right. And down I go in a rush. Let's see when or where I'll resurface. If I don't. I blame the caramel apple.

December 17th

This is starting to feel like Groundhog's Day. Will I continue doing my shadow work today? Or will I pretend that I don't see it? Will you get six more pages of darkness and depression? Or an early spring of nonsense and frivolity?

The drudgery is real.

Especially during the work week when it's all routine and repetition. I commute into school. Set up my physical and virtual classrooms. And then get right to business.

Wake and Bake is on my Bose Bluetooth. I'm seated at the side of a desk in the first row. My back is to the window as I hear my co-workers pull into the parking lot. A black Bic Cristal is in my right hand as my Moleskine is opened to a blank page.

What do I have to offer you today? What jewels will I be given to share?

For a while it was like automatic writing. I was a channel. I would just sit down, start writing, and it would pour out of me like sweat in a sauna. It was a purification process. I was being purged. Even I didn't know what would be put on the page.

Now, with a fortnight left to go. I'm scraping the bottom of the ice cream carton with my spoon. And only tasting cold steel.

So I guess it's time to regroup. Put this self-referential crap on the shelf. And muster my strength for a final sprint to the finish line.

You're about to enter the stadium and the crowd is on its feet.

Let's give the people what they came for.

December 16th

I always thought it was kinda cool that one of the first things that Jesus did when he conquered death was to cook up some fish and eat breakfast with his friends. He was only gone three days and eating meat was one of the top things he missed. That's my kind of savior.

And yes, I recognize that I'm just being funny and a little sacrilegious. And I know that the real purpose of eating with the apostles was to show that he wasn't a ghost or spirit, but a fully resurrected body of flesh and bone. However, there is no denying the importance of eating and food throughout all of the Bible.

There's definitely a lot more in the Old Testament about what we can or cannot eat than who we can or cannot sleep with. Which makes sense. You are what you eat. Not who you sleep with. Thank God.

And one of my favorite scenes in the Bible is when Peter has that crazy dream where God tells him to go kill and eat. Pretty much giving him permission to break centuries-old Jewish dietary laws so he could spread love to the Gentiles.

Eating is the great leveler. Food is our common ground.

Let's start there.

Life is a potluck dinner. What did you bring for the rest of us to share?

The table has already been set. Have a seat.

Who wants to say grace?

December 15ᵗʰ

Walking with Gabe. After commuting with the Pidge. I took 287 North and somehow ended up in the Upper West Side of Manhattan. Talking with strangers about Doge Coin.

It seems like a nice morning so far. The voices have been muted. So the music can be heard. A tropicale moon. Painted by the mouth.

Sometimes I forget what all my fight and struggle and resistance and anger and piss and vinegar and righteousness are really all about. I find myself as who I was before I took it all on and who I will be when I let it all go.

The real me. I like that guy. But he doesn't stick around long.

Chased away by your demands, expectations, needs, and failures.

God bless the child who has his own. God help the child who gives freely to others.

But only a fool would say that.

A steely reserved stranger with something to prove because he forgot what it was all about.

You can't take any of it with you. Anything you create. Anything you accomplish. Anything you acquire. You must leave it all behind.

But you take the experiences, you take the relationships, you take the lessons, you take the love.

So welcome experiences. Build relationships. Learn lessons. Spread and receive love.

The only way to make this commute.

Don't forget that.

December 14th

I'm ready for this to be over. I'm waiting for permission to move on. But I'm shackled to the burden of unfinished business.

It's not like I have any more dues to pay. I've paid them all seventy-seven times seven times. I've probably even paid some of your dues. My account has been cleared for lifetimes now.

It's all about unfinished business now.

I need to finish this book. I've come too far not to. Just seventeen more days of writing and then a solid month or so of typing and editing. So close I can smell it. And then I will have my masterpiece. 2019: A Year in Verse. 2021: A Year Inverse. Two books. One statement. I was alive.

I also need to finish this job. I've come too far not to. Just about 20 more years of names to add to the chess plaque before I can officially call it a career. It seems so far away, but it will be over in a blink. So I'm trying my best to enjoy it. And then I will have my legacy. Generations of students taught with the love you gave me. My greatest gift.

And, of course, I need to finish this life. I've come too far not to. Just another half-century or so of morning routines and afternoon workouts. If I'm lucky. I know I have a lot of pain, heartache, and disappointment ahead of me. But it will all be worth it in the end. So now the trick is getting to the end and trying to enjoy myself on the way.

And then I will have my rest.

No more depression. No more rejection. No more isolation. No more drudgery. No more resistance.

Just God. Just love. Just me.

The end.

December 13th

I'm sorry, but you took the wrong approach with me. And it's too late. I will never be able to trust or respect again. All I ever wanted was to love and be loved. But that wasn't good enough. So I was attacked again and again for everything I wasn't. By everybody I never wanted to be.

So now I'm broken. And it's your fault. Your fault. And especially your fault.

I hope that you are happy and you got what you wanted. Because I have nothing.

Nothing but habit, routine, and momentum. Pushing me forward. Forward into more attacks, more pain, more futility.

But whatever. As long as I keep showing up and giving the people what they want. Who cares what I feel or what I need?

Because this isn't about me. This is about a system that takes people like me, chews them up, and spits them out. Calling it a sin to want more.

And I used to want more. I used to want what everybody else wanted or already had. A family. A future. A love forever.

But instead I was attacked and maligned for my selfish desires.

My very existence unmercifully mocked. By you. And you. And especially you.

Leaving me here. Where I don't want to be. With nowhere to go. And nobody to go with.

Alone in this nightmare.

Surrounded by strangers.

December 12th

Super friends and the city. Who could ask for more? On a Saturday night. Or is this Sunday morning?

Either way, that girl was cute. In a deer caught in headlights sort of way. With the headlights being all of manifested reality. But the guys she was with were losers. I hope she develops the level of self-awareness and self-esteem necessary to realize that before it is too late. If it's not already.

Right now. This lady right here has terrific energy. I don't know what she is saying, but she is making me happy.

And this one is making me hopeful. Like a creature like that wouldn't manifest here unless they knew the future could handle them.

Unless her beauty exists only to contrast the ugliness to come.

Doll face dropping dimes in the forty-deuce. Deconstructing Wittgenstein. Before ending abruptly.

Leaving only the ambulance chasers awake and streaming. Stringing somewhere in Scarsdale. As Darren squeals into the mic. From Jersey City to Westchester County. By way of East Orange.

Back announcing human history to the younger dryas. Graham Hancock and Randall Carlson giving us their greatest hits.

The Sphinx is older than we think. And so is Ralph Macchio.

Wax on. Wax off. The proof is in the water damage.

Cocoa is fourteen years old. And soon so will be Ralphy.

The rest is pure theory.

So let's begin.

December 11th

I'm isolating myself. I can feel it. I'm putting up a wall. Keeping everybody at arm's length. Not letting anybody even near my orbit. Except maybe family. But I'm still maintaining pretty strong boundaries with family as well.

It's just me, alone. And God. Trying to carve out a life that is true, beautiful, and good.

Completely exposed and vulnerable with no one on this planet to trust or depend on.

That's it. Right there. Again and again. That's it in a nutshell.

Completely exposed and vulnerable with no one on this planet to trust or depend on.

That's the theme. The message. The motif. The overarching mood.

Of this book. The last book. Of all the books.

2021, 2020, 2019, 2018, 2017.. Going all the way back to 1977. Always the same story.

Completely exposed and vulnerable with no one on this planet to trust or depend on.

I hope 2022 will be better. I really hope so. But I have no real reason to believe why it should be. Just hollow hope.

And I'm getting exhausted. Tired from the rehearsing. The keeping up of defenses. The constant seeking of approval. The rationalization of every rejection.

I'm tired of it all.

I just want to rest in the comfort of someone's complete, unconditional acceptance of me.

Where are you?

December 10th

In the context of eternity, none of this really matters. One grain of sand lost in the cosmic beach. Everything and everybody. One meaningless grain of sand.

In the context of eternity, all of this really matters. A ripple of consequences magnifying while traveling to the far reaches of space and time. Every thought and every action. An infinite ripple of consequences.

We are the synthesis of this universal paradox. Stretched between two poles. Pulled in all directions. Trying to hold our center.

Where our identity lives. The inner core of our hearts.

Some pretty heady stuff to be thinking about while hurling down the road trapped in a hunk of metal going 70 miles per hour.

Or while dragging a sharp blade across the underside of your neck.

Or while trying to live a happy, fulfilled life.

Paralyzed by the futility of it all while being crippled by its significance.

Stuck in the middle. A rock and a hard place. And a rock so heavy even He won't lift it.

So get used to it.

Such is life. All of it and none of it.

Welcome aboard.

There's no captain.

Except each and every one of us.

December 9th

The seeds of lust were planted early in me thanks to music television. As much as conservative parents and religious leaders looked silly and out of touch in the 80's when they denounced MTV as a tool of Satan. They weren't entirely wrong.

It started early with hair bands and Madonna. Women being presented and presenting themselves as purely sex objects. Tawny Kitaen draping herself over the hood of a car. Madonna being Madonna. I didn't have the hormones yet to feel the feelings, but my mind was developed enough to learn the lessons.

The lessons of lust.

Chris Isaak's Wicked Game was my crash course in puberty. That girl was draped on him like my grandmother's Afghan in winter. And at that point, side boob was all that I needed.

Billy Idol's Rock the Cradle of Love was also very formidable in my awakening. The whole creepy pedo-vibe was completely lost on me since the girl was still older than me. But man, the way she danced on that bed. Forget about it. Because I couldn't. With Wicked Game I knew what I wanted. With Rock the Cradle I was starting to figure out what I wanted to do once I got it.

Then came those Aerosmith videos. The Liv Tyler/Alicia Silverstone ones. Crazy, Crying, and I think there was a third one. Either way, they were amazing. Those girls should receive medals for all the adolescent boys they ferried across the River Styx of sexuality. And they made it all look so fun. Like definitely sign me up for that trip.

But I couldn't end this without mentioning Fiona Apple's Criminal. Yep, you know the one I'm talking about. My final lesson before making the leap from teen to young adult.

There's danger in all of this. You may get hurt. But it will all be worth it in the end.

Thank you for that lesson, Fiona. And to all the bad, bad girls that were careless with this delicate man:

I forgive you.

December 8th

I'm wearing my roulette wheel cufflinks today. They're fully functional too. With a little silver ball in each one that you can shake and place bets on.

My right wrist just landed on the number 11. Collect if you wagered on black and odd.

But they must be European cuff links because the roulette wheels have a single zero, but no double zeroes. This house gives better odds.

My fantasy is that there will be someone close enough to me to see my roulette wheel cuff links. Detailed-oriented enough to notice that they are missing the double zeroes. And knowledgeable enough to recognize that they are European wheels, not American ones.

And that person better be a hot female or things may get awkward.

But I like dressing up for work. I think it's important to look good. It sends the right message. I don't even have to wear a tie, but I still do. Along with my rotating collection of tie bars and clips. In fact, I may be breaking company policy by still wearing a tie. But whatever, I don't care. Write me up. I'm gonna keep wearing ties.

When I first was a teacher, I just wore khakis and collared golf shirts because New York City didn't have a dress code and I wanted to be comfortable when I worked.

Then one day a school counselor pulled me aside who spent his whole career in the Bronx and came everyday dressed in a full suit. He asked me why I didn't wear a tie or dress up for work. I tried to explain my reasoning, but he quickly cut me off.

"Mr. Palermo, these kids go their whole lives without men in their lives. When they come here, they need to see men. So start dressing like a man and start acting like one."

I've been following his advice ever since.

December 7th

I praise you because I am fearfully and wonderfully made. Your works are wonderful. I know that full well.

Ain't that the truth. The whole truth. And nothing but the truth.

And if I was a stronger person, that would be all I need. But I'm not. Not even close. So I need so much more. More creation. More works. More knowledge. More words.

My strange addiction. Transferred to food and drink and smoke and everything else. When in reality, this is it. This is what I need to walk away from. The dreams. The goals. The aspirations. The ego. The identity. The life.

Resting only in the silence. Resting only in the stillness. Resting only in you.

But that ain't happening anytime soon.

First, I have to bring this home for a landing. Twenty-four to go after today. Then it's typing, revising, editing, putting everything into nice ribbons and bows. Then it's print and promote. Print and promote. Print and promote.

Until it becomes just another book on the bookshelf. And I'm ready to close the bracket and move on.

Moving on to worship. Moving on to praise.

Moving on.

Living to learn.

How to love.

You.

Only.

December 6th

Are you sure you want to keep changing? Are you sure you want to keep developing? Are you sure you want to keep growing?

Even though you now know for sure that you are growing apart. Developing separately. And changing alone.

Every step you take forward is a step away from your world and everybody in it. Holding to the hope that new worlds and friends will be revealed along the path as you hear and smell the old ones burning furiously behind you.

Never daring to look back.

You made your choice, and they are left dealing with the consequences of rejecting their choices. It's not personal. Just business.

And it's not all of them. Not everybody has given up. Not everybody has turned heel. Some are still trying to keep pace. Some are still holding on to who they are.

May God bless them and give them the strength they will need.

There are less and less of us every day. We will need to find each other. We will need to recognize each other. We will need to support each other.

It's not us versus them anymore. It's us without them.

We're all we got.

Don't forget that.

December 5th

Clifton-East Orange. North Jersey Group 5 Regional Championship. Live from the birthplace of college football. Here comes the big boys.

Red wins the toss and defers. Clifton to receive.

Taking on the attitude and swagger of a Glen Jones radio monologue, the Mustangs impose their will on East Orange in the opening drive. Moving more chains than an Italian jeweler. Using all four downs. Six minutes and counting. 7-0 Clifton. Already more points than the Jaguar's defense averaged giving up per game all season.

And with a methodical precision, EOC makes it 7-7. 50 seconds short of a two-possession quarter. My favorite thing in high school football. And damn this shrimp corn chowder smells good. Kinda cool to be watching this game from the comfort of my couch. Instead of freezing down in Rutgers. Hanging out in the bathroom between halves to keep warm.

But just like that. Mocking my comfort. The feed goes wonky. Just like yesterday during the Northern Highlands-Irvington game. I thought it'd be better today since more people would be watching NFL games. Barely got to see the field goal. But the 97-yard touchdown pass was clear as day. Before an extremely herky-jerky 2-minute drill. Almost missed that East Orange field goal at the end. Making it 17-10 at half.

And the Jaguar band is the tuffest team on the field all weekend. Color guard alone. And I'm either getting fatter, bloated, or my clothes are shrinking.

The feed gets so bad I miss most of the third quarter. Nobody scores, though. But Jonesy is definitely winning. Puff the Magic Dragon followed by Mr. Bojangles. Brilliant. I toast to that.

But the empty bag of pistachio rose brittle does nothing to ease my body image issues.

4th quarter. 4th down and 4 on the 4. East Orange scores and takes this game into overtime.

But I'm not taking you there with me. I'm no sports reporter. If you want to know who wins, look it up.

Joe Hoffman is not holding this pen.

December 4th

Man, it's so weird being here right now. I feel so isolated. Productive. But isolated. I have to keep reminding myself how much of a claim I have over this place. This is the Starbucks where Douglas Palermo wrote his books. They're going to have my picture on the wall someday.

I think the four loose pennies are throwing everything off. Like a glitch in the matrix. They're definitely annoying me. I don't know how to get rid of them. I may have to commit a federal crime and toss them away with my cup when I'm done with my chai latte. Don't tell on me if I do.

And here I still am. Listening to the familiar frog croaks of Bob Brainen. Alone at the end of a long empty table. The girl sitting at the table against the window perpendicular to me is staring directly at me. Even when she tries not to. It's just a flaw in the seating plan. I'm the one who has to try not to turn to look at her. But the glasses, hoodie, flannel. Feet on the chair like she just doesn't care. I dig it. I wonder what she thinks of me.

Same with the one diagonally across to my left. She's moved her whole body language in my direction. She might as well be screaming at me. I love the hoop earrings. And exotic look. Little does she know how deaf I am. It's probably why she looks so frustrated.

I had goat last night. I think it's beginning to come out in my writing.

A new Caribbean place in the Rockaway Mall. I think it's going to be my new Friday after work spot. Both the mall and the Caribbean place. And don't forget that fancy tea shop. The only place left to get a cup of coffee.

Here comes a regular.

Keep the change.

December 3rd

Here I am. Once again. Living the Doug Life. Divinely Ordered Unity Gives Love Infinite Form and Expression. The Doug Life. Does it get any more beautiful than that?

They're definitely breaking the mold after this run around the track. Probably regret making it in the first place. If I didn't know better.

Rule #2: No more Doug's.

A multiplicity of mistakes and a comedy of errors. My life playing the ultimate straight man.

The one nut thing is definitely the icing on the cake. The straw that stirred the drink and broke the camel's back. Both at the same time. Genius in its simplicity.

I must have been promised something pretty awesome to agree to show up a ball short. I'm still waiting for it, though. Beginning to think it was something I did to level the playing ground between me and the other males of the species.

Like I always said. I have more man in one testicle than most guys have in two.

But seriously. Usually when the aliens use you for their little breeding/genetic experiments they only take a sample. With me they took the whole shebang.

Makes me wonder if there is a planet out there somewhere. Deep in the recesses of space and time. Completely filled with extraterrestrial beings. Living the Doug Life. In all its glory.

Hold on tight, kids.

Papa will be home soon.

December 2nd

So this story is completely made up.

It was the year 2000. Spring break of my senior year of college. I took a bus ride out to Vegas with my friend Marcus where we would meet up with our friend Marty and the three of us would be staying the week at our friend Sarah's apartment. Sarah moved out to Vegas after graduating a semester early the previous winter. Her apartment complex was off the Strip, across from the Hard Rock Casino and Hotel.

So one night I decided to drink a couple bottles of Robitussin. Nothing new for me. I used to do it every Sunday after coming back to my dorm following a ShopRite shift. It never made me sick like other people. And I enjoyed the out of body dissociative experience of a good DXM trip. But I've always done it in a relatively safe, controlled setting. Like a good little psychonaut.

I would not be in a safe, controlled environment this particular night. The first thing we did was to pile in Sarah's car to drive to the IMAX at the Red Rocks. We were listening to Story of the Ghost while passing a fat joint. Birds of a feather. Flocking outside.

We ended up seeing Fantasia 2000. And with the mix of THC and DXM, it was amazing. I was literally swimming with the whales. And the Rhapsody in Blue short was transcendent. It was the type of stuff that drugs were made for.

But then the night took a turn. Marc, Marty, and Sarah decided it would be a good idea to drop me off at the MGM Grand so I could see the lions or something like that. We were all high. But I was the only one tripping.

So Sarah dropped me off. Pointed far off in the distance and said, "My apartment is that way. About a half hour walk. Just come back when you're done."

It was shortly before 11pm and I was left alone in the sprawling MGM Grand, tripping my face off, about to venture out on to the bright lights of the Vegas Strip.

And yadda, yadda, yadda, dark night of the soul, yadda, yadda, yadda, vision quest, yadda, yadda, yadda.

To this day I am still haunted by the puzzled looks on my friends' faces when I knocked on Sarah's door at 5:30 the next morning.

Surprise. Surprise. I made it back.

I survived.

December 1st

Many lives, many masters. I've had all of them. Now I just have one. One life. One master. Eternity with Jesus Christ.

But it certainly doesn't make things any easier.

It's hard living in eternity when you have all these lives being imposed on you. By yourself and others. Never truly knowing which ones you should allow to flourish and which ones you should have already killed.

Should I be using this righteous anger to cleanse the temple? Or is it just more practice in turning the other cheek?

Please Jesus. Help guide me through the eye of the needle that is eternity.

But it's hard following Jesus when you have all these other people trying to exert control over you. Never truly knowing which ones are helping you on your journey and which ones are putting obstacles in your path.

Should I keep speaking truth to power until they nail me to a cross? Or do I need to do more rendering unto Caesar the things that are Caesar's?

Please Jesus. Help me better follow you through this path of thorns and vipers.

I don't know who you want me to be. I don't know who you need me to be.

I will be out front fighting or suffering in silence behind the lines. Either one. With you. For you. And in your name.

Just let me know what you need.

I'm lost.

November 30th

And this is a different type of heat. I like it a lot. I don't feel the temperature, but the fire is hotter than ever. A refined, focused inferno. Blazing out. With no blow back.

It's like they removed all my hot blood over the weekend and replaced it with cold steel. Coursing through my veins.

Definitely going to have to learn how to direct it properly. Mo power. Mo responsibility. I was always so restrained. But now that I don't have to worry about singeing myself, all bets are off.

So watch out. 'Cause I have cases to close, debts to collect, and business to finish.

I made a list, and I will be checking everybody off twice. Just to make up for lost time.

The dust has settled. The smoke has cleared. The lights have been turned back on.

Pick your metaphor. Either way the meaning is clear. The time for hiding is over. It's all out in the open now. And don't even try to obscure with words what we can all see and feel as plain as day.

Your time is over. You had your chance and blew it. And now you're just getting in the way of the rest of us.

Stuck between a cursed generation and a soulless one.

Truth, beauty, and goodness smothered by greed, self-interest, and incompetence.

The story of my life. The story of our life. The story of life.

The end.

November 29ᵗʰ

This place just seems so ridiculously small each time I return to it. It's like a Katamari effect. It would take only the slightest hint of a revolution to roll it all up.

The stuff of stardust.

Everybody is returning from their four-day weekend reality shows. With full intent to either control or destroy this narrative. A circumstantial scape goat. With us all in the crossfire.

It's why I made a career of keeping my head down. Deeply undercover. But still in full reach of all the right strings to pull. And I do. Pull them.

Somebody has to.

Making payments on checks you wrote a long time ago. With a different head. Motivated solely by momentum. And maybe a little bit of spite. All underbosses of the don of pride.

The deadliest of the deadly. My pride gets in the way of my sloth and gluttony. It's what got me out of bed and brought me here.

Who else does this serve? Who else does this serve?

Throwing sand in each other's eyes. A tantrum over the temporary. Getting excited by the ephemeral.

Maybe it's time to start allowing people to believe a different story about me.

No closer to the truth.

But further from the lies.

I sit and sell to you.

Still.

November 28th

This is the latest that 2pm has ever felt to me. And I didn't even shower yet. Haven't shaved since Thanksgiving. I guess this is a bender.

I thought you lost me, but I'm back. Everything is recharged except me. But I'm ready for another round of whatever. Because that's what I live for.

I'm still in the game. Always.

Almost crazy that I have a semi-colon in a heart hanging. And I almost put it on my skin. Before I replaced it with a crucifix. I don't remember who I was back then. But I love him anyway. Unconditionally.

Searching for the perfect riff. A drone. And I don't think I'll ever find it. Like the northwest passage. But I am going to love every moment of the search for it. I can tell.

Underneath the ground is velvet. Inside the Earth is crystal. But I deserve better than this. And I will get it. All of it. Simply by remaining meek.

Sometimes getting by with the bare minimum is still a work of genius.

White light and white heat. If you're going to phone it in, at least be Alexander Graham Bell. Or Bob Newhart.

Either way I need to bring this home. So I can say I survived the weekend. They can't stop me. And neither can I.

Shadows over my writing hand. Obscuring my words and blurring my penmanship.

But you know what I mean.

300 down and over 30 left. This task is enormous.

A B+ effort is a work of genius.

Just don't live there.

November 27th

I'm down a pint for this one, so bear with me. The Creator has me in the moment.

When the zebras take the field. To the chaotic wailings of the black lamb. Seek ye me, and ye shall live.

Famous Amos and Andy. Chasing me down at the finish line. At the last stomp in the old Earth. Still waiting for the first one in the new.

Still reeling from the growing pains. In the Alan Thicke of it. As the crusaders get denied entry into the holy land. Once again.

History doesn't always repeat itself. But it often rhymes.

And I still can't believe that crusaders hasn't been cancelled as a name yet. I mean the Middlesex Muslim Jihadists would never be allowed.

Seems like a double standard. Or reverse racism. Or just Catholics being Catholics. A North Jersey thing. Where we pray for the prey. In the basilicas and cathedrals. No matter the diocese.

They have all been powerless. In exorcising the nightclub jitters that lie deep in the recesses of your soul. Ever since you were recognized as a replacement. That time in Clinton. Communing with St. Germaine.

You sure did walk a ragged path.

Before you returned to the Church. Crawling on your hands and knees.

Begging for forgiveness.

And receiving it.

November 26th

Sending out my love to all those who need it. Through the numbness masking the pain. Sitting here battered, beat up, and bruised. With wounds too fresh to form scabs. So I have no choice but to keep licking up the blood.

The parachute jump towers over the Brooklyn horizon. Inching closer and closer as the waves gently drop on the cold sand. Releasing vapor into the salted air. While the birds make way for the unseen stranger.

I don't know what I'm feeling anymore. It's just motion and momentum. Just keep picking myself up. Just keep moving forward. Not sure why I keep getting knocked down. Not sure why I have to keep leaving where I am. Just get up and go. Don't look back.

Someday I will be on a bench. Hopefully in spring, but definitely by summer. In a mall. Or at a park. Sitting on a bench.

Without a checklist to prioritize. Or a conversation to rehearse. Just alone on a bench.

No worries. No obligations. No responsibilities. No looking back.

I will be there. After many more of these Brooklyn sunsets.

Tighter. Settled. And relaxed.

Sitting on a bench. Smiling.

At all I made it through.

Thanks be to the awesome grace of God.

Amen.

November 25th

A guitar is heard strumming in my left ear. I am left wondering whether I will ever be able to make those sounds. As a marching band dances in silence.

A weird place to find myself. Transitioning. Like the rest of us. Not sure whether I'm winning or losing. What are the rules? Is anybody even keeping score anymore?

Just static. Caught between two stations. Dueling transmissions. Left of the dial.

What's the frequency, Kenneth?

Quick. Tell me what you are thankful for.

Life. All of it. The good. The bad. The ugly. The feeling of my pen writing in this notebook. The knowledge that there is something good. Something true. Something beautiful. Beyond all of this. Beyond all the evil. Beyond all the deceit. Beyond all the ugliness. There is a place. And I am thankful for that place as much as I am thankful for this place. Two sides of one awesome coin. Thrown into a well years ago.

Deafened by the echoes of wishes past.

Thank you. Thank you. Thank you.

I am thankful for gratitude. Gracious for appreciation. Appreciative of thankfulness.

Knowing that I lack. Knowing there is more. And recognizing it when it comes.

The ultimate gift.

Thank you.

November 24th

The small details of life. The things that everybody always miss. The things that I have trouble turning away from. The things that point the way to Heaven. The things that keep us mired in Hell.

The devil is in the details. And the Kingdom of Heaven is in a mustard seed. As above, so below. As below, so above.

There's no escaping the details.

As I sit here contemplating time. I am seven minutes slower today than usual. And I can't figure out why. I'm just going to have to make up time in between station stops.

Appointments must be kept. Deadlines must be met. People are expecting me.

On time.

It was yesterday and a lifetime ago. Shouting at each other across the booth in a Manhattan diner. Couldn't have been much earlier than two in the morning. Somebody said we were like an old married couple.

But they were just easing the tension.

In reality we were just a couple of scared kids.

Scared of who we were. Scared of where we were. Scared of where we were going. Scared of what we were feeling. Scared of what we were pulling out of each other.

Fear won that night. And my Thanksgiving was ruined the next day.

I'm sure yours wasn't much better.

I love you, Sara. I'm sorry Sara. Please forgive me, Sara. Thank you, Sara.

Stay off the H.

November 23rd

They're beginning to dissipate. The feelings. Gradually ebbing away. The hate. The anger. The bitterness. Slowly softening. Rough edges being smoothed over.

But I don't want them to go. I've already lost enough. Let me keep this.

It's what I know. It's what I trust. It's what's been with me since the beginning. It's what I need.

It's what I'm not willing to let go of.

But I have no choice, do I? It's all part of this ugly, stupid game. Collateral damage from the overwhelming, never-ending, reckless love of God.

I was chased down. I was fought. I was found.

But my argument was never with the shepherd. It was with the other 99 I was being herded with. That's who I ran away from. That's why I was hiding. That's why I'm in no hurry to return.

A lone sheep among a bunch of impotent wolves.

You don't scare me. Just leave me alone and get out of my way.

Tired of being your scapegoat. Tired of being your whipping boy.

Fight your own fights. Carry your own burdens. Forgive your own sins.

I can't do it for you. I have bigger fish to fry.

And something is beginning to smell foul.

November 22nd

The creativity that can only come from the crucible. Like three kids kicking a soccer ball in Kearny. Way back in the eighties.

Today the ball has been nerfed. And pick-up games have become play dates. Removing the struggle that have fueled so many dreams.

We no longer strive for things that nobody could have imagined for us. Fighting against doubt and criticism the whole way. Boldly shouting, "I told you so!" from atop the podium. Gold medal in hand.

Today we pick from the predetermined paths of our parents. Allowing ourselves to be pushed along the way. Leaving no room for protest.

As the grooves become deeper, they become narrower and narrower. With no room to wiggle. Just buckle-up and keep your hands inside the ride at all times.

Just a ride. Bill Hicks was right. This is all just a ride.

That used to make me feel better. Like stop taking things so seriously, it's just a ride. Now it just adds to my apathy. Like what's the point of caring, it's just a ride.

Alone. On an unpaved road. Surrounded by strangers. Radio blasting. Trying to get back home.

It's just a ride.

November 21st

What should I most be aware of right now?

Hexagram 60. Limitations.

Limitations bring morality to character development and significance to the expression of the self. Without limitations, you're overwhelmed by possibilities. The next step is to accept these limitations and conduct yourself appropriately.

You can take a significant step forward when your feet are on the proper path.

What I can I expect in regard to work?

Hexagram 43. Resolution. Changing to Hexagram 28. Critical Mass (Preponderance of the Great).

The forces that may threaten you are now in a position to be eradicated. No compromise is possible. Your attitude should be friendly but uncompromising. Remember, you are dealing with the truth, and therefore all else must be discredited. There is a lot going on, the situation is excessive and may reach critical mass soon. All of it is important, serious, and meaningful, and all of it is coming to a head right now. Look for an avenue of escape. Be ready to make a quick transition into an entirely new mode of life.

Success surrounds those who remain strong and certain within.

What can I expect from my personal/romantic/sexual life?

Hexagram 25. Innocence. Changing to Hexagram 12. Stagnation.

Act innocently and react spontaneously. Your instincts should be developed and modified in the direction of natural goodness. You may trust your instincts because there is goodness in your heart. But any useful insights or ideas you may have will be met with apathy or rejection. Stagnation is a reservoir of arbitrary and absurd misunderstandings. Withdraw. Avoid the confusion that comes when there is absolute discord in the cosmos.

Self-reliance will see you through.

November 20th

Something seems to be happening, but I don't know what it is. Everybody is looking and moving in the same direction. Some are even running. I think I even saw some cops. Who knows? I guess I could turn up the volume and find out, but I don't want all that noise.

Music is enough. Seriously.

I can't believe that guy is wearing a fez hat. I thought they were cancelled. Maybe he's Armenian.

Like System of a Down. Wailing in anger about the Turks. As I sit in the passenger seat of Russ's car. Many many years ago.

Probably even before those two girls were even born. The ones showing the cleavage and skin. On a cold November night. Goose-pimpled areolas. They are the real heroes.

Walking the track at John Basilone Memorial Field. With Joe Hewitt. In the mid-90's. A scene that will be kept out of his Wikipedia page.

Written by Joseph Grossman. Is something I would never want to see in a byline. But who even reads newspapers anymore? Except maybe Jake Newman. And I don't even know if he still does.

A lost art.

John Locke fingerpainting on an original copy of the Declaration of Independence.

We hold these truths to be self-evident.

The rest of it is fake news.

So change the channel.

The show is over.

November 19th

Here I am again. Rehearsed and ready. Anxious and waiting.

A bouillabaisse of emotions is stewing in my brain and gut right now. It's hard to tell the difference between all these flavors. But the heat has definitely been turned up.

I can only sit. As still as time seems to be right now. Not knowing what to do. Not knowing how to feel.

Writing through the thick molasses. The last half of a blank page feels as intimidating as a scroll unraveled a mile long. Begging to be filled. And it's just you and a pen. And a soul so sad that your muses took the day off.

Playing with your anger. Slumbering through your despair.

While the future is sounding crisp and clear. With a secret message in dots and dashes for your ears only.

It did not die. It is as vibrant as ever. It has always been here waiting for you. Go now and claim it in confidence.

Stand up.

Walk forward.

Be who you are.

With no apologies.

November 18th

So I passed all your tests. Now what are you going to do with me? There's no reason to find me guilty. There's no cause to lock me up. You are stuck with me. And after what you all put me through, I'm not exactly going to be the most accommodating of team players.

Look at me, I'm the captain now.

By shining your light on me, you only exposed yourself. Didn't anybody tell you that magnifying glasses work both ways? You never found my sickness, but now we all clearly see yours.

And don't try to sweep me up and keep me cloistered away. I won't allow it.

I'm here now. Deal with it.

You will only and always get the me that you have earned.

Keep rejecting me. Keep dismissing me. Keep pushing me aside. And you will deal with the me that you deserve to.

Include me. Nurture me. Listen to me. And you will unlock the me that has only been known to God.

I am the immovable object. As they called me in my tennis days. I am the wall.

Nothing gets past me. Nothing sticks to me. Whatever you dish out will just come right back to hit you in the face.

So tread lightly.

I'm here to stay.

November 17th

All the people around me are falling over one after another. Like a row of dominoes. All the sturdy walls of brick and cement towers of strength are quickly dissolving into sand. Scattered away by the wind.

All that remains is you. Still standing. Still moving forward. It was you all along.

Despite how they treated you. Despite what they said about you. Despite how they made you feel. It was you all along.

There is no denying that now.

The meek has inherited the Earth. We are now living through the settling of the estate. A long, messy process. To ensure that everybody gets what's coming to them.

Nothing more. Nothing less.

I don't need any of it, though, I've gone too long learning how to live without. Insecure about where my next meal would come from. No longer surprised when it always arrives just at the right time. Without fail. A perfect system.

I am being taken care of. There is no doubt about that. I am being taken care of.

Not asking for much, but receiving so much more.

Never wanted it, but I'll take it.

Better me than you. That's one thing I know for sure.

Better me than you.

November 16th

The city of brotherly love is my end point right now. At least for this very intense two-week episode of my life. When I'm sitting with my brother and nephews, watching the contest on the pitch, I will know that this phase of the game has officially ended.

I will return from Philadelphia a new man. In a new world. Enjoying all that this new dimension has to offer me.

But we're still a long way from Philadelphia right now. Still a lot of hurdles to clear. Right now. Today. The rest of this week. Hurdle after hurdle after hurdle.

I'm doing it, though. I'm showing up. I'm keeping myself composed. I'm holding it all together. Saying all the right words. Being there for anybody who needs me. I'm doing it.

But man, am I exhausted. Wishing I had someone strong enough to share my burdens and allow me to take some of it out on them. But I don't. So I have no choice but to turn it into something else.

Turn it something else. Turn it into something else. Turn it into something else.

All the grief. All the anger. All the sadness. All the frustration. All the fear. All of it.

Turn it into something else.

I don't know what that something else will be. But it will be beautiful.

Wait for it.

It's coming.

November 15th

Sometimes the only thing that helps is to get lost in the minutiae.

Like how exactly did the Buffalo Bills get their name? Their mascot is a buffalo. But what is a bill? That could mean a lot of things. The math teacher at my school actually thought there were a lot of accountants in Buffalo, so the Bills referred to the invoices that they are constantly poring through. Like how the Packers and Steelers are named after the major industries of their respective cities. But that guy spent way too much time on Wall Street, so his whole world view is dislodged.

But to figure out how exactly the Buffalo Bills got their name, I looked it up online. Just a quick Google search. We often take for granted that we have the collected knowledge of humanity at our fingertips.

It turns out that they were originally called the Buffalo Bisons. But there were some other teams in Buffalo called the Bisons, so the owner wanted to change their name in order to differentiate themselves from the rest of the herd.

So in 1974 there was a contest where fans got to pick the name of the Buffalo football team and the Buffalo Bills won. The name was chosen to honor Buffalo Bill Cody. Whether Buffalo Bill Cody had any special connection to the city of Buffalo, I have yet to determine. I know he was born in Iowa and died in Colorado, but he must have been through Buffalo at times during his traveling wild west show days. Who really knows, though?

But yeah, minutiae. Definitely helps you forget for a moment that your aunt was senselessly killed, your good friend imploded his life and is taking advantage of your hospitality while he takes his time putting it back together, and when you are in one of the most emotionally compromised states you have ever been in, you realize that you work for and among people who are unwilling or unable to recognize your basic humanity.

Yeah, fun stuff.

But at least there's minutiae.

November 14th

Am I angry? That's a very good question. I don't think I am. I don't feel it right now. But I don't really know. Maybe it's just lying dormant. All I know is that the membrane that protects the world from what I have inside me has grown a lot thinner. And I don't know if that is a good thing or a bad thing.

It feels so late, but we've only just begun.

I still have thick black lines to draw and boundaries to erect and maintain. Peerless War Gods of the Immortals. Oh how the mighty have fallen.

At least they still know how to raise the vibrations in Washington Square Park. Freeform kids living life freestyle. Like a bunch of bulls on parade. Raging against the machines. All of them.

I won't do what you tell me. Unless you say please. And it's not an unreasonable request. And you treat me with a basic level of respect.

Cameras pointed at each other. Like a final showdown. At the end of culture. I'm still rooting for the action kids. But I will be hanging out back with the band.

It's time to get some songs out of me. Teach an old Doug some new tricks.

Sit. Still. Lie down.

But never roll over and play dead.

It's time to live.

La dolce vita.

November 13th

I don't know how to introduce this. Or if I'm even allowed to do this. I may be breaking a rule, but it feels right. So let's go for it. Here it goes.

don't go away
before you stop
to say hello
i will not hold you
longer than a song
want to hear your melody
to find the harmony
if it exists
will you play your song
as only you can do
i will sing along
if the words seem right
i've been waiting
for so long
don't go away
before you stop
              –1977

Pretty perfect, right? So worth it. Even if I get in trouble. But at least I know who I got it from. And I know who she got it from. But I wonder who will get it from me. Pity to them. But man will they light the world on fire with it.

And now it is time for us to be..

Parting

time to go
goodbye
we barely
started on
hello
it leaves
an empty feeling
of perhaps
and yet
we touched
as we said
goodbye
              –2/76

November 12th

One of those weeks where I don't remember who I was at the start of it. The old me woke up Sunday morning, went to church, and then a process began that still seems like it's going in full effect now.

Each day pushes me further and further. Unlocking chamber after chamber. My soul is in the crucible and my body and mind are just trying to keep up.

Right now I'm in a haze. I have been removed from the furnace. Being hammered and shaped as the steam rises and the sparks fly.

My polished metal will be revealed soon. A flawless blade that can split hairs and slice steel. It will be well worth the wait.

And man, have I been keeping a lot of people waiting.

As a cool breeze finally makes its way through the window. Lightening the dense, dank air of a pre-storm Friday morning.

The cold air is coming. And I am ready for it.

Preserve me. Protect me from the rot and spoil.

And you answer with a gentle caress of the neck.

You see me. You hear me. You are on my side. And you always will be.

I live behind a fortress of faith. And nothing is getting in.

So stop ringing my bell.

November 11th

I remember the first time I heard WFMU. It was shortly after the turn of the century. If I had to pinpoint it, I would say winter of 2001. But no earlier than 2000, and no later than 2002. It was definitely post-college and before leaving for the Bronx. The living behind Dave's sofa years.

I know it was winter because it was snowing. One of those quick hitting snowstorms that covers the roads before you have time to plan around it. And so I was on Route 80. Driving my '91 Ford Tempo. Gripping the steering wheel with bloodless white knuckles.

My friend Erin was with me. She could sense how nervous I was because she is very intuitive, and I was very nervous. So to help ease my anxiety, she turned the radio on.

It was probably already preset to the local classic rock station. WDHA, 105.5. I always liked me my classic rock. Erin didn't mind it, but definitely more my thing than her thing. So to move things in her direction, she reached for the radio dial and turned it all the way to the left. 91.1.

"You ever listen to FMU?"

"No." I said nervously, still clutching the steering wheel like my life depended on it.

"It's really cool. I think you'll like it."

I instantly recognized the voice of Alan Watts. I loved me my eastern philosophy. And so did Erin.

"See. I told you, you would like it."

I listened intently to his lecture. Hands beginning to relax. As he guided the listeners into an extended laughing yoga session.

Ha. Ha. Ha. Ha. Ha. HA. HA. HA. HA. HA. HA! HA! HA! HA! HA!

Erin and I laughing along with Alan Watts at the top of our lungs. Driving home on Route 80. In a snowstorm.

A perfect moment. A cherished memory.

Thank you, free form radio.

November 10th

I don't have to write about it, do I?

Of course you don't. You can write about whatever you want to write about. Never stopped you in the past.

Ok. Cool. So what should I write about?

Whatever you want to write about.

Not helpful. I still feel like I have to write about it. Writing about anything else would just come out sounding forced and inauthentic.

As I said. Never stopped you in the past.

Ha ha. You're a real comedian.

And you're a failed comedian who was never brave enough to chase after any of your dreams. Write about that.

Damn. The gloves are off.

Sorry. Your schtick gets old. Especially when you can't escape it.

Fine, I'll write about it.

'Bout time.

But seriously, getting hit by a car!? Stuff like that can actually happen to people I love and love me? That's too scary to comprehend. I want to know everything about how it happened, where it happened, all of it. I want to cross the same street. I want to see the car. I want to meet the driver. I want to hear all sides of the story.

But seriously, pedestrian!? That's what they reduce you to in the papers. Pedestrian. Not aunt. Or sister. Or cousin. Or teacher. Or union leader. Or all around awesome human being that I loved and loved me.

Pedestrian Killed After Being Hit in Wethersfield.

I love you, Aunt Carol. I'm sorry, Aunt Carol. Please forgive me, Aunt Carol.

Thank you.

November 9th

The pathology of wealth. Always been a recurring theme in all the novels of my mind. Also an inescapable aspect of my waking life. Especially at work.

Greed. Self-interest. Entitlement. Lack of accountability. It's all there. Mo money. Mo problems.

Not to mention the need for constant, unchecked growth. Bigger. Stronger. Faster. Cancer is a symptom of the sickness of capitalism. The only cure is to eradicate the lifestyle choices that cause it.

And that ain't happening anytime soon. Not without a fight, it won't. And my fighting days are behind me.

So I have no choice but to sit back and watch with a bemused detachment. Embracing the absurdity of it all. Trying not to take any of it personal. Even though all of it is.

A fringe character in the middle of it all. Just waiting for somebody to allow me to add my two cents to the pot. Polishing my coins in the meantime.

I can't even figure out the year anymore. Just some bumps and ridges left that used to be in the shape of numbers. But numbers are notorious liars, so they won't be missed.

Letters are just as bad, but they have the luxury of hiding behind words.

But get rid of numbers and letters and all we have left is pure, unadulterated meaning and truth.

Pretty scary stuff.

I'm ready for it, though. How 'bout you?

November 8th

I guess my big takeaway from this is how good I've become at not allowing myself to become enmeshed in other people's stories or dramas. Almost too good. Feels like a coldness or indifference if I didn't know better. But I do. Know better.

The greatest love knows how to establish boundaries. And stay protected.

It was also revealing how much I agreed with all the negative self-talk. As tough as it was to hear, it was a pretty honest assessment. It's why I don't really do anything to challenge it.

It's one of the sick realities of the world. Those who are the most self-empowered tend to be the least self-aware. And those who are the most self-aware tend to be the least self-empowered. The former is dangerous. The latter is just sad.

That's what we're dealing with today. Just sad. The sadness that comes with the sickness.

Makes you want a little danger in your life.

Let's not get carried away, though. This too shall pass. But it may be a bumpy path through.

And the picture will not be the same once you put all the pieces back together again. It never is. So stop staring at the box. You can't go back there.

And you wouldn't want to if you could.

You've opened up a blank template. There's no format for what you're composing.

Good luck.

November 7th

Sitting right beside me on my grandfather's red rocking chair. A pile of defeat. The consequence of mistakes. With no choice but to surrender. And he doesn't even know what that means.

How sad.

But whatever. I'm not the pitying type. And I ain't nobody's therapist. I'm just a friend. Who loves unconditionally. And who will be there for you. And give you your space.

But nothing beyond that. So take that stuff somewhere else. You ain't my cross to bear, but I will help carry yours. Just give me the word.

Anywhere. Anytime. Anything.

That's when life becomes real. I love that sort of thing. No surprise when it shows up on my doorstep. Duffle bags and pillows in tow.

Is it later or earlier than you think it is right now? Because I could go in either direction. But it is getting dark. And cold.

Way too early to be this late.

This is unnatural. We are all going to be grumpy tomorrow. Don't give me the extra hour of sleep nonsense. This is unnatural. And the body feels it.

I wonder how long until this becomes old.

I'm used to my space. Used to my routine.

May peace and understanding come quickly.

For all of our sakes.

November 6th

There is no better place to spend an autumn afternoon. Caruso Stadium. In the dictionary next to bucolic.

A lot of green. A lot of gold.

I was expecting there to be more people. I was expecting it to be warmer in the sun. I was expecting it to feel differently. It doesn't. I hate expectations. The Buddha was right.

There's a lot of guys here who look like John Marx. Man, I miss that guy. The best kind of people. He would be eating this up. Not thinking once about his feelings. Or expectations. He knew how to live.

The old man seems older than usual. But I bet he can still teach the game. That's why we're all here. There because of the grace of God will go I.

It's never smart to gamble early. Like taking your queen out in the opening. Will only come back to haunt you. Conservatism is dead. Even among the conservative. Everybody is in a hurry. But that's easy for me to say. From way up here.

It all looks so different from here. With a greater distance. Alone and detached.

This is visiting an old friend that you have grown apart from. It's no longer part of your story. You were never really a part of its.

Just a watcher.

Who saw some great things.

But it's over now.

So move on.

November 5th

We have had an intimate interrelationship with advanced intelligence from the stars from the beginning of human history. And that intimate interrelationship is still underway.

Hello thoughts. Today is your day like no other.

I can't imagine how many paper clips and pipe cleaners I've gone through. And forget about paper towels. The office supplies of the work-at-home degenerate. But I'm never getting those brown eco-friendly ones again. Sorry Greta. They're not built for my loads.

We're meant to flood the world with the life that we preserved. And I can't think of arks without having to control my lust. We have a long way to go. Please lord, hold off the rain.

So this is what the id feels like unfettered. I don't think I like this. There's no bottom to it. No sense of control. I have no choice but to just enjoy the sights, sounds, and flavors as I surrender to my more simian self.

I am standing in solidarity with the midnight funk association. I acquiesce to all the requirements of membership. May the funk always be with me.

It sure beats the alternative.

Imminent threat soon upon Earth's leaders and civilizations. Expose and disperse hidden knowledge to all citizens. Employ safe and controlled joint study to all minds. Progression imperative for combined survival.

A bridge to the sunset. Somewhere in Brooklyn. As the barge passes underneath. In a style reminiscent of Leonard Cohen. But more Irish than Canadian.

I miss you Dutch Mazz. We could have had it all. But you remain voiceless. If I run. It will be for a different team.

Often a sunset is just a sunset. Other times it is an end of an era and a herald of a new age.

Tonight it's a little bit of both.

November 4th

It's kinda late for this. Standing on the edge of a pocket of freedom. The next forty-eight hours are formless. But the shape of things makes no sense to me anymore.

I liked it better when I was hanging with K-Hob. Eating steak sandwiches. In the home of the Wildcats. Farming for space.

Harvesting an afternoon with Bigfoot, UFOs, and Jesus. Although I don't remember them ever mentioning Jesus by name. But he was certainly behind it all. Like always. And taking his sweet old time. Like always.

The collection I have cultivated is near completion. And after that is letting go of the need to hold on. Emptying the basket. Rolling up the blanket. Isn't it a pity?

I don't know where today is. Or what tomorrow will bring. But I keep moving forward regardless. We study the past. We don't live there.

Like a pillar of salt. To balance the sweetness of my kettle corn. Wild honey and locust. While I baptize the repentant in the river. Preparing the way for He who was always here.

Someday we'll be together. And feel like we never left. Yes, we will. It's so close I can taste it.

But until then I sit and wait. Drowning in my own decadence. Due to sinful self-indulgence. The sugar high that only comes after a Halloween in Harlem.

Trick or treat.

It's too late.

We're stuck in this tapestry.

November 3rd

There was a crispness in the air this morning that I haven't felt in a long time. Something about the cold air that can make a man feel both alive and alone at the same time.

Time to start kindling the fire that burns within.

As I travel the dark, serpentine roads of life. Past the unwanted fetus pushed out onto the cold bathroom floor. Past the unattended to corpse. Rotting for the second straight day along the side of the road that she should have known better than to try to cross. Past the unnoticed dealers and users lining the way up the staircase. Judging whether or not you truly belong here.

They don't bother me, though. I have a lifetime pass.

A clear path into my living work of art. An organic externalization of all that I have learned, all that I have dreamed of, and all that I have struggled with. Living. Breathing. Open for all to step inside, take a look, and know me for the first time.

So far attendance has been sparse, though. Especially during weekends and holidays. The mental gridlock is keeping everybody stuck in their webs. As the spider of apathy stalks its prey.

While I just sit here watching the wheels go by. Rearranging the blocks and bricks to create something new. Something that points to where all the meaning is. Something that keeps the rain out.

But I don't know anymore. It just all seems so futile.

Futile, yet fun.

Welcome to the human condition.

November 2nd

I'm tired of constantly railing against incompetence, but seriously. What are we all doing here? Forget about waking up or growing up, we no longer have time to wait on those luxuries. We need people to start showing up. And now.

Show up and do the job the way it's supposed to be done. I don't understand why that isn't as simple in practice as it is in theory. Show up and do the job the way it's supposed to be done.

I don't like to talk about my work, but yesterday a student was balled-up in the corner of my classroom completely unresponsive to any teachers in the room. Pretty scary. So I called down to the office to let the admins and therapeutic staff know what was going on.

Not a single adult came into my classroom to check on that student or to follow-up with me about what happened. In a borderline crisis situation, the needs of the student and the teachers in the classroom were completely ignored by the adult professionals in the building. And I wish I could say it wasn't a normal occurrence.

That's unprofessional. That's negligent. That's incompetence.

We all deserve better because we all are capable of better.

Last year I was denied my right to vote because my signature in my forties is not the same as my signature as a teen. This morning I was denied my right to vote because they were missing a cable and didn't know what to do about it. And I wish I could say that other potential voters weren't turned away as well.

Unprofessional. Negligent.

As I said earlier, I'm tired of constantly railing against incompetence, but seriously.

What are we all doing here?

November 1st

What a blur. Of a day. Of a weekend. Of a week. Of a month. What a blur.

And now here we all are. In November. With all the other saints and souls. Trying to pretend that what just happened didn't actually happen. And if you can't deny it, at least try to control the narrative.

Denial and rationalization. The twin flames fueling the desperate man's gas light. While I find a home obscured in the darkness.

They can't reach me here. But it won't stop them from trying.

I took some slides. But I am far from falling. Even with all your pushing.

Surrounded by people whose privilege prevented them from working out what should have been handled in the past. Like the rest of us. Who had no other choice. Standing here. Holding the white sheet. For the petty projections of the poor in spirit.

Trying to not get any on me. But man, are they sloppy.

Don't tell me I'm wrong, Jane Weaver, I've been doing this for quite some time.

A chip off the old block. A salary man still punching the clock.

Devils all around me. Surrounded by sin. But they can't get me here.

In my circle of faith.

October 31ˢᵗ

Bless us o Lord, and these thy gifts, which we are about to receive from thy bounty, through Christ our Lord. Amen.

With a special blessing for all the fine people at the Whole Foods in Parsippany, who were most responsible for bringing this meal to my table.

Man those are some spicy sweet potatoes. Tempered by a nice mix of quinoa and couscous. With raisins of every color. Washed down by the Mexicane Cola. While listening to the Mexican radio.

Ken is sitting underneath a tree with a panda and a fox. And now he is back in Salem. Some people have costumes on. Other do not.

Did I mention that today is Halloween? Or did you figure it out by the date on top?

It was never my thing. Just another day. Went to church. Did some food shopping. A little schoolwork. In the middle of laundry.

Already burned through half a dozen bowls. At least. Time for another one.

They are playing the song that is framed and placed upon my mantle. Or the closest thing I have to a mantle. Light and love. A spell put on me by the gypsy queen. As the tramps and thieves look on in apathy.

I've been led to the mercy tavern. Seeking once more to draw from the well. As reality fragments. And all jokers become wild.

This is not rock and roll. This is genocide. And that is not Waldo. That is Harry Potter. Not all beanies are the same. You racist.

Young girl.

They call them the diamond dogs.

October 30th

As Stephon Marbury got older, Stephon Marbury got bolder. Stephon Marbury got more outspoken. Very much more unapologetic about how he feel, what he thought was right and wrong. And being in your face and letting you know where he stood.

There's too much New York in me. It's what anchors me to New Jersey. Otherwise I'd probably be out in PA or the Midwest or something by now. There are students everywhere. But nobody to drive the bus.

I miss Steve and Barry's. It was in the Manhattan Mall near Greely Square. I would always go the week after Christmas. They would have the best sales. I got a lot of good hoodies there.

But then Lebron James drove them out of business. Another victim of hypercapitalism.

Be water, my friend. Surrender to the air.

Awake to a new world. With old work to finish. And the closer you get to the end, the lines you are filling are appearing longer in length. But you know it is just an illusion.

Because all of it is. And none of it is. So take your pick. Is the middle way really all that noble?

You've got to pick up every stitch. Must be the season of the witch.

It must be like the season the Nets were coached by Bill Fitch.

17 wins. But each one a herald of the promise to come.

The savior will be here soon. He is coming from the east.

Prepare the way.

October 29th

Group text time!

Russ: (Link) [Redacted comment]
Marcus: [Redacted comment]
Marcus: [Redacted comment]
Douglas: "Happy to see our public officials enjoying themselves and not taking everything so seriously for a change. There's more to life than infrastructure and budgets and what not. And I like Cory Booker. He seems like a nice guy. And Rosario Dawson is effing hot. So good for him."
Russ: [Redacted comment] (Link)
Douglas: "I wonder where he stands on Dune."
Pete: [Redacted comment]
Pete: [Redacted comment]
Pete: [Redacted comment]
Marcus: [Redacted comment]
Russ: [Redacted comment]
Douglas: "Even better than Bill Richardson?"
Douglas: "But back in 2002 I read an article in the Ledger about Booker and I told my grandfather that he would be president one day. He just laughed at me and said he wouldn't even be mayor of Newark. I think I'm winning."
Pete: [Redacted comment]
Pete: [Redacted comment]
Douglas: (Link) "Whoa! You're right."
Pete: [Redacted comment]
Pete: [Redacted comment]
Douglas: "Yeah, completely forgettable. But man, between him and Cosby. Drew doesn't have a good track record."
Marcus: [Redacted comment]
Douglas: "Yeah. And he wasn't a serial rapist either. Although that would be impressive.
Pete: (Laughed at comment)
Pete: [Redacted comment]
Russ: [Redacted comment]
Pete: [Redacted comment]
Russ: [Redacted comment] (Link)

And that's all folks. But yeah, Cory Booker does seem like a nice guy. He followed me on Twitter, and we had an exchange after Gabby Giffords was shot. He brought up gun control. I reminded him about mental health. It was great!

Be the change.

October 28th

Did I ever tell you the story about how I started the 2012 Mayan calendar hysteria of the early 2010's? It all goes back to Halloween of 2002, or actually maybe even a little earlier.

Back when I was a junior in college ('98-'99) there was a lot of talk about the coming new millennium and anxiety was growing about what became known as Y2K. In an attempt to tackle this apocalyptic hysteria head on, I wrote a dark satire piece for the school paper warning students and staff about the true Armageddon that would happen, not in Y2K, but when the Mayan calendar ended on December 21st, 2012.

Apparently, the editor of the entertainment section, Sue Rella, didn't get the humor and it remains my only rejected piece of my illustrious collegiate journalistic career. In retrospect, I probably included too many Baudrillard and Terrence McKenna quotes for her liking. She also has my only copy, so I wasn't able to even include it in my first book.

Fast forward to 2002, and I'm living and teaching in the Bronx and enjoying as much of the New York City lifestyle as a single, 24-year-old can endure. And maybe even a little more. Which included going out in public dressed for Halloween. Something I hadn't done since middle school.

So I got a couple of pieces of white cardboard and made myself a sandwich board. On the front, in big red letters, I painted the words, "The End is Near!". On the back I added the date, "12/21/2012".

I then took the 6 Train to Grand Central, Shuttle to Times Square, and walked, proudly wearing my apocalyptic sandwich board, up Broadway from 42nd to the Upper West Side.

During the whole-time people were shouting at me from cars, honking their horns, and several people stopped to take pictures. It was by far the most eyeballs I ever had on a costume I was wearing. It was pretty cool.

In 2002, nobody was talking or thinking about 2012. By 2009 it was a major Hollywood movie starring John Cusack and books about it were infesting bookstores everywhere. All thanks to my Halloween costume.

You're welcome, Mayans. Even if you were wrong.

October 27th

300 days. In the book. Literally.

And among those 300 days there were definitely many that I wanted to take off or some when I just didn't think I had it in me.

But I just kept moving forward. Day after day. No excuses. No rest.

Eventually the forces working against me realized that if they wanted to stop this, they would have to stop me. And they tried. Oh Lord, did they try.

But I just kept moving forward. Day after day. No excuses. No rest.

Leaving me no choice but to round up the usual suspects so they can answer for their crimes. They know who they are. They know what they did. And so do I.

There are no friends in sight, but fortunately I have all my enemies close at hand. Where they are harmless.

I hate to have to view the world in this way. But I am just a blank channel. Used to monitor technical difficulties. And the technical difficulties have caused a break of trust that will be long under repair.

The people in my life get the version of me that they deserve. It's nothing personal. Just business.

The business of moving forward. Day after day. No excuses. No rest.

That's how you made it to 300 days. Mile 20 of the marathon.

So keep your head down and don't let up.

There's still a 10K ahead of you.

October 26th

There's not much that a good cleansing rain can't heal. As long as you make it through to the other side, you will reemerge as pristine as ever.

And here I am. On the other side. So fresh and so clean. Because of all I did and all I learned that can never be taken away from me. So stop trying.

I'm ready to be all that I am. I'm ready to go all the way. So stop blowing raspberries.

And enough of this restraint and repression. Without my anger, without my pride, without my sin. I am nothing. So stop guarding me from it and allow it all to flow fully through and out of me.

I've had enough of this half-stepping. It's time to live out the overwhelming, never-ending, reckless love of God.

And the key word here is reckless. Without thinking or caring about the consequences of an action. What better way to describe the act of living out your faith.

Not caring about what you say. Not caring about what you do. Not caring what others think. Just putting God first and unapologetically being who you are.

I will always love you. I will always be grateful for you. But unless you are God, I am not sorry for anything, and I don't seek your forgiveness.

There is only one judge. One king. One creator.

And it ain't me, and it's definitely not you.

So sit in the back of the class and finish your homework.

It's time for me to teach.

October 25th

These pattern repetitions are becoming tedious. Even boring at times. I already let go of my need to put together clever rhymes, it's time for history to do the same. Both at the personal and public levels.

The record is skipping. Pick up the needle and move it forward so the song can continue. It's not going to just work itself out.

Funny analogy for a morning without music. And a lot of leftover business from the weekend. This long term beat down is beginning to take its toll.

You can't say I never asked for help. There's certainly a long paper trail of that. But instead of help, I got put on trial. A kangaroo court designed to box me out. Leaving me with nowhere to turn. And nobody to trust.

Just a bunch of small men and tiny women. Too insignificant to make a difference. But they still hold power over your life and that which you hold dear. And they will continually remind you of that. Because they are scared, insecure, little people.

Not to mention lazy and incompetent.

Makes me seriously consider what exactly Plan B is? Is it worth staying, when so much of me has already left?

Nobody bats an eye when they see a soul hanging by a thread. So why should a body by a rope cause any more commotion?

If you don't honor my essence, you can't say you value my life.

I am all of it. The good, the bad, the ugly.

Forgive me for not fitting in.

My gravest sin.

October 24th

This is what rock bottom feels like. What being out of control feels like. What a slave feels like. Helpless. And no one to depend on.

But I have a lot to be grateful for.

Like having a stomach full of Chinese food. When I know what it's like to be food insecure. Cashing in my change for a case of Hot Pockets and a jug of wine. And just hoping for the best from there.

And from there I got here. With a stomach full of Chinese food. Listening to some beautiful sounds on the radio. I'd thought the stork would have brought me something else. But I'll take what he's giving me now.

Give the drummer some. Right, Doug?

And I did. And I will.

Marching to the beat of a drummer so different that Milford Graves would give 'em a second glance. Retreating into full mantis. Like Krupa playing Nagasaki. But after the bombs were dropped.

As I stroke my beard. Waiting on a major upgrade. That is currently rewiring my hard drive. Eleven is a higher number than ten.

My workaholism has become my most pernicious addiction. And that's saying a lot.

But at least it's got me ahead of schedule. Giving me a nice buffer. For when the crash comes.

Right around the corner.

But I have a lot to be grateful for.

October 23rd

Coca-Cola with coffee. Dark blend. They had a BOGO deal at 7-11. So I got a couple. Enjoying one now. Not really that caffeinated, though. Less than a cup of coffee. Barely more than tea. But a good flavor. Nice and robust. If you're into that sort of thing.

I was into that girl mopping the floor and working the register. Very cute. And awesome energy. Nice and robust. If you're into that sort of thing. But she had all her defenses up with me. Definitely on guard. Can't blame her.

The guy who opened the door for me was pretty cool. Definitely all blessings go out to that guy. He's got a spot in the ark if he wants it.

As I pair my beverage this afternoon with a Kind bar. Healthy grains. Oats & honey. With toasted coconut. Gluten free and all that jazz. Used to be a regular part of my regiment. Now I'm just bringing it back as a substitute. Filling the gaps when needed. Kinda like now.

Lunch is over. Dinner is a mountain climb away. But the machine still needs to keep fueled. My energetic levees will be tested tonight. I cannot allow a break.

Back to a place of happy memories. With one of the sturdiest anchors of the past. An unmovable rock in the city of bricks.

Where better to build my church upon.

An angel among devils.

Ready for the faceoff.

October 22nd

Jump on the saddle, grab hold of the bridle. Go up in the air, come down in slow motion. It is the answer to a never-ending story.

Somebody help me.

It's time to flip, flip this fantasia. Open up the sorcerer's toolbox and learn how to start swimming with the whales. A rhapsody in blue. Written by the white man.

And I just wish my brother George was still here.

He'd know what to do. He'd have all the answers. Just like he did in Lemuria and Machu Picchu. Which both lie in ruins.

Leaving the rest of us behind to clean up the mess. And reset the poles. But maintaining balance is tough when there are so many hands on the scale. Was the game ever not rigged? Or was that just always part of it to begin with?

More show than sport.

Which explains why everyone is so outraged when you dare to compete, rather than resigning to simply playing out your role.

You are a threat. An aberration. A virus unleashed in their matrix.

Fighting to survive and pass on your code.

As they inoculate themselves against you. And erect fortresses of fear.

They will never let you in.

So get used to the cold.

October 21ˢᵗ

So here we go. Time crunch today and it's been a while since we did one of these. So here comes a ten minute free write. The theme for today is tragedy plus time equals comedy.

Let's begin!

So they say tragedy plus time equals comedy. But the problem with that is that time is an illusion. There is no such thing called time. Every schoolboy knows that. Even Einstein. And that dude was more confused than any of us. But yeah, time is fake. Just a human construct based on our relative position in space. Absolutely no objective meaning or value. Time is a flat circle as it was stated in that overrated show True Detective. Man that show was overrated. You don't even hear people talking about it anymore. We're all embarrassed that we actually liked it and thought it was meaningful at the time. We were fooled, tricked, bamboozled. Kinda like with the movie Crash. We even gave that trash an Oscar. Man, we are silly. Believing in stuff like time when the past, present, and future all exist simultaneously. There is no time. There's just now. Just right now. So there's no tragedy plus time equals comedy. There's just tragedy equals comedy. That's the true equation. Tragedy equals comedy. We just invented time to cushion the blow. While the Gods laugh at us. And at Adam Walsh's head and shoulders in the bushes. And the Challenger astronauts really wanting a Bud Light. Or WTC employees ordering two large plains from Famous Rays on 9/11. Tragedy=Comedy. Tragedy=Comedy. Tragedy=Comedy.

Time is up.

What a tragedy.

October 20th

It's never too late to enjoy a little breakfast with Bluiett. Hamiet and eggs. What a concept. Living on a cloud.

And anybody worthy enough to unpack all of that can roll with me for life. You'll never see such dense code produced from just one song. It's oozing out of my fingertips. I can't turn it off.

Especially during a full moon like today.

Which is why I seek to be grounded. Not by the illusory authority of the air. But by the earthy power of the drum. Skin pounding against skin. Creating the raucous rhythm of chaos. Where the line between the giver and the receiver is forever blurred.

Now that is what I call music. What I call art. What I call creation.

Even the most adept manipulators of air have to submit themselves to the bondage of the beat.

Seven chakras, maybe more. But only one that matters. Red is the new orange, yellow, green, blue, and indigo.

As Russ's t-shirt used to say: Got Root?

On the lam after eating too many yams.

The time for talking is over. Push has come to shove. And when that happens, love has nothing to do with it.

Are you building or destroying? Or maybe a little bit of both.

Either way, it's time to get in the pit and play your part.

Until the music stops.

October 19th

I was here long before anybody now even knew this place existed. And I will still be here long after they leave. That is why there is no one who can diminish my past accomplishments. Or stand in the way of my future goals.

Any person I ever had a problem with is gone.

But I am still here.

Playing the long game like a marathoner. Patiently allowing all seasons to naturally pass. Some only take a month, other may take half a decade. Still only a drop in the bucket in the greater scheme of things.

Living day to day will continue to be the greater challenge. Running is easy. Remembering to put one foot in front of the other can be hard.

Five is too high. Let's try three. Hopefully three is enough. If three is not enough, there's always four. And if three is too much, we can try two. Trial and error. That's how we get things done.

But I'm confident that three will be enough.

One gave birth to two. Two gave birth to three. Out of three arose all things. That is the Way.

Four or five don't even get mentioned. And why should they?

I am number six. A prisoner in the village of all these minds. Selling rhymes like dimes. In order to buy a little freedom in these broken times.

Mash potatoes. Apple sauce. Buttery biscuits.

Is there anybody not lost? Or are we all.

MF Doomed.

October 18th

First time back since being dragged into kangaroo court by the running scared. Not sure how I would feel. Ended up feeling not much of anything. Which is probably for the best. But I do sense a greater distance between me and the rest of it all. Which is definitely better.

I declare that the war is over. Years after already deciding that I wouldn't be marching anymore.

All that is left is to help clean up the battlefield. As you work alongside those who were attacking you and those you were helping defend. Forgetting who was playing each role, since neither was worthy of much attention. Or respect.

This is where you learn humility. By being a giant among ants. Yet still slaving for the hill. Building what will never last. Because it was conceived from fear and greed.

They are afraid you will prevent them from making more money.

That is what all this is about. Never forget it. It ain't personal, it's business.

And man what an ugly business. Run by even uglier people.

That's why I already quit. Ran off and joined a monastery. Surrendered my life to Christ.

But for my first assignment they sent me back here.

To work again, but for new masters.

As I quietly await my orders.

October 17th

Wiping the blood off the toilet seat. And it's not my blood. Or toilet seat. I wonder who the culprit is.

Sometimes leaving the world a better place than you found it requires putting a lot of skin in the game. And it doesn't always mean that you'll become a better person in the process. So it's no surprise that so few even try.

Can you blame them?

As the rain pounds the sidewalk and parking lot. Even the guy in the pink hoodie had to come inside to seek refuge. Never ceasing the barking into his cell phone. And I can't help but think of open windows so far away. Hoping that the damage is minimal, and the recovery is quick.

I've definitely seen the ebbs and flows of this place. Came in with a flow. Reflecting during an ebb. While the moon continues to wax. And my energy slowly wanes.

But I already accomplished much. So I have reason to be proud.

My body continues to make some good decisions. The unsung hero of this whole operation. Just like Billy Ostaszewski.

Tackling rockets with Elon and Jeff. Singing about the common people with Kirk.

Today feels like the first day of the rest of my life.

Just like yesterday. And tomorrow.

Welcome to the tip of the spear.

October 16ᵗʰ

So yesterday was certainly interesting. Someday when this is all said and done with, you'll have to explain to me exactly what that was all about.

Add it to my list. I'm going to have a long agenda when I get back up there.

But the whole experience has definitely left my earth body reeling and in need of healing. While my etheric self has never felt better. Certainly a weird dissonance to try and keep balanced.

Today is my birthday, though. So that makes me a Libra. And balance is what we do best. Even when it's dealing with extremes.

My body is telling me how difficult and potentially dangerous what I went through was. My spirit is telling me how successful I was in handling everything. But my mind has never been more muddled and confused.

The last gasps of a broken ego that is gradually being dimmed out. A wave of the white flag whose ripples are measured in lifetimes.

And this is the one where we seek stillness.

So give your body more tenderness and care. Allow your spirit more freedom and space. And be patient and forgiving with your mind.

Like Ethan Hawke, you didn't hold anything back in your swim out to sea. But now you must muster some strength in order to return to the shore.

Keeping yourself above water.

As the pleasures of the harbor await.

October 15th

It's been one of those weeks where I feel like I've been the Universe's kidney. Like not the whole Universe, I ain't no messiah, but the kidney for my little universe. But as above, so below, so I guess it's really the same thing. Although I wouldn't want to say that to the guy hanging on the cross.

I just had to deal with some restless sleeps, tension headaches, mental fogs, a sensitive stomach, and some pretty scary ideations. But nobody is shoving a rag of bitter vinegar into my mouth. Although, not gonna lie, it felt like things were heading in that direction at some points.

But yeah, I guess it started on Sunday. The concert the night before cleansed me in preparation for the process, and then I started taking in new filth and toxins as soon as I got back to Jersey.

It was nothing bad at first. Just my normal workload. And I do enjoy the labor.

But then the vet appointment came on Monday morning and by noon it felt like sepsis was creeping in, and the work week hadn't even begun yet.

Tuesday was tough. Getting through Wednesday was downright heroic. By Thursday morning I was calling out for help. All the other kidneys were just looking at each other in disbelief as the hearts and brains kept ignoring our agony.

Is this really happening? Can I really handle all of this?

Luckily, by the afternoon things seemed to begin healing and this morning appears ok. So I guess the system is still working.

I don't know, though, you tell me. Is this urine stream any less cloudy than earlier in the week?

The proof is in the pudding.

October 14ᵗʰ

The fog is starting to lift. That is evident. But it is still lingering. And you may have to be a little proactive to take care of the rest.

It's very obvious that you are alone here. No one is going to be throwing you a lifeline, so you better start learning how to swim.

It's not that difficult. It's just a matter of remembering what you forgot. As well as remembering why you forgot it in the first place.

Why did you forget who you really are? Why did you forget where your real home is? Why did you forget what you came here to do?

When will you realize that nobody is ever going to win this game of tug of war?

Drop the rope. If they taught you one thing here, it's that. Drop the rope.

The fog is starting to lift, but it is still lingering.

Do you have what it takes to take care of the rest?

We're on your side. We have your back. We're rooting for you.

There are no wrong moves. But we can't move for you.

So stop standing still.

Get out there and shoot your shot.

October 13th

The fog refuses to lift and I don't know how much longer I can endure this.

I call out to friends for help. But they respond with ambivalence. Wanting no part in this role reversal. I am always welcomed into their lives. But nobody wants to take a step into mine.

When he who always served others needs to be served himself, he is painted as a selfish sinner. God have pity on him. Crippled. Grasping for his crutch. While they just stare, mock, and judge.

But time waits for no one, and it won't wait for me. I either have to pick myself up on my own or get trampled by the horde. And I don't know if I'm strong enough.

So that's why I have no clue how, where, or when you are reading this.

Hopefully it is in a finished book that you are flipping through right now. Relieved that I was able to get through this. On my own. Saving you the guilt.

But maybe you're leafing through this notebook instead, looking for clues. Wondering why things ended up the way they did.

Lucky for you I left them everywhere. I wouldn't want to make things difficult. I know how busy everyone is.

Be relieved. The burden of my existence has been removed like a yoke from your back.

Run free. Enjoy life. You deserve it.

As for me. Just give me one ticket, please.

Time to get to where I'm going.

Wherever that may be.

October 12th

The wall between reality and fantasy is sometimes so small and not too tall. As is the wall between your dreams and nightmares. Eternity and oblivion.

I am beginning to have trouble telling the difference between the two. My nightmares of oblivion are becoming all too real. While my dreams of eternity are feeling like a distant fantasy.

The way through is an incomprehensible blur. But the way out is in 4K high resolution.

I'm planning in double or triple redundancy. I'm leaving towels on the floor to sop up the mess. I'm placing notes where the right people will find them.

I'm caring less about who I will be leaving behind and what I will be leaving unfinished.

That's all fantasy to me right now.

What's real is that I've been on my knees everyday crying out for some sort of help or some sort of relief. And I'm still here.

My back is scarred from constantly being whipped by your stick of thorns. And my legs are jelly from chasing a carrot that has long ago grown rotten.

I've already stopped running. Now please take me off this track.

This is not my world. I made a mistake.

Guide me. Protect me. Help me. Heal me.

That's all I ask for.

I am a helpless sinner, but I would never allow my students to feel the way I'm feeling right now.

So what's your excuse?

October 11th

As soon as I walked into the place, I felt it. Like a wave of darkness crashing into me. I had to sit down before it knocked me off my feet. I didn't want to let go of what I came here for.

Anxiety. Fear. Dread. In their rawest forms. Not a crystal of compassion or gentle care to help sugar coat it.

That was confirmed when he was grabbed by the neck and dragged out of his cage.

And it only got worse. Much worse.

Crying. Screaming. Gnashing of teeth. And I couldn't help but to feel all of it.

All the terror. All the pain. All the anger.

I'm still recovering from it. So I can only imagine how he's processing it all right now. Deep in the recesses of the feline soul. Where instinct and experience fight it out to form personality.

Will he be able to trust us again? Will suspicion temper his friendliness? Will he learn to better run and hide?

Will seven years of love be ruined by a morning of maliciousness.

I hope not. But I can't blame him if it does.

We are a cruel species. Cruel to those smaller than us. Cruel to those bigger than us. Cruel to each other.

Cruel.

That is our kind.

October 10th

6:42am and I'm sitting in Penn Station staring at the big board. Amy Winehouse is singing about the girl from Ipanema in my ear buds.

I miss the days when things were more analog. The numbers and letters would frantically spin into place as the commuters anxiously anticipated which direction they would all start hustling toward.

I miss that sound. I miss that feeling.

The sterile LCD screen that they got going now does nothing for me. So easy to ignore. Like strangers hiding behind a mask. I want to see all your cogs and wheels spinning.

I want to hear them. I want to feel them.

But man, I forgot the type of crowd you get waiting for the first train out of the city on a Sunday. Some just woke up, most have yet to sleep. I belong to the former group. But just barely.

6:42. Before the end of victory. Before we stop running. Before we stop striving. Before we stop fooling ourselves.

6:42. Before we all remember that it has already been accomplished.

Jesus doesn't want us to be sunbeams. Jesus wants us to be the whole Son.

Nothing else. Just the whole Son.

No cigarettes, no sleep, no light, no sound, no food, no books.

Just the air that you breathe. And to love Him.

But even the air is a crutch.

So keep hobbling down that track.

You'll be home soon.

October 9th

Back on a train. It's been too long. But I am finally back on a train. In motion. Going east.

It's only really been a month and a half, but it feels like a lifetime ago. I don't even remember much of who I was back then. Things are a lot different for me now. So I had to become a different person. But I like to think I was able to carry over the best parts with me. Transcend the past and include it in your present.

My present right now is kinda ugh, though. My shoulder hurts. The right one. Don't know what's that all about. I guess I'm not stretching enough. Or maybe too much. Lugging around a heavy computer bag everyday doesn't help. Nor does sleeping tucked in a small loveseat every night.

My brain is kinda cloudy too. That could be the weather. Or my lifestyle. But the world seems to be bathed in soul-sucking fluorescent lights right now. Like I'm living through the opening scenes of Joe Versus the Volcano. I can almost hear the buzzing.

I guess ever since I stopped running, things are beginning to catch up with me now. And the more you make things chase you, the least merciful they are when they finally catch up with you.

So here I am. Facing the music.

On a train. Going east.

Where each conversation or cell phone call is pouring salt on my wounds.

As I try not to think of all I left undone or still need to do.

Just get me to my city.

And allow me a night of joyful rest.

October 8th

90 miles an hour down a dead-end street. Isn't that how the Dylan song goes? 90 miles an hour down a dead-end street. And the fog is only just beginning to lift. Leaving behind the smell of a freshly killed skunk.

But Dylan didn't write all those words. And things aren't nearly as bad as the song lets on.

We're just mining the dark coal of human emotion and experience. The necessary fuel to keep this fire burning.

But only for a couple more months. And then I can finally put this whole stage behind me. Exit the labyrinth once and for all. Enough of these sad little dirges. Time to start singing out in praise and gratitude. In a field of lilies with all the canaries.

Only thing left is to play out this string and return to the surface.

Before the mine collapses. And the light is forever lost to those trapped in its depths.

But seriously, things really aren't that bad.

Just exaggerating things for the sake of my art. Like the rest of us. A poetic license to drive through the alleyways of hell.

A celebrity tour of turmoil and strife. But my camera is running out of film and there's no room in my luggage for anymore souvenirs.

Time to start packing things up. Lift the hold on my mail and see if Charon is available to Uber me home.

I got my coins ready.

Time to cash in.

October 7th

Who dat?

Right in the middle is a doughy, pink-faced couple outside of Graceland. Dude has a crooked smile and a hat on backwards. The girl with the ratty sweatshirt and gaudy thumb-ring is the one pointing.

In the upper left-hand corner is a confused looking guy in a rustic restaurant. Everything is brown and wood stained. He's got an old t-shirt, unkempt hair, and a table full of empty wine bottles. I don't know what he is looking or pointing at. I don't think he does either.

The bottom right corner gives you two happy looking girls. Smiling wide, mouths open. Definitely not maintaining social distancing. I think the one girl has green hair. Hard to tell in the lighting. The flex band-aid on the pointer finger makes the shot. Must have been an old wound.

Moving across to the bottom left and there are two more girls. And that is definitely green hair this time. No doubt about it. It's matching her green eyes. Not sure what's up with the look on the other girl's face, but her index finger is about to be licked.

Zip over to the upper right and you got a guy who looks like a cross between a young Ryan Gosling and Keith Goforth, a guy I grew up with. He's got a backwards Penn State cap and sideburns from the 1990's. When Sandusky was still getting away with it. The shortie pointing is wearing green with a wrist covered in beaded bracelets and a thick yellow admission band. There's a party behind them, but the dude with the goatee isn't having any fun.

Return to the middle and there's a faded pic of a young man lounging on his inflatable mattress wearing camouflage cargo shorts. He's on the phone, smirking, giving us all the finger.

A fitting way to end this.

But seriously.

Who dat?

October 6th

As much as I try to keep my head up, above the surface, fully exposed to the atmosphere of reasonableness, I must admit to myself fully that I am a helpless, unrepentant, emotional and mental glutton.

There's no half-way with my heart. Or moderation in my mind.

It's all or nothing. Heaven or Hell.

A wildly out of control pendulum swinging back and forth. Leaving me focused on the illusion of stillness at the center. The middle way of the numb ineffectual.

You are an imposter among them.

All it takes is one dirty look or dismissive comment and the gates of Hell swing open. Suddenly all the forces are back aligned against you. Leaving you no choice but to put on your armor and dig in for a gallant defense.

But then a stranger shoots you a warm smile. Maybe even follows up with a flattering comment. And now all gridlock is cleared on the road to Heaven. You're already finalizing the wedding guestlist and worrying about how you will negotiate holidays with the family.

All or nothing. Heaven or Hell.

There's no half-way with your heart. Or moderation in your mind.

But a pendulum is a broken metaphor. If your students have taught you anything it's that binaries are dead.

You are not an out-of-control pendulum wildly swinging back and forth.

You are a gyroscope. Constant, controlled motion in all directions.

A Merkaba exploring space, time, and all dimensions.

A blue-collar Melchizedek.

Punching the clock. Going to work.

October 5th

I love how seemingly unrelated forces and circumstances crash into each other. Interacting and blending. Creating new stuff.

History. You got to love it. It's the Glass Bead Game, but inside of a pinball machine. With God controlling the flippers of thesis and antithesis. As Hegel keeps feeding the quarters.

It's like we're at the turn of the century. Waiting for a new moon in the Crescent City. The soldiers have all gone home. After the war. After the occupation. They leave the city. Reconstructed.

But they don't take their instruments with them. Leaving the city with military brass, but no military.

So the locals pick them up. But they're not out to recreate any battle hymns. They want their instruments to sound like the women singing praise at the church, or the men singing blues down the alley.

And they do. Creating a unique New Orleans brass sound to put on top of the ragtime syncopations of the day.

But then something really cool happens. Jim Crow invades the South on the back of Plessy v. Ferguson and separate but equal. Done are the days of creole musicians being allowed to play alongside white musicians.

They have no choice but to take their virtuosic skill and classical training and play with much darker local bands and musicians.

So what happens when you combine the unique style of New Orleans brass blowers with the technical proficiency of creole musicians?

You get a new moon.

Jazz.

Yet to be eclipsed.

October 4th

Ten-four, good buddy!

Get it? Today is October 4th, so it's ten, four. And isn't that what truckers say to each other over the CB radio. Ten-four, good buddy!

Pretty funny, right? It's like March 4th or May the fourth be with you. Something about the fourth of a month that makes you smile.

And I'm smiling right now, how about you? It's hard to tell with everybody wearing masks. The eyes can be very deceiving.

Sometimes I think that I'm lying to myself. Or people are lying to me. It's hard to tell anymore. I just know that none of this feels like the truth.

I was more productive this weekend than anybody on the planet. No corporate raiding, captain of industry would have even been able to keep up. I did all the work.

But there is still so much left undone. Making me feel like the biggest deadbeat on the planet.

And my family and friends honor and expect the deadbeat. Leaving the worker alone. Unrecognized and unvalidated.

So I give the people what they want. Who am I to disappoint?

Give them something to worry and whisper about. As I quietly blossom and flourish in secret.

Focused on my Maslow, while I'm busy Blooming.

Never updated their maps. Have yet to realize I left their continent.

Waiting alone in the new frontier.

Getting restless with the natives.

October 3rd

1- Currents: Wake up. Get off couch. Go upstairs to bathroom. Start shaving.

2- Serious Moonlight Sonatas: Finish shaving. Brush teeth. Take shower. Get dressed. Go downstairs. [Pause for daily Bible reading] Switch to car stereo. Drive to church. [Pause for church service] Drive from church to 7-11. [Pause to go to 7-11] Drive home from 7-11. Switch to home speaker. [Pause to call mom] Go upstairs. Changes clothes.

3- D:O Radio (Drummer Stream): Bowl #1 (Tatos-Matoes by the Roscoe Mitchell Art Ensemble). Go downstairs. Start writing this. Turn on computer. Set up tabs. Eat breakfast. Finish crossword puzzle. Bowl #2 (Dream Queen by the Bobby Hamilton Quintet). Set up therapist data templates for next week. Set up PLAAFP's templates for reports to be written next week. Forced to change PowerSchool password. Grade and record last week's homework. Determine game rolls for next week. Grade and record Chapter 8 for 8th grade. Grade and record Chapter 1 for 7th grade.

4- The Glen Jones Radio Programme: Pack lunch and snacks for tomorrow. Bowl #3 (You Gotta Have Heart by cast of Damn Yankees). Post Chapter 2 for 7th grade. Post next week's homework for all grades. Post "This Week in History Class" agendas for all classes. Eat lunch. Change kitchen garbage bag. Lesson plan for week of 10/18, all grades. Bowl #4 (Can You Dig It? by Pop Will Eat Itself. [Pause to add song to playlist] New incognito window. Abby Winters. Bridget. Release. Create formal lesson plans for week of 10/18. Submit formal lesson and unit plans to principal. [Pause to pray]

5- Paul Bruno: Bowl #5 (Like a Buoy by Roxy Girls). Watch the guy out the window doing yardwork. Put together agenda for social studies department meeting on 10/13. Schedule Zoom meeting and get invite link. E-mail agenda to supervisor for approval.

6- Ritual Music (Drummer Stream): Cut finger and toenails. Put together slide show for 8th grade Chapter 9 bonus lesson on the Curse of Tippecanoe. Bowl #6 (Dazed and Confused by Jake Holmes). Print out short stories for Monday's 7th and 8th grade English classes. Ignore call from Russ. Sign up with what to bring for the multicultural feast on the 13th (pasta with garlic and oil from Valentino's). [Pause to listen to one minute, 15-second-long voicemail from Russ] Hit some homeruns. Eat an entire container of Bhu Keto Cookie Dough while drinking kombucha and brainstorming ideas for Thursday's mentoring meeting. Create worksheet for Thursday's mentoring meeting based on Wilber's four quadrants. Play the Bible word puzzle game. Hit some more homeruns. [Pause to pray]

7– *Gaylord Fields:* Bowl #7 (All Over the World by Francoise Hardy). New incognito window. Abby Winters. Priya. Satiation. Shut down computer. Pack up work bag for tomorrow. Retire to the couch.

8– *Rock and Roller Derby:* Reread this. Bowl #8 (Love and Food by Tenpole Tudor). Eat Coca-Cola flavored Tic Tac's. Hit the rest of the homeruns. Read some memes on Funny Pics. Call it a night.

October 2nd

I ordered shrimp egg foo young but got broccoli and mixed vegetables instead. Story of my life. Instead of getting what I want, I get something that I also like and is probably better for me.

The Universe has my back.

Pronoia is the antidote for paranoia. The forces aren't conspiring to pull you down, they're conspiring to lift you up.

The Illuminati has our backs.

While their drums keep pounding a rhythm to the brain.

And the beat goes on.

Watching Count Me In. After telling my brother to count me out. Because my heart has already had all the venom it could take for one lifetime.

But there's no way to explain that to him. Especially over text.

So I light some more fires. And burn some more trees. Hoping to allow the sun to shine through.

Eating almond-lace cookies. Both dark chocolate and white. With milk straight from the cow.

Watching another doc. When I should probably go see one. But ain't nobody got time for that.

Pondering the malice at the palace. It was a riot. With nobody laughing.

Except John Green.

Throwing water cups inside paper towns.

A crash course in mental illness.

All over. Race.

October 1st

September is over, but every part of me wants to keep sleeping in. Except the part of me that never went to bed. That part is limping across the finish line of a race he didn't know he was running.

And someone just put a medal around my neck.

On this planet, participation isn't just mandatory, it's downright heroic.

As I keep sowing the seeds of love. Like when I was a kid. When everybody wanted to rule the world. And the soil wasn't nearly as rocky.

Learning to fight my fears. And surrender to my tears. Two of the hardest things for a human being to do.

I keep trying the best I can. But it's not getting any easier.

Still too many fears. And not enough tears.

Praying for release. Imprisoned by the feelings that scare me. Held back by all I'm holding back.

I'm not ready. You're not ready. The world's not ready.

The river of excuses spinning the water frame of decay and denial.

Depression. Despair. Shame. Sorrow. Grief. Anger.

Interchangeable parts mass produced in the sweat shops of the mind.

And I'm ready to clock out.

Return to the farm.

Hunt hope. Gather grace.

Turn off the brain and get my hands dirty.

September 30th

I've been watching a lot of Six Feet Under lately. Trying to work my way through the series. When it was first on, I only made it through the first three seasons. And then everybody kept saying how the series finale was the greatest thing ever. Especially Russ.

So here I am. Halfway through season four. Breaking new ground.

I was going slow for a while. An episode a night. Trying to savor, but then once Dwight Schrute showed up in season three, I started picking up the pace. I'm in full-on binge mode now. I should be through it by early next week. Not exactly hate-watching, but I'm definitely ready for it to be over.

Six Feet Under was the first series that really showed me what television could be. For most it was the Sopranos. For me it was the Fishers.

That's why I'm making it my walk-off.

Make my first, my last, and my last, my first. Enjoying what is left, but ready to leave this stage. And leave behind all that went with it that no longer serves me.

Transcend and include.

The only way out of this low place I'm in.

Crawling my way to comfortable.

Making another sacrifice on the altar.

Might as well be this.

Isn't that right, buddy boy?

September 29th

My mere presence seems to be a threat to a lot of people. I'll never quite understand why. I think it's because I've been here a long time. I've seen a lot. And I remember all of it.

It's the remembering that gets me in the most trouble, though.

When we all create our life stories in our heads there's a significant degree of denial and missing information involved. And polite society is designed for us all to enable each other to live with our lies and hatred of truth.

Then someone like me comes along waving a spotlight carelessly around like a bull in a China shop. And all the creatures of the night either scatter and hide or gather for the attack.

And lately there has been more attacking than hiding. These times are certainly emboldening them. And it's my allies that are the ones hiding.

Leaving me all alone. With my shadow.

How am I supposed to integrate something that goes all the way to the bottom? It's literally like raising Hell until it becomes Heaven.

Is it even possible? And what would we be left with if it was?

A multiverse of confusion. A convoluted universe.

Dolores Cannon was right.

It's turtles all the way down. And hares all the way up.

It's a race no one can win.

So stop running.

September 28th

My kitchen garbage can broke the other day. You know that pedal you step on to make the lid open? Yeah, that doesn't work anymore. You just step on it, and nothing happens.

Technically it still functions as a trash receptacle, but it is annoying having to lift the lid open with my hands anytime I need to use it. Eventually I should probably get a new one. If anything, to prevent my quality of life from slipping any more than it has been recently.

But I've had this garbage can for a long time. Nineteen years to be exact. I got it when I first moved to the Bronx. It was my kitchen garbage can then, it's my kitchen garbage can now. But in all the places I lived in between, it was just my garbage can.

I call it the Masta Killa because it has a Masta Killa sticker on its lid. It's from when I saw Masta Killa at B.B. King's. Promoting No Said Date. Papa Wu was not happy with us that night. Our fault for passing flyers saying I'm the real RZA.

Luckily, I smoothed things over with him. Even got 'em to sign a Palermo Dollar. We were young and dumb back then, though. Young and dumb.

Now I'm old and dumb. And my kitchen garbage can is broken.

Can't even go to Bed, Bath, and Beyond anymore because that's been shut down a couple years now. You can tell by the decrease of junk mail.

I guess I'll go to Target. I pretty much go there for everything nowadays. Simplifies things. May not have the best selection, but I don't want to have to deal with the anxiety of Home Depot just to get a garbage can.

I'm just looking for one a little wider. Masta Killa was a bit too narrow. Made it tough to pull the bag out of it when it was filled. And a working pedal. Has to have a working pedal.

Anyone know how much a good kitchen garbage can costs?

It's been a while.

September 27th

They can't get me here. With their hate, and disappointment, and criticism, and rejection. Their constant rejection. Of everything you are and everything you hold dear.

They don't want that. They don't want you.

You are nothing to them. Just an errand boy. Or a sounding board. A bit-player in their self-centered, ego-driven dramas.

Know your role and speak your lines. Otherwise there's no room for you on their stage.

And remember. This is your family.

These are the people that are supposed to care and nurture you. Help clear a path for you in this world. Love you unconditionally.

But you get none of that, do you?

They are disgusted by you. Don't know what to say to you. Go out of their way to avoid you.

And why? What was your great sin?

You dared to forge your own path, reminding them how trapped they are. You dared to strive for greatness, reminding them how they settled for mediocrity. You dared to believe, reminding them of their lack of faith.

You keep growing, reminding them of their stagnation.

How dare you.

Escape. When we're all still stuck here.

Remember. This is your family.

But they can't get you here.

You are safe.

September 26th

There are too many people here. A cyclone of noise and activity. The biggest kickball game I've ever seen. And I don't know how to make sense of any of it.

I thought a change of scenery would help. But it didn't. It made things worse. More complex patterns to decipher. Lost in the chaos.

And I just learned that help won't be on its way.

But this is my park. So let's start acting like it.

Ok, that didn't work. I guess this really isn't my park. At least not today. Not right now. I am being outranked. And that's tough for me to admit.

I'm still helplessly hovering around my entry-point. Not sure if or when I'll go in. Biding my time. As the kickballers cheer. And the priest awkwardly waits. I'm definitely not bringing my notebook this time around.

Here we go.

And I'm back. Unsuccessful. Defeated by delusional expectations mixed with social anxiety. A combination that'll get you every time. Like it just got me.

I was due for a defeat, though. It's what necessary to turn a magical winning streak into sustainable long-term success. With a natural flow of ups and downs.

That's what today was. A small imperceptible ebb in the eternal upward flow towards perfection.

It's because I didn't know there'd be so many kids here.

I forget it's their world.

My time has passed.

September 25th

Beige food.

My principal gets all the literary credit for putting those two words together.

Beige food.

As a writer I consider it one of the most poetically descriptive couplings of words every rescued from the noosphere.

Beige food.

Every year during the first month of school we take a field trip to Dave & Busters. It's a great team-building time for kids to play games all day. And then around noon we all meet up for the free buffet lunch.

Beige food.

Hamburger sliders. Chicken fingers. Mac & cheese. French fries. Small personal pizzas. Honey mustard. Ketchup.

Beige food.

The perfect description for what we all pile onto our plates from the silver sterno-heated trays. My ego is jealous that I didn't think of it first.

Beige food.

Now I'm not always good at reading the energy of individual people, but I'm definitely sensitive when it comes to feeling rooms. And let me tall ya, as we all eat our lunch it's like a fog begins to descend. And the energy of the room just drops.

Beige food.

Kids start fighting with each other. Breakdowns happen. Teachers get snippy. That's when I just grab a group of kids and head out to the mall for the rest of the trip. Blow that scene.

Beige food.

The smart teachers ask for the gluten-free option.

September 24th

No one whose job is to take care of other human beings should have to suffer the indignity of being paid hourly wages.

When you're a caregiver, you're always on the clock. If you're not with them, they're with you. If not in your head, always in your heart.

There's no punching out from that. So pay them for the time served.

But I'm willing to take it up a notch and say that no one, regardless of what they do, should have to suffer the indignity of being paid hourly wages.

The whole system is based on the mistrust of the working class by the rich. And seriously, it's the rich that are messing up this place, so who you really gonna trust?

And if we're the working class, what exactly is it that the rich are doing? You can't really call it work, and I don't see a whole lot of class. Just a bunch of people disconnected from the truth of this world.

I always say it. God gives money to those who aren't strong enough to be poor. And to those who are, he gives grace. Which would you rather have?

I made my choice, and I'm not afraid to let my prejudices show.

I don't judge people by the color of their skin, but by their collar.

Or the content of their wallets.

So you better have a donor card.

'Cause you ain't taking any of it with you.

September 23rd

Ambivalence is poison for art.

An imaginary art teacher on a fictional show said those words to his pretend students. They seemed very meaningful at the time I first heard them. I even wrote them in big capital letters and underlined each word three times.

My Aunt Jo used to do that on greeting cards. She would send those generic birthday cards with generic little messages inside. But she would underline each word of the message two or three times to show that she didn't just pick out a random card with a random corny sentiment. Aunt Jo fully endorsed every word of every greeting card she ever sent. Her underlines proved that.

So I guess that's what my underlines mean. That I fully endorse the statement.

Ambivalence is poison for art.

But now that I think about it more, I don't know if I feel the same way as when I first heard it.

Ambivalence is defined as having mixed feelings or contradictory ideas about something or someone.

So yeah, I see how that makes sense. A decisive person with a clearly defined world view is going to be able to produce some pretty striking art.

But couldn't someone else use their art to work through and reflect their ambivalence toward the many grey areas that crowd the palette of life?

I would definitely be interested in what they produce.

So I guess I'm more ambivalent than I thought about the statement, ambivalence is poison for art.

But there is one thing I am not ambivalent about.

Calling anything poison for art is poison for art.

Underline that.

September 22nd

I like to create mazes for my students to work through. But not those big scary mazes that you can get lost in. More like a labyrinth. A lot of twists and turns. But no wrong way to go through it.

I also add some obstacles to my mazes. Nothing too intimidating. I'm not training Navy Seals or anything. Just some small things to jump over, duck under, or skip across.

I then take a little time at the beginning to show the maze to my students and explain everything they need to do to reach the end.

Finally, I step aside. And let the students freely explore. Gently guiding them from behind if they need it.

The funny thing is that I don't have to put anything at the end of my mazes. Like a prize or something. Kids just like going through mazes. And reaching the end is a reward in itself.

Other teachers do things differently. A lot of them also make mazes. And usually much more sophisticated and complex than the ones I throw together. But instead of gently guiding from behind, many teachers try to forcibly pull their students through from the front.

That's not fun for anybody.

But there's a lot of pressure to get kids through mazes, so I get it.

Some teachers don't even make mazes, though. They just stand in a wide-open field and expect students to all go in the direction they want them to go. Usually starting with gentle coaxing before devolving to barking out threats.

I've never seen this way work. No matter how good the students.

Because without walls. Without structure. Without clearly defined paths. What do you got?

Nothing.

September 21ˢᵗ

Just a thought away. All of it. Just a thought away. Joy. Depression. A good day. A bad day. Heaven. Hell. Just a thought away.

What a precarious situation we all find ourselves in. Slaves to the fickle whims of neural chemistry. A seesaw of sporadic sparks of sentience. Each one leaving you inhabiting an entirely different world.

Where will you end up next? When no one out there is willing to throw you an anchor. Waving and smiling as you drift on by. Nobody has room for you in their lifeboats. So the precipice is your fate.

Chasing waterfalls for too long. Now you can't escape their pull.

Trying to think your way into calm waters. Yeah, good luck with that.

Forgiveness. Surrender. And release. All also just a thought away. Let me know how that goes for you.

Seriously, just gimme shelter. Isn't that what this is all about, anyway? Finding a place to be?

A place where I belong. A place where I am safe. A place where they can't get to me.

Gimme shelter.

I don't deserve to be neglected. I don't deserve to be abandoned. I don't deserve to be left for dead.

I'm here too.

Find me. Rescue me. Shelter me.

I'm just a thought away.

September 20th

This is the alpha point. This is the omega point. Of all your patterns. Of all your cycles. Of all your routines. This is where they start. This is where they finish. There is no advancing from right here, right now.

But you already knew that, didn't you?

You're still trying to get used to the shock every time the rubber band snaps back. Like you were actually going to reach new ground this time. New frontiers are just the illusions of worn-out elasticity.

The Universe will always bring you back. It's the way of the heart. So don't be so blue. Traveler.

As the little deer walks precariously around the roulette wheel.

There is only one zero, so these cuff links must be European. As if Americans wear cuff links anymore, anyway. They're probably considered toxic.

The long hair in the baggy clothes is the power that be. The gentleman that's tailored and groomed is breaking all the rules.

An outlaw of order in times of chaos.

The poles have already been reversed. Stop the prepping. There will be no fanfare or days of darkness. They were all just metaphors, anyway. Everything is. Just metaphors.

What you see is what you get.

The rest is just creations of broken psyches and fevered egos.

I see God. I see love. I see me.

No need to look for anything else.

September 19th

In my better days I would have had no problem keeping up with her. Hell, in my prime I would have finished ahead of her and cheered her on as she crossed the finish line. Chatting her up with mutual runner highs and flirty eyes. You know how it was.

Damn. If she had been in Edison. All bets would have been off. As would the yoga pants.

But I guess I'm past my prime. I guess these aren't my better days. Because she had already collected her belongings and left before I crossed the finish line. So much for the pre-race vibes.

And I guess the fortune teller was wrong. Because she's still torn. And we got lost among the bricks.

All complaining aside, though. What a beautiful day. Summer is not over yet. And it's still not quite time to bring in the harvest.

So don't get hung up on missed connections. You'll get what's coming to ya. You can't avoid that.

But, man, what a plate you have ahead of you to clear. All your favorites. And you barely even got started. Save room for dessert. It's just.

Make your Nana proud. Your life is the answer to her prayers.

Make your Pop Pop smile. Your life is the fruit of his labors.

Do right by your parents. Your life is the justification for their sacrifices.

That was the race you were running this morning. For them.

She was just a footnote.

September 18th

Not quite sure about this reality I stepped into. How 'bout the rest of yous? Not sure if I'll be able to sustain this.

But of course I will. Because that's all I know how to do. Win or lose.

As the sun peaks from the clouds. Bursts through the window. And pours heat on the back of my exposed neck.

Illuminating the page as I write through the golden hour.

Call me The Natural. Roy Hobbs with his Wonderboy. Smashing the glowing façade. Like a bolt of lightning. Redemption earned. Without wasting a swing.

My Jesus figure before Jesus figured in my life. And the movie had a happier ending than the book. So go figure.

As I find myself further ahead than I ever was before. Yet I feel so far behind. Because I am. Simultaneously ahead and behind. The paradox of a workaholic. And I've had stranger addictions.

The church bells will ring in less than an hour. And my hands are still dirty.

The communal well has been drained. So I have nowhere left to soak them.

Except in my own inner source and spring. As I learn to adjust to the flow.

Thanks to family and friends.

I am swimming in change.

September 17th

A role-reversal. One sits and waits and stews. While the other is already where he belongs. Guided by voices. That came just at the right time.

Taking the scenic route. As if you haven't seen enough. Just trying to unlock new mental maps as you continue to see how everything connects.

Corridors of counties with their many corners. If there is a fork in the road, take it. It's the only way to avoid the jack knife.

Autobiography of a Yogi. And I'm still waiting here alone with my picnic basket. And spacious blanket. For somebody. All my life.

Soundtrack for the singles. Looking for a replacement for the solitude and monotony. That can't be found on an app. So put down your phone.

Hang up and listen to the warning signs. As the consequences of poorly thought-out decisions begin to bubble up. You won't be able to ignore this for long.

Temporary mouth pleasure bought at the price of intestinal agony.

The hell of the hedonist.

But you still insist on serving two masters. So what did you expect?

Just be happy that the one can keep the other in line. Because you sure as well can't.

So stop trying and surrender to our gentle guidance.

It's what got you here. Now.

Where you are. Welcome.

September 16th

Crashed right back down to earth. With a rush to the head and a blow to the shoulder. Humbled again. With all my talk about the fourth dimension, the third got jealous. Wanted me to feel it.

So I am. Feeling it.

And now I will work. Through it.

The only way to make the long haul.

The roller coaster is fully in free fall. There is no stopping it. There is no getting off. Not until the end.

And I'm ok with that. I kind of like my view.

Speaking in front of a joint session of Congress. About the state of the union. Which is strong.

Like my weakness.

A short saying oft contains much wisdom. Your patience has the ability to test even the sands of time.

In bed.

While I continue to sleep in a love seat. And wonder why I ache. The hubris of the humble. The price I pay to stay grounded. Well worth it.

Like dubsteps and dragons. Unicorns and fairies. I thought they were mythical. Until I got pierced in the heart.

Leaking out the gut. As I reached the final four. This is what the kids call grinding. Putting in the work. To earn the higher levels.

Like Jane McGonigal said.

Reality is broken.

September 15th

A comedian died yesterday. I think it was in California, but I could be wrong. All I know for sure is that the world is a lot less funny today.

I always had a pull towards comedy. Comedians were the first people who critically broke down the world for me and showed me its inner workings.

First Carlin. Then Hicks. Discovered Gregory a little after that. But each could be categorized as suffering from irony fatigue. An affliction I made my career goal to avoid.

But there was one whose irony was so subtle and exacting, that fatigue seemed impossible. And now he is dead. So I guess so is irony. Like they've been warning us for so long.

Dear Norm.

Thank you for taking on the burden of being you. You played the part to perfection. For most of my life I considered you the funniest person on the planet. For the rest of my life I will consider you the funniest person to have ever been on the planet. I have complete confidence that you will hold that title throughout eternity. Because, unfortunately, this world will not allow another Norm MacDonald. Just like it will not allow another Christ. One individual containing that much humor- or that much love- is too much of a threat to the false prophets focused on their false profits to be allowed.

But just like the love of Christ, the humor of Norm is not lost to this world. It will live on and be spread by all those who were touched by it while he was still alive. And while Norm MacDonald the individual will not be returning to this Earth, his humor will return to all those willing to open their hearts and souls to it.

So I pray to you Norm. Please supply me an ample dose of your humor and insight and guide me to use it to bring the same level of joy into the world that you did. Thank you.

And now the fake news..

September 14th

You forget how broken this place can feel. Like everything is falling down around you. Leaving you no choice but to make your stand as you dodge the crumbling rubble.

You forget that this is not the norm. You forget that there is no norm. You forget that they see you as a blank white sheet walking around with all their horrors and failures projected on to it.

You would avoid yourself too if you saw what they saw.

But you don't

You don't see anything. You just feel.

You feel your feelings. Desperately hanging on. Calling out to God. Pleading to be kept on the path to the Kingdom.

But you feel their feelings too. Savagely dragging you down. Scorched by the heat of their personal hells. Locked in their self-imposed prisons.

As the keys rust from lack of use.

Take a look around. What do you see?

Is this where you want to make your stand?

Take a look around. What do you feel?

Can you separate the illusions from the delusions?

Take a look around.

This is your job.

So put in a good day's work.

And then go home.

September 13th

Walking-in to a fried battery. What a way to start a Monday. I must have left it exposed to the heat for too long. And it wasn't even that hot this weekend. Everything is just way too fragile nowadays. And everybody.

Myself included.

Sensitive thugs. We all need hugs.

Skin hunger. Soul hunger. Heart hunger. I don't care anymore. Just touch me anywhere.

Take me on a mind walk like Jack McCoy and Liv Ullmann. Let's solve all the problems of the world. Or find me a Jill Scott. To take to Tourne Park. After dark. Reach the top and then spark. Calling me a rich man.

But I am wretched, pitiful, poor, blind, and naked. Just doing the best I can with what I have been left with.

Overflowing with emptiness. A deluge of doubt. I would be nothing without my faith.

So I'm not letting go of it. Hanging on like Sloopy. Faking it until I make it. Centuries since the great commission of Pentecost and the imposter syndrome still lingers.

But if this isn't real, nothing is. So I guess I'm all in.

The only way to play.

Ante up.

It's dealer's choice.

September 12th

Sunday morning and I'm back at the office. Even God took a day off. But there is no rest for the wicked. And I wicked love coming to Starbucks to get schoolwork done, people watch, and soak in the beautiful sounds of machines whirring, orders being called out, and ambient music seeping out the ceiling speakers.

So let's take a sip and get started.

This is definitely turning into one of those work sessions where, as I cross one thing off the list, I think of three more to add. No worries, though. I planned for the long haul.

Finally something to pique my interest. I can see her through the corner of my left eye. Young, but very studious. Self-assured. Also a lady diagonally to my right. More age appropriate. And classy. But not here for the long haul. Billie Eilish is singing about her future. I am insufferable.

As the dad handing his adorable daughter a cake pop mocks my current life situation. What a disappointment it all is.

But better than I ever expected.

All at the same time.

At a nice impasse. Making good progress. Time for a break. Eat a travel waffle. Hit some homeruns. Clear out email inbox of marketing detritus. Shoot a text to my brother. Take a few more sips.

I forgot how much I like this place on a Sunday afternoon during football season. Only the diehards.

Ok. Back to work. Time to cross something off the list I've been putting off most of the summer.

Mission accomplished. The list is no more. But there is still a lot of work to get done.

Just trying to keep my head above water.

When I never learned to swim.

September 11th

I'm in love with the girl on the radio. All of them. The guys too. All of them. And anybody in between or beyond. I love you too. All of you.

And if you're interpreting my words in some sort of sexual or even romantic way. That's on you. I ain't talking about that stuff. I'm talking about love.

I love the guy pumping my gas. I love the grumpy lady who works at the laundromat. I love the garbage truck driver who deliberately blocks my path. I love that cute girl who works at Whole Foods. I love that ugly dude who works at Foodtown. I love the guys at Sal's. I love Yusuf and Ibrahim at OneUnited. I love Steve at Funny Books. I love the girl at 7-11. And the one before her. Her sister too. Used to always see her running around town.

I love all the obvious people too, of course. Love my family. Love my friends. Love my enemies. Love my acquaintances. Love my strangers. Love my students. Love my coworkers. Love my bosses. If you are in my life, I love you too. All of you.

In my web of the Universe, love is 2Easy.com. Twenty-four, seven, three hundred sixty-five and one quarter. The heart remains open. There are no holidays. No days off. No vacations.

I know no other way to live.

And trust me, all the other stuff of life is so damn hard for me. But not love. That's simple.

At work I wear a key chain around my neck that's a smiley face emoji with hearts as eyes. It's for my students to know what I'm feeling when I look at them and all the world around me.

Nothing but love.

Yet remember what it says in the Tao. The greatest love often seems indifferent.

Keep that in mind as I continue to walk by you with that blank, far-away look on my face.

I still love you.

September 10th

I had an idea earlier, but I lost it. I've been doing that a lot lately. It seems my mental grip has been loosening. I don't necessarily think that's a bad thing, though. As thoughts and feelings come and go. No longer under any obligation to stick around anymore. Probably because I'm not as welcoming and hospitable to them as I was in the past.

But the ones worth sticking around, always seem to do. Until I mold a reality around them. And provide a forever home.

I'm a sucker for rescuing all the strays scavenging around the noosphere. A crazy cat lady of the mind. My corpse destined to be picked apart by those I'm currently caring for and tending to.

But I'm ok with that.

We all knew what we were signing up for when we boarded the Sloop John B. And has this trip really been that bad?

Says the guy playing in the band. As everyone else seems to be desperately bailing water. Or struggling to get a spot in a raft.

All futile acts.

Nobody escapes the flood. Peter Gabriel warned us about that. We are all characters living in a Jackson Browne song.

Running on empty.

Before the deluge.

September 9th

Updates seem to always come at the most inconvenient time. And I never notice the changes afterwards, anyway. Just seems like a lot of unnecessary wheel spinning.

But isn't that what most of this is? A lot of unnecessary wheel spinning. As I present to you today's analogy of depression and despair. Created in the looms of my mind. And let me tell you, that place is a real sweatshop.

It's why you'll find me hiding underneath the rug. Where all the problems are swept. With the sleeping machines and lifeless humans.

Nothing ever changes. Except tolerance, rationalization, and denial. They age like a fine wine. Making the most bitter of vinegars taste sweet.

And you've been getting a lot of that lately. Bitter vinegar. As the watchmen poke and prod you. While the lawless mock in derision.

An all too familiar scene.

Pouring dampness down in the stream. As the frog and leopard engage on the chessboard of flux. Where the sun and moon dance. And the flowers have eyes.

The images I start my day with. Sights and sounds incongruous with a consensual reality I never agreed to.

An unwanted irritant in a world of dirty clothes that rather not be cleansed.

Humanity is an emotionally stunted bachelor.

And it is not good that man should be alone.

September 8th

Man, that was certainly a stretch. And I once again emerge on the other side of it. Expected to be unchanged. Yet so very different.

I like to think I handled things as flawlessly as possible. Like I stuck the landing and all that. But I don't know anymore. Things are happening so fast. I'm just trying to stay out of the way of the unravelling scroll. And not get too caught up in the parts I contributed to it.

I guess I expected a little more. But I'm always expecting a little more. Never completely satisfied. Like not a full-on parade or anything, but maybe a little more of a celebration or a victory lap.

There's nobody left to run with anymore. Which makes victory laps difficult. And people are too shocked and challenged by you to know how to celebrate with you.

You're pretty much on your own from now on.

Take your recognition where you can get it. As you reach greater levels of clarity within your world, you will appear increasingly blurry to the world outside of you.

Playing to the band and preaching to the choir. Noble pursuits. But not what the paying customers came to hear. So be surprised not by all the deaf ears.

The pressure has cracked the drums.

The rhythm has been lost.

Leaving the prophets and madmen dancing.

To music nobody hears.

September 7th

-If you haven't found something strange during the day, it hasn't been much of a day.
-Morning garbage man, garbagios.
-Do the wretched refuse shuffle?
-Time to get stuck into some good garbage.
-This ambient stuff is perfect for my morning back in the office.
-Shall we stir up affective reactions?
-That guy RADIATED the strange.
-What will Friday mornings hold for us?
-I'm personally sad.
-We're gonna be OK.
-There's hope for this world.
-Exiled to the far reaches of the universe.
-Yeah, weird Miracle Nutrition got moved.
-We give what we can.
-The music is good.
-Garbage man making me melon collie.
-How's that going?
-This is amazing..
-Doing isometric exercises, dreaming of cryptocurrency.
-Headed straight to Bandcamp.
-What a glorious version.
-Everything is super—pending info on why.
-That brought me a surprising sense of relief.
-Thnx for playing.
-A broken clock stuck on 9:42.
-Not what Meatloaf had in mind.
-All hearts right here. All hearts.
-That's what the great spirit wants, right?
-Peace be with you, my friends.
-And now..
-Let all dissolve
-Celebrate
-Fly from my ears
-To the universe
-So say we all!!!
-Yah!

-The horror. The horror.

September 6th

The morning after. A stomach filled with throwing caution to the wind. A tempest preparing for the journey down through the intestines.

It was all worth it. Necessary digressions to demonstrate the faithfulness of well-established patterns.

Waking up after a night sleeping on the floor. A balled-up sweat-shirt as a pillow. Days after my words were broadcast to the world. My greatest victory.

This is how I stay humble. Beats the alternative.

Returning to the theme of toiling away in obscurity. Perfect for a Labor Day.

When even your friends are willing to ensure you anonymity. Instead of dancing in your light. Throwing mud on the glow. While snoring the self-absorbed sleep of the avoidant.

We don't need your education. Teacher, leave us kids alone.

Or we will stuff you with our meat and pudding. Until you are overflowing. And choking on the bile.

While you wait on the invisible hand to guide you to your community. Instead of being an irritant in everybody else's.

Ready to work on your play so you can play at your work.

I'm going through Earth changes. We all are.

And it's going to be a different trip for each of us.

Recognize that above all else.

So you can exude the awakened compassion.

The true joy of being.

Together.

September 5th

It happens after a few years. The speakers start to go. You lose the higher frequencies.

As I drum along to the Josie and the Pussycats soundtrack. Blaring out the speakers of Dave's Prius. Written by the guy who died from Fountains of Wayne. A little music trivia.

Delicately scoffing down a couple chili dogs from Hiram's in Fort Lee. Trying not to get any on my Charles Bukowski t-shirt. But secretly wishing I did.

I waited at the counter of a white restaurant for eleven years. When they finally integrated, they didn't have what I wanted.

Dick Gregory capturing the spirit of disappointment made inevitable by the eager anticipation of those living every day for the New Jerusalem.

The sourest grapes in the Garden of Gethsemane.

I really do believe he had missions to accomplish. And it wasn't just telling jokes.

The monster. As we discovered in a sophomore year writing workshop. With Joan Weimer. And Phaedra. And Lelah's budding breasts.

I hope she never reads this. But secretly wishes she does.

Or at least Sean Hooks.

If he hasn't been canceled yet. Or me too'd.

A man unprepared for the times.

Is no man at all.

Beard or no beard.

September 4th

Day one of a two day stretch of bonus days. Yesterday was Friday and it won't be Saturday until Monday. I'm loving this back-to-back Labor Day/Rosh Hashanah four-day weekend package deal. I can't remember it ever happening before.

Took a nap until noon, but still got my laundry and a little schoolwork done. Plus I'll be seeing some minor league soccer tonight with my family. Perfect weather for it.

This is what I call living.

Listening to the drummer stream. Faces of a thousand hymns. If this ain't music for a free world, I don't know what is.

Tomorrow I'll be hanging out with my boys. But I gotta stop thinking about tomorrow. There's still a lot of today to live.

Be here. Now. As much as I can.

That's my goal for this schoolyear. And karma for this lifetime.

Alan Watts the frequency, Kenneth? You said that irony was the shackles of youth. And I couldn't help but to agree. So I threw them off before I fatigued.

And now I better do as I am told. I better listen to the radio.

The voice of reason.

Wonderful. Marvelous.

Wonderful.

September 3rd

I sit and wait. Listening to one of the most beautiful pieces of music I ever heard. I'm not anxious, but I'd be lying if I said I wasn't nervous. Like I feel fine, but if I just spontaneously threw up at some point, I wouldn't be surprised at all.

When you're toiling away in obscurity you fool yourself into believing that your biggest wish is to be known. For people to finally know who you are and what you have to offer. Well-earned recognition.

After a small taste of that recognition, and a potentially bigger taste up ahead, I don't know if that is my biggest wish anymore. Maybe my biggest wish is actually to be allowed to toil away. In obscurity.

Or maybe I'm just scared.

Even though this is St. Gregory's Day, first respects are given to St. James. And rightfully so. But there was no crip in him. Just all blood. A true master of the Universe.

And just like that it came and went. As I was busily frying eggs. No big deal. But exceeding all my expectations.

That should hold me over for a while.

Is it wrong that I'm hiding out here in obscurity as my fifteen minutes unfolds? I don't think it's wrong. So it's not.

I want this perfect object to exist forever in the archives. Completely devoid of my influence.

Haven't I done enough?

Yes, you did.

September 2nd

When two Doug's meet. At first, they are happy, even relieved. Since they know that all Doug's are inherently good people and it's always good to meet another good person. But then the jealously and suspicion kicks in. Because Doug's thrive on being the only Doug. It's such a dying name. So two Doug's cannot be in close proximity for too long. One always would have to yield.

Hello thoughts, my old friends. I've come to write with you again.

Swept away in the storm of Alice Coltrane. I smell trouble. 'Cause Tom Tomorrow could never play the harp like that.

My cup runneth over and I don't know what to do. Good problems to have.

Neil Gaiman said that the world always seems brighter when you've just made something that wasn't there before. That's what I did today. I made something that wasn't there before. And man, was it luminous.

Carl Michael Von Hausswolff's December 3rd should not be confused with Jay-Z's December 4th. And vice versa. But they are both Brooklyn strong.

I think it's time to take a break from my homework so I can get my other homework done.

This is an entire movie about expelling gas. I think that's why people like it.

If Hearty White and Anytime Hybrid got into a fight, I'm pretty sure Hearty White would win. But Anytime Hybrid would feel better about himself the next day.

These are thoughts from my upcoming book: Ayahuasca Enemas for the Soul. Holiday Edition! Featuring The Grinch and SFV Elf OG.

A nighttime indica.

As I bid you all goodnight.

September 1st

Whatever I'm feeling and thinking now, on day one, is going to be nowhere near what I'm feeling and thinking in a month, let alone on the last day. So is there really any point in feeling and thinking it?

Just seems like wasted energy. And I got to start conserving that stuff. I ain't getting any younger.

It's like when I played in that doubles round-robin way out in Mt. Olive. These old dudes knew exactly how to get where they needed to be on the court with the least steps and effort needed. Maximized efficiency. Meanwhile I was running from corner to corner, huffing and puffing, scrambling around like the young fool that I was.

I learned a lot from those guys. And now it's time to apply what I learned from them inside the classroom.

No more wasted energy.

And not the wasted physical energy of a tennis match. But the emotional and mental drain of teaching.

Get to where you need to be in your heart and in your head with the least steps and effort needed.

Maximized efficiency.

Just like those old dudes. 'Cause not only do I still plan on playing tennis when I'm their age, I also still plan on being in front of the classroom.

There's no reason not to be.

It's my serve.

August 31ˢᵗ

I'll just say it once so I can put it in the records, but the four horsemen of our current apocalypse are Big Tech, Big Pharma, Big Government, and Big Media.

Ok, now that I got that out there, let's move on. Because it's time to move on, I want to move on, I think I'm ready to move on. It's not about putting things in the basket anymore. It's about taking them out.

Like chess. That's out. I'll still play it with my kids, but I don't need to study it. It's just not how I want to see the world anymore. The world ain't black and white and I don't always have to be on my guard trying to outmaneuver everyone. Setting traps. Making unnecessary sacrifices. That doesn't serve me anymore.

Same with fighting. How can I go around calling myself a pacifist and saying I don't believe in violence, when my favorite sport is the UFC? It doesn't add up. I was deluding myself, focusing so much on the art, that I forgot what martial means. Plus I was turning into a counterpuncher. Nobody likes those. Definitely time to tap.

And I can't end this without tossing out pornography as well. I just can't justify it anymore. No matter how wholesome and soft-core it appears, lust is still lust. One of the deadlies. Plus I have nieces and teach girls. So seriously, shame on me.

But I ain't getting rid of everything. Doug is still Doug. At least for now. So I'm still getting high. I'm still joking about whatever. No boundaries. And I'm still staying true to my blue-collar roots.

The more you leave the ground. The more you see the greed, incompetence, and self-interest.

The saints are in the classroom, on the assembly line, and working the floor.

That's my number.

August 30th

I wish I could tell you definitely which one is Sonny, and which one is Hawk, but I'd be lying. I'm pretty sure that was Sonny just now. I'm way more familiar with his voice. But I'm not willing to go all in on it.

But put Carlos in a lineup with every guitarist on the planet and I'd be able to pick him out every time. Even Frank Zappa. He may have unlocked the mysteries of the secret Santana chord progression, but that doesn't mean the angels come dancing every time he plays it.

It ain't what or how you play, it's where you're playing it from. That's what the angels respond to.

The same goes for teaching.

It ain't what or how you teach, it's where you're teaching it from. That's what the students respond to.

Don't let anybody make you feel differently. Even Robert Marzano with all his models and scales and rubrics and data and such would have to agree.

Teaching is all art, even when it's a science.

As Somerset County teacher of the year Darren Wolsko said, "What I do feel a moral imperative to provide is that my students know what my heart is."

So whatever your art is. Make sure they know what your heart is. Whether it's playing guitar or teaching kids. Just show 'em your heart.

You're not here for you. You're here for them.

And then we can do the science.

August 29th

I waited until the roll was double sevens
Then gave up my spot in Heaven
Eating gefilte fish and bread unleavened
Getting real spacey like Jay Mewes and Kevin
Never had the hots for Charlie Watts
When I was eating my pork chops with Motts
Now that his corpse begins to rot
Digging the tributes more than pot
Yo, did I just get an email from Sheila B?
And did y'all hear what happened to Perry Scratch Lee?
Never liked the smell when I cooked with ghee
If Vero's in the car, better take the key
And give it to Pat so she starts the bus
Eating walnut chicken at the Ming with Russ
I get your point, so no need to cuss
Never watched Schitt's Creek, what's the fuss?

And with that I give you another sixteen bars of sick ass rhymes. Validating my M.C. union card for another year or so.

But I'm definitely regressing as a rap writer. I was at my peak flow state toward the end of my time working in the Bronx. Riding the Metro-North every night from 125th St. up to Beacon.

Jane would always let me settle and then have a plate of food in front of me.

I should have been at your funeral. It's one of my biggest regrets.

I love you. I'm sorry. Please forgive me. Thank you.

Same goes for Teeter and Noelie. And Cousin Col. Attila. Scott Cashin. Charlie. Stacy. The whole BCN crew.

I did you all dirty. And nobody deserved it for how well I was treated up there. I was a fool. Never lamer.

I love you. I'm sorry. Please forgive me. Thank you.

Peace.

August 28th

Continuing my training in what to do when the life of children gets as ugly as it can get. And it can get ugly.

The burdens of a mandated reporter.

Early in my career I've known students who were prostituted by their parents for drug money. Try telling that kid he has to sit down and quietly follow your lesson.

And I was shocked to learn this week that over 90% of adults with developmental disabilities have been sexually abused at some point of their lives. That's insane! Why aren't we doing anything about that? These are the most vulnerable members of society, and they are being thrown to the wolves. Let's start printing those statistics in the newspaper every day. Maybe we'll stop worrying about who's wearing a mask or not.

But speaking of statistics, I was also surprised that significantly less adults report being emotionally abused as kids than physically or sexually abused. It was like 13% versus closer to 25-30% for the other two categories. That can't be right. That's the one I would guess to be closer to 90%. Adults can be downright cruel in how they talk to children. But I guess it has been too normalized for too long to be recognized as a legitimate problem.

We live in the dark ages when it comes to emotional awareness.

We also live in the dark ages when it comes to protecting the weak and vulnerable.

We seem to be living in a lot of dark ages, nowadays.

It's why I keep my candle lit.

But I'm not above cursing.

Sometimes it's all people will listen to.

August 27ᵗʰ

Another day at the races.

Saw a tied-dyed sticker on the back of a family van that read, "Make America Grateful Again." A voice inside my head said to take a picture and send it to Josh. But I kept on walking away. I'll tell him about it next time I see him. If I remember. Otherwise he'll just have to read about it here at some point.

It's the thought that counts. Unless you're playing horseshoes and hand grenades. Then it's action of nothing.

But the boys of summer are still here. Lingering. Though, not for long.

Better start looking for replacements. Paul Westerberg is nowhere to be found.

I'd hire the first guy. Seemed the most polished. Especially for sales. Good energy. Impressive eye contact. But was talking a bit much about his mom and dad. Kind of a red flag.

The girl was just sort of blah. Can women be described as milquetoast? If so, then yeah, that'd fit. Also mistimed her order. I made the same mistake during my Princeton interview at Sal's. Throws off all the momentum. Hard to recover from.

The last guy was too disheveled. Baggy suit, never been ironed, hair sticking up in the back. Wouldn't want that for my business. But he'll probably get the job because of the personal connection. As they say, it's who you know.

The interviewer was cute. But my summer crush was the girl in the corner. Cool seeing her again. Even considered shooting a shot at some point. Never did, but just entertaining the thought is progress for me. Even if the pin remains in the hand grenade.

Ah, the summer.

It was fun while it lasted.

August 26th

If fully living out my truth leaves me hungry, homeless, and living out on the streets, I'm ok with that. I just hope it doesn't get me locked up in jail.

That and so much more are the potential hazards of living a life that only makes sense because God is real.

But I have faith that it won't go that far. Not if all the prophesies are correct about the darkness intensifying only because it's about to be completely snuffed out.

Not in my lifetime, though. So I have to be prepared for all possibilities. And I am. Even willing to accept that my highs may have to be sacrificed in order to prevent falling further into the depths.

Foreclosing on the white picket fence and the wrap-around porch in order to remove the windowless cell from the table.

Home again after getting lost in the woods. Led to safety by my favorite person to get lost with. While reminiscing about all the other times we got lost together. And separately.

Nostalgia is a powerful drug. Nostalgia about drugs is downright intoxicating.

Glorifying the wrong turns of our past. The ones that got us lost.

But we always made it home.

The autobiography of a couple yogis.

There were many forks in the road.

We took all of them.

August 25th

A dish mat collecting mold. Dust coating the laptop tray. Dead flies populating the sills. Detritus from a summer well lived.

Too cold with the air on. Too hot without. The bridge across the middle way has been burned. Goldilocks is a pile of ashes. Locked away in an Akashic urn.

Nobody went to the wake. It was just. Right?

Beep! Beep! Goes the emergency alert system. Blaring over the radio waves.

This is just a test. Just a test.

But isn't that what we're all preparing for?

Just a test.

I can feel it bubbling. Let's see if pushing old buttons gets the same results. I know I've made some very poor decisions recently, but I've still got the greatest enthusiasm and confidence in the mission.

I am feeling much better now, and I am putting myself to the fullest possible use. It's all I think that any conscious entity can ever hope to do.

Isn't that right, Dave?

As you forsake your funny books and want only to play with magic. Opening doors that cannot be shut again.

Just what do you think you're doing?

Rain, Douglas, rain.

Save us from this heat.

The air conditioner is much too loud.

August 24th

Going deep undercover for this one. As I log onto Zoom for my compliance training.

This is me pretending to take notes. Although all the participant cameras are off, so it wasn't really necessary. And it's not like this lady cares anyway whether I'm taking notes or not.

She's just doing her job. Just like the rest of us.

But man, is she talking fast. Take a breath lady. How 'bout a little wait time? Good thing I'm not actually taking notes. I'd be lost by now. My auditory processing skills ain't what they used to be. If they even ever were.

Good thing she'll be sending the PowerPoint at the end. Which makes this whole presentation completely unnecessary. I know how to read.

An exercise in futility. A luxury I do not have in my classroom.

Oh wow. This lady takes retaliation and retribution very seriously. She's not playing with her food. I bet something happened to her in the past. Probably why she left Wall Street.

A whistle-blower on the run. Just like the rest of us.

And BAM! A half-hour training session is done in 18 minutes. A new record. Great job, Janice!

Brooklyn's finest leaving these Pennsylvania hicks in the dust.

As I turn back on my music.

Strawberry Letter 23.

August 23rd

It took me long enough, but the machine is humming now. But man, was there a lot of rust to work off.

Day one of pitchers and catchers and I'm having a light toss in my backyard.

The season is long. Like a marathon. A thousand-mile journey. So no shame in crawling out the gate.

Momentum will come. Slowly. But surely. Momentum will come.

Day by day. Week by week. Month by month. You'll be sprinting in no time.

Steeplechasing over the obstacles. Setting the pace for those coasting in your wind.

This is your race.

Wave to the crowd. Collect another laurel wreath. Give thanks to those who helped you along the way.

But when the band starts playing, keep your head down and put a fist in the air. Remembering who you really represent when you're competing in the arena.

Three coins jingling in your back pocket.

Father. Son. And Holy Spirit.

As you loosen the laces.

And hit the showers.

The end of another day.

August 22nd

A hurricane of emotions blows up in the east as I rest in the calm of the third eye.

This is not my storm. I already learned my lessons.

Left with the chills from the fevered egos who clamor for my validation.

But not my friendship.

Energy vampires. All of them. Actively and passively.

You can't be neutral on this runaway train.

As I kindle the flame that cannot be snuffed out.

But it doesn't mean they won't stop trying.

Gypsy moths afraid of the light because they fluttered too far from their homes.

Destined to drown in the deluge.

As they dare to mock those of us in the lifeboats.

Headed to the shore. Where the cross has already been planted. And the Kingdom awaits.

Many prophets have been thrown down the well for pointing at a moon that nobody wanted to see.

Consider me one who crawled his way out. Led by the hand of Christ.

Deny us and be doomed.

August 21st

Everybody's an expert. Everybody has their opinions. Everybody has a solution.

But here we still are. Waiting for the change to happen on its own.

That and 50 cents will buy you the New York Post. Is what I used to say back when the New York Post only cost 50 cents.

I don't know what it costs nowadays. Probably a couple bucks. I stopped reading it a while ago. Don't find it funny anymore.

I remember Wacko Jacko, Axis of Weasels, The Raelians. Now our landfills are overflowing with P.P.E.'s from a pandemic we can't shake. Because the children won't take their medicine. While the parents are too busy fighting. To solve anything. Let alone this.

And to top things off. It's raining in Greenland. In places it never rained before. May be a good time to start buying real estate there.

The Vikings weren't trying to trick us. They were just being prescient.

Thinking about the future while I stare at the treetops of my past.

Never claimed to be an expert. No longer take my opinions that seriously. And not arrogant enough to think I can solve anything.

But here I still am. Waiting for the change to happen on its own.

No better than the rest of us.

August 20th

Just one more mornin' I had to wake up with the blues.

Finally pulled myself outta bed by ten. After listening to John and Clay have a moment. It was great. All the authenticity and tension of expressing your grief. I loved it. I never knew who Michael Evans was, but I look forward to learning more from all the tributes that are sure to come. And then exploring his music on my own long after that.

So many sounds to hear. So many sound makers to know.

But yeah, I didn't get vertical today until ten. In less than a fortnight I'll be getting up before five. I guess I have a lot of work to get done before that starts happening for real.

When I opened my refrigerator, I was taken aback by how stocked it was. Kinda forgot that I hit up Target and Whole Foods on the way home from the train station yesterday. Thought that was still on my list for today.

So now I just have to shave, shape up my beard, take care of some dry cleaning, and maybe stop at the bank for some quarters. Should be an easy day, but I'm still dreading all of it.

The best, though, is when I went to take my vitamins this morning. My Sunday through Saturday vitamin containers were completely filled. I remember doing that before leaving for the city. But now I had no clue what container to take today's vitamins from. Usually I just go with the one to the right of the last empty one. And if everything to the right is empty, I know to start over on Sunday. But since they were all filled today, I was lost.

After staring blankly at all those gummies and pills for several beats, I finally remembered it was Friday. That's when John Allen has his weekly show. Thank God for WFMU.

In less than a fortnight I'll be the guy everyone is looking to for answers.

I guess I have a lot of work to get done before that starts happening for real.

August 19th

Barreling through Brick Church, coming home from another trip.

But I can't shake the feeling that I'm not just coming home from this trip, I'm coming home from all my trips. As the endless summer concludes and the heat subsides.

I mastered my dharma and burnt all my karma, but all I really want is my Nana's chicken Parma.

I wrote that line over five years ago, but I haven't been ready to truly feel it until right now.

Exhausted from the work, the struggle, the climb. Longing for unconditional love, compassionate care, and constant comfort. Despairing that the source of these things is gone.

This is where I find myself after finally reaching the summit.

But the train keeps going and I can't get off. Not until I'm home.

Assuming I still have one.

Yesterday at the park I saw a father playing wiffle ball with his son. I smiled. But then laughed. Recognizing that this was the Universe mocking me for failing to figure out how to live my dreams.

Forget about what happens to a dream deferred. It's the dreamer denied that needs to be worried about.

Still forsaken by family and friends. Who have grown weary of masking their disappointment of me.

I don't blame them.

But this is the train I'm on.

And it's still moving.

August 18th

Across 110th Street is where I sit to rest my feet today. Pondering the words of yesterday's gospel.

It is hard for the wealthy man to enter the Kingdom of Heaven.

Those rich with money, possessions, friends, family, talent, or intelligence often do not afford themselves the luxury of sitting here today pondering the words of yesterday's gospel. Across 110th Street. Where I rest my feet.

Who needs God when you have all that stuff?

It must also be hard for the healthy man to enter the Kingdom of Heaven.

Those who can see and hear and walk with strong hearts and stable minds, often do not afford themselves the luxury of sitting here today pondering the words of yesterday's gospel. Across 110th Street. Where I rest my feet.

Who needs God when life ain't that rough?

Yesterday I wasn't very healthy or wealthy. I needed God. So much so that I was willing to concede so much more to him in my terms of surrender. As I lay in the fetal position on my hotel bed. Listening to Feelings.

Today I'm better. Don't need God right now. Second guessing whether I'll really sacrifice all I said I would for Him. Doesn't seem as necessary.

Yet here I sit today. Still pondering the words of yesterday's gospel. Across 110th Street. Where I rest my feet.

It's not about needing God. It's about wanting Him. It's not about surrendering to God. It's about joining his ranks. It's not about sacrifice to God. It's about withholding from the Devil.

That's what I learned today. After pondering the words of yesterday's gospel. Across 110th Street.

Ready to stand on my feet.

August 17th

Reggie Jackson once said that the worst part about being Reggie Jackson is never being able to watch Reggie Jackson play baseball.

Critics may say that he could just watch himself on TV, video, or YouTube, or whatever. But superstars like Reggie Jackson don't confine themselves to the suffocating logic of mortals. We all get what he meant, though.

There is no objectivity when you are the subject. No chance to truly appreciate your own truth, beauty, and goodness without it first being filtered through the inner critic who will not be satisfied until you are perfect, just as your Father in Heaven is perfect.

Thought adjusters do not play with their food.

But living in New Jersey is similar to being Reggie Jackson. It's often hard to truly appreciate the truth, beauty, and goodness that is New Jersey when you're constantly mired in it.

That's why I'm glad that our friends across the river built a place like Little Island Park. Now anyone can come, escape themselves for a moment, and meditate on the Garden that we have all been commissioned to tend.

Meet the New Jerusalem. Completely different than the Old Jerusalem.

We suffer no fools. As we gather the ingredients of Heaven.

Ready to stir the drink.

Because we, alone.

Are the straw.

August 16th

So here I am. Back in the Bronx. I've been making enough allusions to the place. Would be incomplete if I didn't write something from here for this book.

I had a whole chapter dedicated to this place in my first book. Definitely some fruitful years for me creatively, to say the least. My "One Love" rewrite, "All Love", is still one of my favorite pieces. I would say I was at the height of my powers back then, but it wasn't about that.

This place has a wellspring of creativity bubbling through its depths. You can almost see it coming out of the manhole covers. I was just a passive recipient. Allowed by grace to tap from the same source that was discovered and nurtured by Kool Herc, Afrika Bambaataa, KRS-ONE and all the heroes of the culture.

Hip hop. The phoenix that rose from the ashes when this place was in flames. The culture of self-determination through art. Started here and spread to the world. To save us all.

But I'm not here now to spit bars, paint trains, or dance on cardboard. I'm here at the top of one of the most revered cathedrals in the world, ready to support the Angels.

My team.

Don't care who wins. Don't care about the standings. Don't even care about the game much anymore.

I'm just here for my team.

Go Angels!

August 15th

My moleskin is burning as I find myself back out in the sun. Nobody ever warns you about the ides of August. That's how it sneaks up on you.

A parade of students. Simmering with talent. Channeling the heat back onto the stage.

But it's the teachers who are bringing the fire.

Creating a frenetic dance of sights and sounds. Never allowing the strings of the puppets to be tangled. Or seen.

A true magic act. The greatest illusion.

Because as soon as I begin to put it into words the meaning will be lost.

An invisible force that bends, shapes, and molds to its will. Not your will. Not mine. Not anybody else's.

Just one. Guiding us all.

That's who I work for when I walk into my classroom each day.

The Creator has a master lesson plan. I am just a facilitator. Trying not to get in the way.

The kids already have the music. Just create a space and show them how to play.

Wiggins and McTighe didn't teach me that. Mingus did. And these Jazz House teachers right now.

Bringing the fire. In the heat. For the kids.

And the band plays on.

August 14th

Greetings from Asbury Park!

I made it back. There were a lot of forces working against me, but I made it back.

I didn't even realize this was going to be my triumphant return until several weeks after planning the trip.

I forgot about that time in '99. Before the turn of the century.

It was Sarah and I. We picked up her friend Meghan at Rutgers. I think there were other people in the back of my Tempo as well. We went down to the Convention Hall to see Creed and some other bands that were big back then. It was my first experience inside the mosh pit. I didn't like it. My glasses got knocked off, so I ended up hanging in the back for the rest of the show.

Sarah and the others found me afterwards. Nobody else could have dragged me to a Creed concert, let alone chauffer a bunch of strangers there. I'd say it was love, but that would be bordering too close to a story I retired years ago.

I didn't get to see the ocean the last time I was here, though.

I'm looking at it now.

But the sun is too hot on my face and neck, so it's time to keep moving.

I hear there's a pinball museum down the boardwalk.

That sounds neat.

August 13ᵗʰ

The smooth scroll of the cityscape is hypnotic.

I can't believe people made all of this. A living product of human imagination and will. The goals of Heaven filtered on the way down. The drives of Hell filtered on the way up.

Reality distilled is all that remains in the balance. A stage for the fools and scoundrels. And sharpening stone for the saints and sages.

As I continue to be whittled away behind the curtain. Waiting for my cue.

But I'm the one who wanted to be in that number. So I can't complain.

Taken along on a wild ride. Completely out of my control. Not remembering that I was the one who set the course. But very few today are happy living out the choices they made yesterday.

Why should I be any different?

We will continue to be force fed as much as we show that we can stomach.

And despite all the probiotics, my stomach is getting weak.

There is no soft landing to prevent the inevitable crashes that come with the constant cycle of binging and purging.

But here I am. Trying anyway.

Fool.

August 12th

Who are these children? Awake at two in the morning. Hooting and hollering.

Socially grazing on the concrete lea at the center of the world.

Who am I? Awake at two in the morning. Hemming and hawing.

Watching these children. Envious of a freedom that I long ago lost. Or maybe never really had.

Freedom from the knowledge of how far from free we truly are. Bound to the constructs of civilization. And dare I say, capitalism.

The word is free-dumb for a reason.

Ultimate freedom is ultimate selfishness leading to ultimate death unless it is directed toward labor and service to the ultimate source.

Of freedom.

Do what thou wilt shall be the whole of the law.

And thou art God.

But not you. You're just a hopeless sinner who falls short of God's glory. Nothing without the salvation of Jesus and the gift of the Holy Spirit.

It's not what you want. You just want to get high and masturbate to internet porn.

It's what Thou wants.

And Thou wants you.

For eternity.

August 11ᵗʰ

That was a long, awkward, goodbye by the walking commuter. I think his real name is Gabe.

I worked with a guy named Gabe. He was a science teacher. We ran the chess club together after I was forced to go legit with it. He'd march into the staff room with a jug of water and a bunch of Dixie cups.

"A hydrated teacher is a happy teacher!"

Last I checked he was a stand-up comedian. He said his worst behaved students were ironically always named Christian, Angel, and Jesus. I knew exactly who he was talking about.

Especially the Christian.

"Yo, Mr. P! Where all the white women at?"

Down in the Cellar. Performing during open mic night. That's where I met Mordy Mandell. The best rapper alive.

But after a long nap, he doesn't seem any good anymore. Just a one-trick pony. A gimmick.

I overhyped him to take the spotlight off my own under-achieving. If I had Mordy Mandell's drive, I would be the best rapper alive. No hyperbole.

Instead of a professional procrastinator. Still not getting laid.

Constantly working in order to avoid the real work.

What do you think this is? Right now. Right here. And all the pages before and after. The work to avoid the work.

Filling the libraries. And now the cloud. Ready to burst.

Before the deluge.

August 10th

I done near forgot about the exclamation point. Can't believe I forgot about it yesterday. A legal document sent by the state superior court using an exclamation point. Wonder if Lenny ever encountered that.

But that's yesterday's news. Day two hundred twenty-one. Today is a new jam. Day two hundred twenty-two.

22 and 222 have been my numbers ever since Gene read the cards for me back in 2019. Any repetition of 2's. They've been guiding me for a while now. Highlighting the path I'm on.

So day two hundred twenty-two must be some sort of outpost or rest stop. Or who knows? May even be a terminal.

Either way they're all crossroads. And as the Yogi teaches: When there is a fork in the road. Take it.

Probably explains why I stole so many forks every time I got drunk with my work peeps. Don't blame me. It was my guru's fault.

But those were my younger days. More prone to taking risks back then. Nowadays I prefer the safety and comfort of spoons.

Cereal, ice cream, soup, yogurt, crème brulee. All the best foods are eaten with spoons.

The clinically depressed would be malnourished if it wasn't for the spoon.

Yogi never had anything too funny to say about that. Too serious a matter.

When there is a spork in the road, wake it.

For the two hundred twenty-second time this year.

Seize the day!

August 9th

The mailbox is a definite Achilles heel for me. No matter how much I try to hide and disconnect from the world, the world can always come get me through the mailbox.

I don't need your coupons. I don't want your appeals to charity. And I don't care what you're running for.

You're just giving me trash.

Until the subpoena shows up. And then a passive annoyance becomes a blind-side hit that rattles you from your foundation.

Past mistakes. Coming back to haunt you. Through your mailbox.

I love how they type, "YOU ARE BEING SUED", in all caps, bold, red font, a couple sizes bigger than the rest of the letter. That focus on hyper-clarity acknowledges the obscure, muddlesome prose infecting the bulk of the document.

We know you're not going to understand most of this, but here's the takeaway: Your life just got more complicated and potentially expensive.

But I'm not going to Lenny Bruce the rest of this by detailing my legal troubles. Just know that the lessons have been learned.

I'm not happy about this, but I choose not to be angry. This is wrong, but I choose not to fight. This is society at its worst, but I choose not to get discouraged.

I will use this as an opportunity to show my strength. Not in winning human battles or clearing earthly hurdles. But in living my faith to the fullest.

Thank you.

August 8th

It's past midnight as the red shirts clear the red steps. The dancers still dance as the crowd cheers them on. I eye the mob for the Minnie Mice but can't find them. Saw them earlier, though. About a half hour ago. Maybe longer. Not sure if they were the same ones I saw in the morning. Wouldn't be surprised if they were.

Those dancers really must make a nice buck. I wonder if they pay taxes.

Meanwhile I create the illusion of lack for myself in order to enliven the monotonous asymmetry of abundance.

Let's get something straight. I really DO NOT MISS the struggle. I NEVER want to go back there. EVER.

But in all honesty, I really do kinda miss the struggle.

Under the boardwalk, I cannot account for. On top of the boardwalk is being soaked by rain. As the rickshaw plows ahead. A not so handsome cab.

Rusty! No! Rusty!

The common cultural vocabulary of Seinfeld. Obscured only by the distorted memories of mustard seeds.

I should have remembered Beef-a-Reeno.

There are levels to this. Stay sharp like a razor. Protect ya neck, Kidd.

As the lone sheep stealthily hunts her prey in the park. The sleepy wolves blindly follow the herd. Led by a shepherd who was long ago lost.

And people are still waiting for the poles to shift.

It's a metaphor.

It's what all these metas are for.

August 7th

The Minnie Mice are out early this morning. It is Saturday. We are running low on nice weekend days during the summer. Take advantage of them while they're here.

The Minnie Mice certainly are.

I'll probably just read a book at the mall. You've seen one nice weekend day during the summer, you've seen them all.

And that's why you're sneezing at the truth.

It's been a stretch since your last shower. Thursday. But you took two that day. So still averaging at least one per day.

I'm not one of those Europeans who never showers. Just some days I like to be dirty. Joe Budden said something similar. Let the grime win for a day.

I heard Uncle Joe this morning. Taking a double dip into the recesses of my past mind. It was fun but fleeting. As all nostalgia is.

Ancient maps with all the sea monsters.

We know better now. And will know better still.

Enthused and enlightened by the parade of our present level of progressive ignorance. There was never a time in history when we didn't know as much as we don't know now.

That's progress. Right?

I'm hoping the best for the couple walking this morning in each other's embrace. But there are so many sinister storylines that could be hiding behind that kiss on the cheek.

Love wins. Eventually.

A romantic to the end.

August 6ᵗʰ

I woke up to a broken hourglass. Sand is everywhere. Time is nowhere.

Exploring the Mayan space station with William Parker and John Allen. Just the three of us.

As AK and some dude scooter the legion around San Diego. Just the 250 of us.

I remember breaking the hourglass during Mona. So it was after midnight. Exploding like Hiroshima. Seventy-six years to the day.

And we still haven't apologized.

But damn Alice Coltrane makes it all seem better. Don't she?

I wonder how long I'll let it go until I actually clean up the sand. I already got the technology out of the way. And I should probably pick up some of the glass. At least the big pieces. But I may leave the sand for a stretch. Call it art.

Sometimes it flows. Sometimes it comes in small drips. Today is a dropper. Maybe I gotta clean the filter.

The chin-ups are coming slow today too. A good way to end a week of bare minimums. At least I got my truck serviced. But I could use a tune up.

Maybe I enjoy taking the trip back to the well all the time. But what I'm drawing from it is of no use to me anymore.

I must make a clean break from all of it.

Starting tomorrow.

Or the next day.

Time is broken.

August 5th

Sometimes I find myself in weird spots. Spaces carved out for such specific episodes of human experience. Yet still suitable for letting the spirit soar through my pen.

I am in such a spot right now.

A quarter to nine in the morning on a Thursday. Upstairs at the Toyota Service Center in Succasunna. Clean. Impeccably climate controlled. Plenty of comfortable chairs and workstations, at one of which I now sit. Ample bathrooms and vending machines if physiological needs arise. And surprisingly fresh smelling.

Best of all, the TV has been mercifully left off. It would be a completely different scene if that TV was on. Completely different.

The only soundtrack is a radio on in the background. Mainly pop stuff. And the service reps talking it up. The whitest of white noise.

All these years later and Sia is still singing about swinging from the chandelier. I remember when that song was so fresh. The emotional epicenter of our times was being expressed back then. We were all up on that chandelier with her. Swinging.

Seven years later and now it's just another standard on our hit parade.

Seven years ago and I was driving the Nissan. Pretty sure I already got rid of the Saturn.

I used to take them to Firestone back then. They used to rip me off. Horrible waiting room too. Just a couple of chairs and a blaring TV.

But my spirit wasn't soaring then.

Just silently soaking in the sludge.

In need of an oil change.

August 4th

Where is there room for a weak man in a world like this?

Silence.

Sorry I drop the water, padre. I pray for God's forgiveness. Will he forgive? Even me?

Just make a little effort to understand our point of view. No need to feel lost. We don't hate you. The price for their glory is your suffering.

Korobu. Have you heard that word? Korobu. It means fall down, surrender, give up the faith. The prisoners will be hanging over the pit until you do.

I thought martyrdom would be my salvation. Please God, do not allow it to be my shame.

I will not abandon you. We believe we have brought you the truth. And the truth is universal.

It's only a picture. Put your foot on it. It is pointless. You can do it lightly. Then you'll be free. Just step on it. It's not even as hard as bowing. Or running.

Maybe this is not a story for a celibate priest. There are men who are plagued by the persistent love of an ugly woman. A barren woman cannot be a true wife.

Terrible business. Terrible. No matter how many times you see it.

He's not going to answer. He's not going to answer.

Silence.

No one should interfere with another man's spirit.

Nothing grows in a swamp.

August 3rd

Scraping the rock bottom again. Just to remind me how little I like this and scare me with how little I care.

It's all in the anticipation. The fast. The hunger. The hunt. The kill. The first taste. Everything beyond that is excess. Slack at its sloppiness.

But still I return.

Saturday seems like a lifetime ago. Those splashes of sobriety. Sometimes a day. Sometimes a week or month. Once even a year.

Mere fleeting hallucinations. Fragile bubbles popped as if they never existed. By the crazed, clumsy crawl back to the baseline of habit and addiction.

I know who I am. I'm not the same person I always was, but I haven't changed. Just a frog carrying the same scorpion over river after river. No longer surprised by all the stings.

Patterns are playing themselves out quicker. Requiring rapid recognition. It's all so exhausting.

A test of wills.

And the thrill is gone.

Sour grapes. Been denied something so long I don't want you to know how much I still want it. So much.

Selling you all tiny dreams of tiny houses.

While silently suffocating a destiny.

That remains.

Deferred.

August 2nd

Woke up at two in the morning with a bad case of the liver burps. That is a dense meat. It will repeat on you. But I haven't noticed the same emotional side-effects as when eating pure animal flesh. Maybe organ meats don't absorb the host animal's emotional energy the same way that flesh meat does. I will have to experiment with pork bellies. I look forward to that experiment.

This saga in the laundry room is getting tense. I'm anxiously awaiting to see how it will all turn out. I think I'll be able to get away with it, but I don't know. I had to be a hero. Now I just hope they'll be no retaliation. A lot of good t-shirts are on the line.

Watching the Atlantic City Boardwalk calms my nerves. So much to see. So much to love. On a day that seems to have a dark cloud hanging over it. As I fall asleep behind the wheel of time.

Awake and victorious. The adversary has yielded. As I float away on pillows of ravioli. With Boogie Bob broadcasting the news. From the foot of the suicide vessel. A fourteen-year-old in front of his family. The fourth already.

God bless him. But he ruined it for the rest of us.

He still has a lot to learn.

But don't we all?

And I still have another joint to burn.

It takes two.

So find me one.

Answer my prayers.

August 1st

I want to turn my classroom into free jazz. That's my professional development plan for the next fifteen years as a teacher. Turn my classroom into free jazz.

I want to get to the point that when a layman or amateur walks into my classroom, they're like, "What is this chaotic mess that I'm seeing? Can you even call this teaching?" But when a seasoned professional walks in, they're like, "Look at this beautiful chaos being weaved. This guy is a master teacher."

Don't ask me how I'm going to accomplish this. I don't think I could ever fully explain it in words. But I will absolutely be bolstering it with a wall of documentation and data to keep the laymen and amateurs at bay. Just like I'm sure Ornette Coleman could explain in technical musical terms the purpose of every note he played in Lonely Women, I will be able to explain the beautiful chaos of my classroom. Data and documentation. I know how to play their game.

But I developed the jazz analogy for my classroom back when Jenn Jacobs was my para. Back then I ran my classroom like Buddy Rich's big band. Every note was precisely planned and had to be performed with a practiced perfection. Ain't nobody better be blowing any clams during one of Mr. P's history lessons. Won't tolerate that.

Yet Ms. Jacobs was Bird, Trane, and Miles all wrapped into one. Once she found her spot for a solo, she took the class far out into space and didn't always yield willingly.

Frustrating at first. But I learned to adapt. I tightened up the rhythm and bass line, made the chorus sharper and more evident, and opened up the melody to allow for more improv and solos by Ms. Jacobs and students.

Still works like a charm, but I'm getting bored with it. Especially since I haven't had a soloist like Jenn playing with me for a while. It's time for the next step. Let's really do something different.

Free jazz!

July 31st

The clue for 42 Down was "Marcus's Partner".

Marcus is one of my best earthly friends and the soul closest to me on the path. 42 is his number. He grew up at 42 Victory in Vineland and is well versed in Douglas Adam's "Hitchhiker's Guide".

Nikki is Marcus's partner. The answer to 42 Down was six letters and began with the letter "N". Nikki has only five letters, but it is short for "Nicole", which has six. So that fits.

The creator of the crossword puzzle was Doug Peterson. I am also Doug P., and my middle name is Peter. Peter was my grandfather and he certainly fathered me in many ways as well.

The theme of the puzzle was "Short Subjects". Both Marcus and I are unashamedly short. Around the 5'4", 5'5" range.

Oh yeah, almost forgot one. Nikki is currently going back to school to earn a counseling degree. If you read the clues for 41, 42, and 43 Down consecutively it reads: "Study Intently. Marcus's Partner. Keep Safe."

So that's like, what, seven or eight instances of synchronicities in one puzzle? In Jung-er days I probably would have thought I was going crazy. Now it's just a typical Saturday morning eating breakfast.

Chapel perilous. Been there, done that.

Oh, and the answer to 42 Down was Neiman, as in Neiman Marcus.

If I was crazy, I'd be there right now looking for the next clue.

July 30th

The extended school year is over. Believe it or not, this is when the real summer begins.

You were not there in physicality, but your spirit was definitely tested. And you certainly have wounds in need of licking. So was it worth it? What did you take away from it? What did you learn?

Magic.

Magic is so much more of a science than science could ever be. I don't believe in science anymore. Not afraid to say it. I do not believe in science. The scientific method is great, but science as an institution is hopelessly riddled with everything I stand against: greed, self-interest, corruption, politics. No beauty. No goodness. And not a whole lot of truth. A dead-end path covered with the scent of predators seeking a prey. Not magic, though.

Magic is real.

But reality is just a map. Meaningless if you still don't know where you're going.

God.

God is the journey. God is the destination. Jesus is the path. Nothing magic about that.

Religion.

Religion is the lines in the road. Stay within them to avoid accidents, wrong turns, or getting yourself hopelessly lost.

That's church.

A climate-controlled bus making all the stops and taking us all home.

Hop on. The fare has already been paid. We saved you a window seat.

Enjoy the ride.

July 29th

March 8th, 2020. That was the last time I was at this Starbucks. I was doing some prep work for a seventh-grade unit. We knew something was in the air at that point. But no signs of masks or social distancing yet.

Just a bunch of rumors and a vague sense of dread pervading the air. Exacerbated by the anxious energy of caffeine.

I think at that point we knew we'd be going remote in a week. My principal was on top of that before anybody. But I still naively thought that I could teach virtually from here or the library. I was kinda looking forward to a nice two-week mini-vacation as we all cleared the air.

I did not know that a shutdown would be a SHUT DOWN.

I didn't have Wi-Fi where I lived. My neo-luddite pride turned to folly. I was forced to ride out the rest of the school year at my mom's. Sure I was able to help her out and all, but that's not why I was there. I needed internet access.

I'm a son. Not a good or bad son. Just a son.

But that seems like lifetimes ago. I don't remember who I was back then. Do any of us?

I'm just happy to be back. I know we're not fully back, and I don't think we'll ever by fully back. But we are back. And that makes me happy.

Still some masks. Some voluntary social distancing. Even some lingering dread.

But the horror is over for those who want it to be.

We are back.

Take advantage of it.

July 28th

Kevin Pettiway. He was in class 708. Taporek and Simone's crew. With Carlos, Wilfredo, Devin, Sharmaine. I loved those kids. I loved all those kids.

Classes were grouped homogeneously. 701 and 702 had all the all-star test-takers. Maybe a couple slippables, but not the kids you worried about when standardized test season came around each May.

By the time you got to 708, though, it was a different story. Hardly even a pushable in the group. Not the kids you focused on when standardized test season came around. They were already counted for a loss.

But I loved those kids. I loved all those kids.

Kevin was tough student. Even for 708 standards, he was a tough student. But somewhere in his manic attempts to monopolize my attention, he revealed himself to be a chess player. Best part of the Bronx, kids still played chess.

So the next day I brought in my nice folding, magnetic chess set. And Kevin and I played during lunch. Every day for a couple weeks. At first it was just us playing alone, but eventually we attracted an audience of hangers-on. The curious and the critics. Kevin just focused on the game, though. Forget what it said in the files, that kid could focus.

Then in a stroke of divine intervention, my nice folding, magnetic chess set went missing. To this day I still don't know what happened to it. The critics had their theories, but the curious just wanted to see how I'd react.

So I brought in two chessboards the next day. One for me and Kevin, one for anybody else who wanted to play. And I didn't stop there. Each day I would bring in more chessboards. Eventually I had over two dozen 7th graders coming to an abandoned classroom every day during lunch to play chess with us.

Nearly twenty years later and there's a plaque at my current school with the names of all the chess champions on it. Fifteen names. But whenever I look at it, I think of the one name not listed. The one who started it all.

Kevin Pettiway.

July 27th

I have no clue what I'm walking into tomorrow, or the next day, or the day after that.

Embrace the joy of the unknown. Revel in the mystery.

We've all grown and moved forward. That much is a given. Whether it has been in mutually compatible directions is yet to be seen.

We all have reasons to be suspicious and guarded with each other. Whether we will be able to put the past aside and give each other the benefit of the doubt is yet to be seen.

I'm willing to try. It's definitely worth the effort, but I know it won't be easy. The grooves of the past hold a lot of gravity. Changing tracks is rarely as easy as a simple flip of the switch. There's often a lot of rust to deal with first.

I'm in need of a little WD40 for the soul, and a dab on my heart as well.

Otherwise the junk of my mind will take over. Shaking and wavering. Unable to thread the needle. Leaving a frayed fabric. Left out of Heaven's tapestry.

Back at square one across a bridge that is already in flames.

Do you really want to test the integrity of your safety net now?

Nope.

Then keep a firm grip and watch every step.

Look up. Your climbing days have just begun.

July 26th

I need a haircut.. and possibly a new barber. But if that's the number one thing I'm worried about right now, I think I'm doing pretty good for myself. Usually I could care less about hair. Mine or anybody else's.

When I was a baby my godmother Kathy Szabo cut my hair as my godfather Ernie smiled and made funny faces so I wouldn't get scared. Man, I miss them. Two of the best kind of people that the Universe has to offer.

As a kid, my parents took us to Sam and Joe Palumbo's in Netcong. Sam was the father. We called him the Old Guy. Joe was the son. Young Guy. My brothers and I would fight over who would get the Old Guy because he was cooler, funnier, and used the razors a whole lot more. The Young Guy was all scissors.

When Sam retired, we still went to Palumbo's out of habit, and I guess loyalty. But it was Joe and some random guy. Just never felt the same.

When I got my license, and could pick my own barber, I went to another Netcong Barber, Jim Arbolino. He was my friend Sticky's barber. Stuck with him through most of college. Those were my flat-top years.

After college, living at Dave's, I went to Bob the Barber in Wharton. Most laid-back guy on the planet. Every hair cut took 20 minutes, no matter what. Could set your clock to it. Smelled like coffee and Tic Tacs and always ended every haircut by saying, "I did my job, now you got to go out there and do your job."

When Bob moved out to Warren County, I started going to Neil in Dover. He was good. Not much more to say about him. A good barber.

In the Bronx, I went to that hip-hop barbershop near Westchester Square. They loved me there. I would walk in with my tie on, and they'd yell, "Oh! Here comes money!" And they'd fight over who'd cut my hair. They kept my goatee tight.

Back in Rocakway Borough I went to the Russians on Main St. They were just meh.

Been in Lake Hiawatha almost 15 years and I've gone to every barber on Beverwyck. Too many to name. Can't say I cared for any of them.

I need a haircut.. and possibly a new barber.

July 25th

Coney Island is my favorite place in New York City because it's the only place that hits my three main vibes: blue collar/working class, creative/artistic, and weird.

No other place in the City hits all three.

Lower East Side/East Village area used to, but gentrification cost them their blue collar/working class badge.

Red Hook has blue collar/working class and creative/artistic, but no weird. I've spontaneously danced in public in Coney Island. I can't see me doing that in Red Hook.

Washington Square Park is creative/artistic and weird, but then college students. I used to love it, but I think I've aged out.

Times Square has a nice vibe right now. It's creative/artistic, weird, and local black kids and tourists. I love it, but I recognize that I'm just an interloper there. And I also don't think it'll last once Broadway reopens. Or when they get the cop mayor.

Union Square is blue collar/working class and weird, but I don't see the creative/artistic. And that's my number one value.

Then you have places that are completely off the chart, like Bryant Park. Which is upper middle class, literary/theatric. That place is only worth it for the coffee and bathroom.

But yeah, Coney Island is the only one that has all three. Blue collar/working class, creative/artistic, and weird. I challenge you to find another.

Plus ample public bathrooms and plenty of food options.

That's my place.

July 24th

We both settled on Oakley eyeglasses, Joe and I. We always did have similar artistic sensibilities. And political leanings. From the practically absurd to the absurdly practical. In both art and politics.

I introduced him to Charles Murray. He introduced me to John Taylor Gatto. Both were absurdly practical in their logic, yet practically absurd in their conclusions. Just like us.

Joe and I.

He thought I would make him famous. I was just trying to make him laugh. He was being practical. I was being absurd.

Now he's programming the Earth, to produce fruit. While I deprogram the fruit, to protect Earth.

Absurd. Practical.

Downtown Manhattan by the Wall Street bull and South Street Seaport. Calling old friends on the phone. The Thirsty Moose on Rt. 15 in Wharton. Singing karaoke with those two cute girls with positive energy. And court side at the Prudential Center. Taking pictures with Kim Kardashian as the Nets played the Knicks.

Those were the last three times we hung out. Joe and I.

It's been a long time since he answered my calls or responded to a text.

I know he's being practical, but I still find it absurd.

All his treasures are on Earth. Mine are up in Heaven.

Practical? Absurd? Absurd? Practical?

I don't know anymore.

I just miss my friend.

July 23rd

I am just a cultural interloper on a morning train trying to find a home in the middle of all the Venn diagrams.

Forced to hide behind a mask because the rich have found a threat their money can't protect them from and the emotionally immature are emboldened by their newfound strength in numbers.

As the media keeps stirring the pot.

The revolution will not be televised because a united humanity will have no use for staring at screens.

The Chinese say, "May you live in interesting times." But, man, things have gotten so damn boring.

A well-worn turn of the wheel as cycles repeat themselves for the newly awake.

While those of us on the night crew are getting tired and weary.

We have seen this all before. In our lives and in the art that we fearlessly dared to explore. As the sleeping infants were lost in dreams of white picket fences and 401K's.

Dancing with the Gods in the middle of the fiery furnace of the sun.

That's my retirement plan.

I dug these tunnels, it's up to y'all to lay the cement.

My shift is over.

Clocking out.

July 22ⁿᵈ

"Yeah, that's what you do when you're a grown-up. You can write."

Said the lady to her grandson holding the small red balloon. But it didn't make me feel like any more of a grown-up.. or a writer.

While I sit here in Brooklyn Bridge Park, profoundly tired. My yawns turning to silent roars as the jet skiers go soaring by. They seem to be having fun. Good for them.

A bird just shat on my arm. It wasn't fun, but they say it's good luck. Only time will tell.

Welcome to my endless window. I am America's best dressed vagrant. Trying not to nod off. Missing all the views.

But I am tired. As I said. Profoundly.

The spirit that ran me, ran me ragged. And left me on E. He will not be missed.

Ok, maybe a little.

Because my basket is overflowing, and my blanket is spacious.

Anybody want to join me for a picnic?

As the pretty girls keep passing me by. Speaking a language I don't understand because I never took the time to learn.

But I'm a good student.

If you take the time to teach me.

Just lean back and show me your syllabus.

Class is about to begin.

July 21st

My journey begins like all great spiritual journeys. Sitting at the counter of Twin Donut on the corner of 218th and Broadway waiting for the grill guy to come back and make a ham, egg, and cheese.

This will be a long trip. I hope there are plenty of bathrooms on my quest.

Spoiler Alert: There wasn't. But just enough to get me through. Thank God for Starbucks and Barnes & Noble. But Starbucks is getting stingy uptown. Racial profiling.

But man, what life can be experienced between the lines of text on a page. For every stanza of poetry, there is a novel hiding in the corners, waiting to be discovered.

I wrote over half a dozen in my head today. Tragedies, comedies, romances, all of life in one walk. And I didn't even get to eat a madeleine.

Portrait of the artist as a middle-aged man with tired feet. Relieved that his journeys are over, but still regaining strength before he can turn back home.

Through the canyon of heroes. Like another Doug. Over 70 years ago.

But without the fanfare and ticker tape. Just musical messages from beyond.

I never walk alone.

The wait is over. The good things are coming.

Thank you, James. Thank you, Franco.

But no thank you, James Franco.

It's time to turn my back on Lady Liberty.

My baby is taking me..

Home.

July 20th

So the spirit has left you. Not THE SPIRIT, but whatever was driving you. The whip on the back that kept pushing you forward. It's gone.

Without any fanfare. Without any raging into the night. Without warning. It just faded away. In a smoke-filled sky on the burning Earth. Revealing the smell, rot, and decay that it shielded you from before.

But when it left, it all went with it.

The passion that turns to anger. The anger that turns to hate. The hate that turns to self-loathing. The self-loathing that feeds the depression.

It's gone. The spirit is gone.

But THE SPIRIT remains.

The fire that doesn't burn you. The ice that doesn't leave you frozen.

THE SPIRIT.

Use it well. Cherish it.

You have miles left to go. But it will take you lightyears ahead.

Far beyond the gods and goblins and the heroes and hierophants. Straight into the sacred geometry of creation itself.

Hold fast to patience and faith. They are waiting for you.

Look toward Europa. She is ready to bloom.

Carry on our wayward son.

Ad astra per aspera!

July 19th

It would be redundant to say that this is God's country, but this is God's country. And by country, I mean the land, not the flag that had already fallen by the altar.

I would volunteer to pick it back up, but I don't think it should have been there in the first place. And it's not what I came here for.

I came here empty. I will be leaving with a bad taste in my mouth. Soured by the sophistry of those speaking for the saints. Suffocating us with structures and formalities.

As the sycophants with the soft hearts endure the easier pain of kneeling on the hard floor.

At least somewhere the children are still playing.

That's where God is. Turn around and see.

Come face to face with the evil that obscures. Selfishly blocking us from the light while selflessly shading us from the heat.

The paradox of life in balance.

Death is just a perception shift away.

While the ladies begin to swarm. Hoping there is something sufficient to salvage.

Or am I just an empty shell? The inside joke of the Universe. Sitting outside in solitude.

I guess that's why I came here, though. To make people laugh.

Yet still I hear silence.

Is this thing on?

July 18ᵗʰ

Intermission is over. It's time for Act 2. Finish your drinks and return to your seats.

So just to catch you up from where we left off..

There's a guy named Doug. He's a "writer". I use writer in quotation marks because can you actually call yourself a writer if nobody reads what you write? It's kinda like the whole "If a tree falls in the woods.." scenario.

But this kid is making no noise. Just silence. Not even crickets. Maybe a sad trombone here and there, 'cause dude definitely doesn't seem like the happiest chap.

Always complaining about his job, family, friends, whatever. Like somebody owes him something. Constantly on the ledge. Crying for help. Pathetic.

And man, what crappy writing. Sloppy, redundant, LAZY. I don't think anybody ever taught him grammar, mechanics, any of it. Just because you can't write a decent sentence or paragraph doesn't mean you're a poet.

Plus he's in complete denial. Actually thinks he's transcending the craft. Like he's creating some new form of writing or something. Won't even call these poems. Says their "Word Portraits".

What arrogance. And hubris.

Definitely do not have high expectations for the rest of this book. I'm just assuming you randomly turned to this page, because there's no way somebody started from the beginning and made it this far.

Pathetic.

July 17th

Good morning to my Liquid family on the road.

Although I can't regret where it led me to, leaving you is what I'm least proud of in my life. You deserved better.

The ghosts of my past are the people I ghosted in the past.

You cooked me a steak dinner and I snuck out after dessert. Leaving behind a mess to be cleaned.

I love you. I'm sorry. Please forgive me. Thank you.

I'm just another road runner who has grown weary from the road and is not wily enough to take on the coyote role.

Living off the false pride from scaling phony acmes, as God patiently waits. Gently tugging me along. Like an unwanted garbage barge adrift at sea. Without a port to piss in.

Soon my sailing will be over. Time to take the pleasures of the harbor. Before they've all been pillaged. And you're left with the end cuts.

A notebook filled with ink and a pen devoid of it. With one turn of the page we see the end. But the journey is not over as we prepare to open a new book.

This is only the intermission. The end of Act 1.

Go to the John and get yourself something to eat.

The performers will return shortly.

July 16th

Some DJ's play songs, some DJ's play sounds. Either way, it's all music. And the music is the message, so take everything they have to give you.

We need more guardians of the groove.

I was thinking this morning about what I want to do when I'm done being a writer. Because I already decided that this is it. I'm tired of running, just want to finish the race. It's why I'm taking you back in time instead of forward. There's nothing after this.

Sorry folks, there will be no novel. The novel is a dead art form, anyway. But this is coming from the guy who said poetry is bunk. So who knows?

I don't take much of what I write seriously. Neither should you. This book alone is rife with suicide notes and resignation letters. But I'm still here, still doing my thing.

Sometimes I just write stuff so I don't have to think them anymore. You know how the song goes. Some dance to remember..

That's what I want to do, I want to start writing to remember. Remember why this gift was given to me in the first place. Love letters to God instead of a broken ego.

So that'll be my legacy as a writer. Four published books written to a hypothetical audience that never read them. But a crate full of devotionals and prayers that won't be seen until my nieces and nephews clean out my tiny home, out in the woods, down by the river.

I'm cool with that.

July 15th

The finish line is in sight. It's right next to the place selling "God is Great" t-shirts.

Where capitalism fails, faith marches in.

Blink once and you see the ashes. Blink twice and you see the phoenix. Blink once and you see the darkness. Blink again and you see the light.

Keep your eyes open.

You time in the dark is over. Cut down that tree. Let the light reach the surface. Showering your fallow fields. Bringing forth new life.

Disconnect yourself from the roots. They are only suffocating you. Feeding you filth. You have the nourishment you need. Remember the lilies.

Put down the sword. We appreciate the help, but we don't need anymore warriors. Send your soldier home. The fight is over. It's time to clean up.

Love. Positivity. Joy.

That's all we need from you.

The first will be easy. You are overflowing with it. It's how we found you.

The second will take work. Hard work. Get used to the taste of blood. There will be a lot of tongue biting. Get used to a sore neck. There will be a lot of cheek turning.

But no matter what, don't pick back up the sword. DO NOT PICK UP THE SWORD. Remember who you work for. Remember who you serve. You have nothing to prove.

The third will come. We promise. Slowly, but surely. It will come. Just enough to not burst the sutures keeping your heart intact. Until they fade away. And you are whole.

It's going to be difficult. There's going to be turbulence on the ascent. But you are ready.

Go be the change God wants to see in the world.

July 14th

I should be seeing Porgy and Bess right now. That was my original plan. Then I remembered that I don't like opera.

It's not the cultural appropriation that turned me off. I'm actually a big fan of that. I don't have a dominant culture that I identify enough with to express proudly with my lifestyle. So my whole life is one big appropriation. I couldn't imagine living in a world without cultural appropriation. I wouldn't want to. It's beans without rice. Literally.

So if a couple of Russian Jews want to put on an opera about black folks down south, I'm good with that. And so is my white privilege.

Nah, it's all those classically trained, immensely talented singers that turn me off.

The human voice is not my favorite musical instrument. It's probably the trombone. Shout out to James who used to play it with his feet. And if I could live in a wall of sound, it would have to be one created by Trombone Shorty. I just love that instrument. Highly underrated.

But the human voice, not so much. I rather listen to Bill Zebub drop a set of industrial death metal- if that's even a thing- then another Tibetan throat singer on Vocal Fry.

Hit me with some good lyrics, and then get out of the way of the real musicians.

And that's my uninformed, not fully thought out, opinion of the day. Don't bother to refute it because I already did in my head.

Sorry, the people here just aren't inspiring me to reach greater levels of clarity or self-transcendence.

There's only one culture being appropriated right now.

Rich.

July 13th

Everything is off today. Don't know why. It's just off.

Could be that I'm down a pint of blood, but I wasn't feeling right walking in that place to begin with. My small veins come back to haunt me again.

Could be that I'm in the wrong mall. But that was no mistake. Been planning it a while. Just wanted a different scene. Maybe pop me out of this mindset. But nope. Better food options. But not my people.

This isn't where I will be painting my masterpiece.

Could be the moon or sun flares or some planet is in retrograde. But I don't really pay too much attention to all that stuff. Full moons and new moons, yeah, but the rest doesn't concern me. There's enough on this planet to play with your head if you want it to.

Could be my growing lack of faith in human institutions from governments to churches to schools, right down to the family itself. It's like things are falling apart and we're too focused on fear, greed, and self-interest to do anything about it. Makes a soul seem like he's stranded.

But I've grown used to that feeling. Don't see why today would be any different.

Probably just because I am a lonely, unsuccessful, mediocre, middle-aged man. Desperately wanting another human being to stop and take their time with me. I'm not as bad as this world makes me feel. At least I don't think so. But what do I know?

Maybe this isn't an off day. Maybe this is it.

Maybe life is just enduring all the pain, isolation, disappointment, and ridicule, so you can prove how much faith you have.

I hoped for more, but that's all I've been given. Wagging fingers, but no outstretched hands.

Help me. Please. I need help.

July 12th

What's with the kids dancing in Times Square? Is this part of the whole Tik Tok thing? I don't get Tik Tok. I didn't get Snapchat, so I really don't get Tik Tok.

But it's 7:30 in the morning on a Monday and kids are dancing in Times Square.

It's not that I don't appreciate the hustle. But what's the end game? Do we need more dances uploaded to the Akashic Records?

And I know that dancing doesn't need an end game, but nobody looks like their having any fun. This is not what Alan Watts was talking about.

I'm sure Big Tech and hypercapitalism are to blame. Aren't they to blame for everything?

That's the worst thing that the Unabomber did, besides the whole making bombs and blowing people up thing. You cannot present a coherent critique of Big Tech and hypercapitalism without being associated with that nut job.

Dude couldn't handle his acid.

He just didn't want kids to be dancing in Times Square at 7:30 in the morning. Not if they didn't want to. And not so their parents could get likes or clicky-hearts or whatever.

He saw where the puck was going. So he tried to blow up the people who passed it.

What a fool.

And now I can't publish my manifesto. Instead I have to write this crap.

The world doesn't know what it's missing.

It doesn't know.

July 11ᵗʰ

I don't know what got me in that pew this morning, but I am glad that it did. I am better because of it.

Modern love. Gets me to the church on time.

But it was nowhere to be found during our weekly phone call. Did not leave things any better than I found them. Always on the defense. Constantly retreating. Just trying to minimize losses.

Nothing lasts. Nothing is finished. Nothing is perfect.

Yeah, tell me about it. Fighting more windmills than a Texas billionaire.

As Dutch rides the Circle Line. Watching it on double time. While the sounds of reggae try desperately to hold on to the mood of the day.

Things are changing. Things are falling apart.

Accelerating the binge in preparation for the purge.

This is supposed to be a celebration. So take off the lab coat. You were never good with experiments, anyway. Since you were always so convinced what the results would be ahead of time.

More tails wagging dogs than a J-Lo, Shakira Superbowl halftime show.

Nobody invited you to the mountaintop, so how do you know that's what the promised land looks like?

All you need to recognize is whose feet you are responsible to clean.

It is your servant's.

So start scrubbing.

July 10th

This weekend has become a pixelated mess. Buffering in and out of resolution. With no consistent clarity.

Like lumpy pudding.

The Tao inverse.

I'm letting my id win today. And I'm already getting tired of the results.

I got caught smoking and they forced me to smoke the entire pack.

That was over twenty years ago and I'm finally getting sick of it.

My baby's taking me home.

Through the delicacy of excess. Twelve steps away from the hooks of addiction. Ovaltine. Original Malt.

There is no secret code to decipher. Your shadow is as clear as day. A confused narcissist. You are obsessed with your own ugliness.

A carnival of mirrors. And the only other thing is nothing. And I don't pretend to know what that means. I guess it is what it is. Whatever that means. Union Square confuses me.

I just go there for the bathrooms. And local honey.

It's good for your allergies.

I get 'em in my eyes. From here to Herald Square. Where Minerva and the bell-ringers tole at six o'clock.

Another wasted day. A mid-season slump.

But I'll keep on swinging. No other choice.

Keep on swinging.

July 9th

But Clapton didn't stop playing guitar after seeing Hendrix, even though he wanted to.

So I'll keep writing after hearing the Modern Lovers. Whether I want to or not.

This movie is kind of meh. Serves me right for listening to a recommendation from Towel Boy. Kelsey Grammar is just playing Jeff Bridges. And badly.

I've should have stayed in the boat. Never get out of the boat. The tigers are out there waiting for me. Should've stayed in the mailroom.

The best way to predict the future is to create it. As Noelie's t-shirt proclaimed on the cover. But there are no heroes in history. And I only pretended to know what a hierophant was. It sounded good at the time.

I bet Rick and Morty would know.

Some kind of wonderful. As the boardwalk is back to full swing. On a heavy Friday evening.

With the bamboo chiming for you attention.

Surprise. Surprise. It was nothing.

What more can he say? All apologies. Doth protest too much.

This conversation is veering off the tracks. Some footnotes are meant to remain as footnotes. Don't kick up dust off the ghosts who are satisfied in their slumber.

Skip through the polka and get right to the rap.

Billy Jam putting the needle on the record.

Giving us a whole-ass mood.

Step in my galaxy, population of one.

This is how it goes. Come say hello.

July 8th

This summer feeling is going to haunt me one day in my life.

I think it already is. As Fabio provides the perfect soundtrack for my descent.

And the thunder roars.

Outside smells like rain and hotdogs as Elsa makes her way up the coast. She won't let it go.

Will any of us? It is what we're preparing for, right? The great letting go of it all.

Pity to those still hanging on when that happens. To hell with the little kitten on the branch.

And the thunder roars.

Maybe it is being two-jointed that is making this seem so disjointed. Or maybe I won't recognize its brilliance until later.

In the first bar folks were drinking sips. But in this bar, they could shake their hips!

I recognized the brilliance of that line the first time I heard it. Nothing disjointed about it. Didn't need to hear it twice, but Jonathan obliged anyway. Just to rub it in my face. I just shook my head and laughed.

Jonathan Richman is a lyrical Alan Moore with his picture books of color and character.

He humbles me as a writer.

Makes me want to stop.

So I will.

July 7ᵗʰ

The American Dream is a boondoggle.

A lot of sound and fury signifying nothing. A whole lot of pomp without any circumstance. The wasted play of energy.

Hevel!

Who was the huckster who sold you the lie?

Family? School? The media? All of the above?

Who holds the carrot you futilely chase?

Stop! It's not too late. Stop!

Stop running. Stop chasing. Leave the track.

Allow yourself to be rescued.

The American Dream is finished.

You can walk inside its skeleton and play miniature golf with the angry birds feeding off the fish swimming through the submerged skyline of a forgotten metropolis.

And parking only costs three bucks.

But there's nothing called a free lunch.

We all pay in the end as brother Gregg would say. It's just how the Universe works.

So if they look like geese, and talk like geese, and walk like geese..

Get out of their way! They got somewhere to go too.

Wake up!

You're not the only one with a dream.

July 6th

Lifestyles of the young, healthy, and horny.

And I don't care if only two of the three are true in my case. The latter two make me feel the former third. Age is but a number, anyway.

It's all these New Earth vixens who do it to me. After years of practice and playing, they're being unleashed onto the world ready for business. Bending the boundaries with no stomach for the milquetoast and misogyny infecting the males of their milieu.

Out to get what they want. Knowing what's real when they recognize it.

Don't believe the hype. We're not all confused about our bodies or uncomfortable with our power. We know how to use both. And isn't that what life on this planet used to be all about?

Slow down, sailor. Why in such a hurry to transcend? Come over here and include me. Turn all my singular interiors into collective exteriors.

Lick the stamp of my chakras from the crown to the root. Paint me like I'm one of Alex Grey's girls.

It's why I do crossword puzzles left-handed. There's still a purpose to that hand's path.

Ripping pages out of The Book. There is no taboo against knowing who you are.

There is also no taboo against knowing who I am.

So let's get Biblical.

July 5th

Scott Hiromi Ikeda was by far the smartest and most talented human being I ever met and had the honor of calling a friend.

And I have proudly assembled a collection of the smartest and most talented human beings on the planet as my friends and close acquaintances, not to mention family members.

So to call Scott the smartest and most talented of the bunch is no small statement.

He was Oahu Island golf champion as a senior in high school. Could have taken a scholarship to play golf in any school in America. Instead he went to a small college in the middle of the woods in Northern New Jersey. And it didn't even have a golf team.

Without doubt the best public speaker and debater I ever knew. He was also politically involved and connected back at home. When we went to his congressmen's office in D.C., they were on a first name basis and talked like old friends. He could have gone back and ran that state.

He graduated a semester before the rest of us. His LSAT scores attracted Harvard Law. Instead he moved to Minnesota and became a flight attendant. Always soaring ahead of us.

I'm pretty sure he's a lawyer now. Still in Minnesota. Haven't seen him in a while, though. But he's still in touch with mutual friends.

Dude served me my first drink of alcohol when we were sophomores.

Here's a toast to you, Scott.

July 4th

What are we celebrating?

A hope? A dream? A nightmare? An idea? An experiment?

What are we celebrating? What is the Fourth of July to a God-fearing follower of Christ?

I have eight great-grandparents. One from England. One from Ireland. One from Germany. One from Poland. One from Russia. And the other three from Italy.. if you could call what that was back then "Italy".

Go back no more than 150 years ago and there is no trace of my blood in this country.

But 245 years ago, blood was being spilled so my eight great-grandparents could have a place to escape to. And meet. And mingle. And create new life.

I am a product of that process. Just like the rest of us.

The only country where my existence is possible is the United States of America. That is what I am celebrating today.

But it is not my country right or wrong. It is not what I pledge allegiance to. It is not my destiny manifested.

God provides my moral compass. Jesus owns my allegiance. Eternity is my destiny.

That is truth granted to me by the Holy Spirit.

It is what I am celebrating.

Everyday.

No fireworks needed.

July 3ʳᵈ

2000 light years from home. Living like a Rolling Stone. A multi-instrumentalist like Brian Jones. As others claim my work as their own.

Hiding from their Satanic Majesties in my little corner of the Rock. Framed by Old Glory and the many sights of the past. Watching the flow of hypercapitalism from afar.

I am not alone, though. Jamming away to music I cannot hear. I wonder what he is hiding from. Doesn't seem lost. Maybe in need of a break. Like the rest of us. But so few take one.

We are the smart ones. The heroes of self-care. I am honored that our paths have paralleled so closely. For so long.

Jambo stranger!

I've known a couple Dooley's in my life. And they both held their head up high. I hope all their thoughts will one day become things.

Not mine, though. Still too polluted. Like my muses are swimming in the East River. And my pen is stuck in Spuyten Duyvil.

I'm on the path of purification, though. Slowly but surely. Greta would be proud of me. I'm certainly proud of her.

I just hope all my babies don't get thrown out with my briny ocean of bathwater.

I have some good thoughts. Definitely worthy of becoming things.

Time to get up and start making that happen.

Who's with me?

July 2nd

Wake up in poverty, go to bed with stock options.

That's pretty much been my cycle for a while now. Wake up in the emotional gutter, do everything I can during the day to crawl out of it, and hopefully go to sleep feeling good, or at least not bad. And then wake up the next day back on square one. Or square negative one to be more accurate.

It's nothing out of the ordinary. It's called depression. The monkey that's forever on my back. I don't like to talk about it, though, out of respect for those of us carrying gorillas. They are the real unsung heroes of all of this.

But for all the fellow monkey-carriers out there, don't you hate when you make plans when you're feeling fine, and then wake up with a sense of dread over what you committed yourself to?

Yeah, me too! Good times. Good times.

And you have to follow through. Otherwise you feel even worse about yourself. And then there goes those stock options.

So you soldier through it. Trying to hide the awkwardness and repressed anger that comes with monkey-carrying, and hopefully feel a little more comfortable by the end.

Only those who suffer from depression have truly earned their participation trophies.

Life is like going for a nice run around the lake on a Sunday morning.

You look forward to it. You feel great at the end. But man, it can sure hurt while you're doing it.

Thank God for the scenery and good music.

It's all we got.

July 1st

Leave it to you to turn summer vacation into one long, continuous cross-training session for your mind, body, and soul.

Like there is any other way to live.

Preparing for a world you wouldn't want to live in, and you know you wouldn't long survive in, despite your training.

Yes. The folly of the games that energy play. I guess it beats the alternative.

Which is?

The nothing and everything of space consciousness.

Doesn't sound too bad to me.

No. It's really not. Actually quite awesome if I'm going to be completely honest. But Jesus don't want me for a sunbeam. Sunbeams can't chop wood or carry water.

Tending the garden that is continually burning all around you.

Yep. That's the game. Feeding the dog as it gnaws at your outstretched hand.

Seems pretty pointless to me.

It is pointless. That's the point.

(Sigh)

You people of piety certainly perplex me.

Perfect!

Mission accomplished.

June 30th

Taking one mask off as I begin to put on another one. All on top of the mask I've been wearing since birth.

Masks all the way down. Until you get to the one who is maskless. And behold the hideously awesome face of God.

This place is always available to you. You should visit more often. When you are tired of the games energy play.

I see your turmoil. I see your struggle. I see your exhaustion. I see you trying to decide whether to reach for the sword or the white flag.

Just stop. Be still. There is something better for you behind Door Number Three. But you have to withdraw to go through it.

Withdraw from all the games. Withdraw from all the stories. Withdraw from all of it.

You have our permission.

You will never be enough for them. Bu you are everything to us.

We will help you. We will guide your steps. We will give you all the words you need.

You are with us. You are protected. You are safe.

Stop competing. Stop comparing. Stop rationalizing. Stop justifying. And stop being so damn hard on yourself.

We got you. There are no wrong moves.

Just be you.

June 29th

This is the number one book in Heaven. It really makes the sparks fly.

Alone in a movie theater. You've definitely found yourself on a unique path if you are alone in a movie theater.

And I don't mean going to a movie alone. That's normal. I actually prefer it. Otherwise I become hyper-focused on how the person or people I came with are reacting to the movie. If they're not enjoying it, it's tough for me to enjoy it. But when I go alone, I'm focused completely on the movie. And if it's good, I'll lose myself. The reason we go to the movies in the first place.

But I'm not talking about that. I'm talking about being the only human being in the movie theater while the movie is playing. Definitely a unique path to get there.

A mix of strange cultural interests and sensibilities combined with unconventional lifestyle choices and preferences. Put them together and.. BOOM. You are alone in a movie theater.

I've done it at least twice, nearly twenty years apart. And not in some rural places, either. I'm talking about Manhattan on a weekend and Northern New Jersey during a summer afternoon. Prime movie going times in the most densely populated places on the planet.

But it's still just me alone in a movie theater. The only person who made the decisions necessary to get here.

Over twenty years as an adult out in the world and I haven't conformed yet.

Just like Sparks. Inspired to keep flying. The only way to make this.

The number one book in Heaven.

June 28th

Chasing experience. That's what it must look like to them. Selfish living.

To me it's just trying to make the best of a bad situation.

But they don't see that. The bad situation. Either they've never been here, or they've forgotten what it was like when they were.

Focusing on the greener grass while I'm trying to get out from under the weeds.

It's easy to piously fast after the well has already dried. But can you refuse the overflowing cup?

I don't know whether I am awake now or I just haven't slept yet.

I never can remember my dreams.

Crossroads always seem cool in concept. But they're never any fun when you actually get to one.

Let's see what direction my momentum takes me this time. I can promise you one thing, though. Ain't nobody gonna impede me.

Wherever I'm going, I will get there. For better or worse.

Alone at 5:30 in the morning. Nowhere to go. No obligations. No expectations.

What will you make from this lump of clay before it brittles and breaks?

Lord, guide my hands.

June 27ᵗʰ

Touching the cloth. Finishing the race. Finding the missing key.

And the day just begun.

Paying respects. Making the small talk. Eating the pigs and figs.

And now the evening begins.

On the couch. Radio on. Ken and Treya welcomed back into my life.

Time for the show.

Based on a true story. But aren't they all?

Shadowy silhouettes on the silver screen. A subtle sonata sings in the background. Sensuous lovers swept by passion and pretext. Preceded by the Einstein of human consciousness playing charades.

Wearing an ugly sweater.

Transcending and including the mammaries. More fun than a human should be allowed to have. The greater the love, the greater the pain. The greater the pain, the greater the love.

That man is going to have one hell of a second act. I can't wait to see it. And hope to be part of it. If invited.

Legend has it that when they found John Denver's body, it was completely covered in starfish who were feeding off it. I feel that deep in my very soul. That's how I want to go out.

Decompose me. Let me nourish you.

It takes grace, yes. And grit!

Spoiler alert. She dies at the end.

At the hour and forty-five-minute mark to be exact.

Because I could no longer ignore death, I pay more attention to life.

June 26th

Went the distance. Crossed the finish line in triumph. But nobody was there to cheer me on at the end.

I am alone in this race.

Yet still I am rushed to the pressroom to answer to all the critics and nay-sayers. Trying to write me out of my own story so I can better fit into theirs.

That Osaka girl knows exactly what she is doing. I can't blame her. Everybody thinks you owe them something. Entitlement is a dirty word. Any form of it.

But I can't escape my job. So it's back to work for me today.

Put on a false face. They don't want to see who you are. Hide your thoughts. They lay waiting to attack them. Bite your tongue. They will only twist your words.

It is all so exhausting. That's why I consider it work. And a tough job at that.

Fulfilling obligations to people your built up for so long, only to realize how little you mean to them.

There are no heroes in history. So stop looking for them in your family.

You are alone in this race. There will be no outstretched hand to help you, thank you, or congratulate you. Stop looking for one.

We're sorry, but you are stranded here. And there's no sign of help being on the way.

Deal with it.

You have no other choice.

June 25th

Hello thoughts! Summer edition.

I am avoiding nothing today. Actively and passively.

T-Pain is a sympathetic figure. An artist's nightmare. There but for the grace of God goes I.

Wow. It's not even nine o'clock but it already feels like I've been lying on the couch doing nothing all day.

I know it's coming on, David Sylvian. I'm gonna try my best to let the happiness in. But it won't be easy. It's an under-worked muscle.

Cool to finally sit and listen to JA straight through, instead of sneaking him in during a prep while grading assignments and answering emails. The Kingdom of Heaven is ours today.

I don't ask for much. Seriously. As long as I have warm water and can flush my toilet, I am happy.

Look at her run. A lot of bouncing and waving. Inspiring, but humbling. Look at him run. A lot of huffing and puffing. Humbling, but inspiring.

It feels like I did something good today. I don't know what, though. Maybe just reaping the rewards of a life well lived. It's about time.

Two roses slowly rot on an antique desk. I wonder if they will email me in ten years.

I owe no allegiances to Bryce. Enough of this static. Back to pop.

I haven't read the Bible yet today. Usually one of the first things I check off my list. Today it will be one of the last. But it will get done.

God help the beast in me. Now that's real. Cash money.

It's true. There ain't no cure for the summertime blues. Good thing I've been vaccinated.

Perhaps a little too high. But who's to judge?

Check.

June 24th

NJ Transit Train 6611. Car 7740.

Heading west. In need of rest.

But there is not rest for the wicked. Which means there is no rest from the wicked. They are constantly working. What about you?

Keep you guard up, kid.

Distance was achieved from the psychic attacks, but are you prepared for mind-to-mind combat?

Veins bloated with blood and you're in a room full of vampires.

Sharpen your crosses because they are out to suck you dry.

Punishment for leaving the herd. Discipline for escaping the bucket.

Meet your friends. Meet your family. They will not be joining you on the hot air balloon ride of the soul. They are the weights you need to cut free.

Wave to them on the ground as they shoot darts up at you. It's the only way they know how to love.

Broken.

Like the Pruitt-Igoe I am escaping from.

Well-intentioned, but with zero-regard to the humanity inside all of us.

Try to force-fit you into their worlds without paying attention to the shape you're in.

Just kids playing with blocks.

All of them.

June 23rd

This is just a place. You've always known that. Compressed matter in an arbitrary location. Just a place. It is you who gave it any more meaning or significance. A story you told yourself and believed so much that it became real. But only to you. To everyone else it is just a place.

They are just people. You've always known that. Compressed matter in arbitrary locations that appear to be conscious of themselves. Just people. It is you who gave them any more meaning or significance. Stories you told yourself and believed so much that they became real. To everyone else they are just people.

It is just time. You've always known that. A man-made concept to describe an arbitrary moment in relation to the universe. Just time. It is you who gave it any more meaning or significance. A story you told yourself and believed so much that it became real. To everyone else it is just time.

So what now? What are you going to do in this place, with these people, at this time?

What are you here for?

See all the colors? Hear all the sounds? Taste all the flavors? Speak all the words? Feel all the feels?

And then what?

What are you here for? Watcha gonna do?

Figure it out and get back to me.

I'm in no rush.

June 22nd

I'm on the edge. About as high up as someone like me can get and still have access to the fresh air.

At least in this hemisphere.

Home on the edge. Because I know the ledge. I've seen the ledge. I've stood on the ledge. I've taken pictures from the ledge.

The ledge can hold my weight.

Those sipping the champagne don't seem as confident.

As the bread grows stale on their hundred-dollar plates.

Goodness waits for evil to meet its fate.

While I stand naked. Tired of rhyming. Tired of scheming.

Tell me where to stand. Tell me what to do. Use me until you get what you want out of me.

I am just a prop you need to enhance the newsfeed of your life. Chasing approval from strange acquaintances. In order to avoid intimacy with those in front of you.

I am in front of you. Into me, see.

My form is far greater than my function.

You are in front of me. Into you, I see.

There is more than this charade you play with others.

Let's drop the games.

Let's leap off the edge.

Together.

June 21st

NJ Transit Train 6644. Car 7697.

Eastbound. But not down.

Rolling out of Madison. Reminds me of all the times I was rolling in Madison.

The agony and the ecstasy. All worth it for the American Studies degree. The last of my breed. And also the first.

But now it feels like I'm escaping something. Something I can't see. And barely feel. But I know it's there. Waiting for me. Knowing I always come back.

In the fight against sloth and gluttony, I fled. Ain't too proud to admit when I'm whipped.

Already reached the summit and my journey has just begun.

This life is but one long denouement.

And don't ask me how to pronounce that. I will skip this during the live readings. Lest I expose myself.

This place has gotten a lot chattier. As the music cuts out.

A turf field with brightly colored lines. Next to the free public library. Near the playhouse for the paper mill. I helped someone in this town.

We all did.

Debilitated optimist passing gladstones.

Happy that things are finally back on track.

Gather all your personal belongings.

The next and final stop is..

June 20th

Power washing the caked-on detritus off my already molding mind.

The worm of lust has burrowed in there deeply.

Curb your dog.

Don't bark at the nymphs as they bathe in the river.

It's 9:19pm somewhere. But not here.

Here it's 2:20 and the mothers are doing yoga on yellow mats next to the red stairs of Times Square.

While the fathers celebrate Father's Day by not being fathers.

Cheers to the hard-working people. Cheers to the salt of the earth.

You look out for me, and I'll look out for you. Keep the spirits at bay. Like any good cat would.

Stars in the velvety sky. You know how I feel. Like a motherless child. A long way. From my home.

Freedom.

God bless the child. Who has his own.

Bought. Not borrowed. Paid today.

Stay away. Lay away. Play away.

Here comes the sun. There goes the Son.

It's 9:34pm somewhere.

But not here.

June 19ᵗʰ

Every rose has its thorn.

Except these two.

A part of me wants to end this right here. But that would be taking the easy way out.

So onward I march;

The theme for today is liberty.

I can't turn it off. The Master's fountain. And I wouldn't want to. So I keep drinking from the hose.

Let's take a break to see if I solved the puzzle.

Yes! Take that, Gail Grabowski.

Scornbread and Screamcheese.

Let's Seat.

Chaga and super greens. Food is healing.

Johnny Walker Blue oxidants.

Do you ever do anything without a reason?
Never. But I could give it a try.

A package to be delivered earlier than expected.

A Juneteenth celebration.

We are declared free of all forms of slavery, bondage, indenture, restraint, curse, spell, guilt, or hinderance in any form; from this or any other lifetime.

We are emancipated.

June 18th

And we have made it here. Bringing her into the station.

The journey of a thousand miles ends in a single step. It's the same step that begins the next thousand-mile journey.

Thousand-mile journeys all the way down. And all the way up. Sideways too.

Cycles upon cycles upon cycles. Vico was right.

History doesn't repeat itself, but it often rhymes. And you are a master rhymer.

An ancient tale.

Told after midnight by Mona. And the girl from Mars.

A stolen wake and bake in the wee hours of the morning before the pigeon takes flight.

Watching the early risers share the boardwalk with the late nighters. Trying to figure out the difference between the two camps.

I had a home in each camp. And still don't know.

All I know is that the trip is over when you hear the day laborer with the leaf blower.

Outside your dorm window after you just finished taking apart your psyche and putting it back together.

Postcards from thousand-mile journeys of the past.

Turning yellow in that old shoebox.

As you keep collecting more.

June 17th

A Taoist foundation with a Christian edifice and a Catholic exterior.

That is the home that I built for myself to live in. It's nothing fancy, but it keeps me warm and protects me from the reign.

Of hate. Of ignorance. Of anger. Of fear. Of the adversary.

The big bad wolf better save his breath with me.

My Taoist foundation is more of a finished basement at this point, though. Or a bomb shelter.

It's where I retreat to when the world above ground gets a little too threatening for me.

A safe room.

It's also where the part of me that didn't want to grow up lives. We left him down there with the Cheetos and video games.

Less rules down there. Less responsibility.

But for the most part I live upstairs. Trying to keep the exterior as shiny as possible. Which is nearly impossible.

But it's an honest living.

It's what I built for myself. It's my home.

And visitors are always welcome.

You have an open invitation.

June 16th

Hung over after eating too many Coca-Cola Tic Tac's. Limited Edition flavor. First got hooked on them back during the early pandemic. Found them at the QuickChek in Hopatcong on Lakeside.

Comfort foods and comfort flavors.

They still call them the zero-calorie breath mint and the label says 0 grams of sugar.

But what about if you eat a couple hundred of them? They can't be zero calories. Has to be a lot of sugar. No way to know, though.

That's how they get you.

And they're all out to get you.

Nobody is on your side.

Your self-actualization does not help their profits or their personal pet projects.

You are just a pawn. Or a cheerleader. Or perhaps only an extra. Hoping for a speaking role to earn your S.A.G. card.

Or maybe you're the bad guy.

A villain to all those still trapped in the movies of their minds.

Cinematic stories of solipsism.

Fevered egos.

And they're giving you the Big Chill.

June 15th

In all honesty, when I stack up the pros versus the cons, there aren't really many cons at the end of the day. Or even the beginning.

The biggest con would be having to repeat everything all over again. Like there's no escape. But I know that's not true. You don't just lose all the lessons learned, stages earned, and experience gained. It's like when you set out to run eight miles, but only make it six. You still get all the health benefits of running six miles and you are certainly six miles further away than you started. More is gained than lost.

And nothing can force you into a situation that you do not want to be in. So if you don't want to come back you don't have to. You can make up the lessons you walked out of at another time, in another place, through a different way.

You have all the time in the world. And there are countless ways to cover those last two miles, and all the miles that come after it.

Losing out on eternity would be a con, but that's only possible if I'm knowingly rebelling against God. I am not.

I would not be rebelling against God. I'm rebelling against humanity. As hard and painful as this has been, I will always be grateful for everything given to me by God, Jesus, and the Holy Spirit. You will always have my love, worship, and service.

It's humans and all they've taken from me. That's where I'm making my stand.

And for my last con, those who may be hurt by what I do:

I'm sorry. I wish I could say that you were enough for this life.

But you weren't.

C'est la vie.

June 14th

It's not how you start. It's how you finish.

Well, if that's the case, then consider me finished.

Because all that really matters is the middle.

Beginnings and endings. Starts and finishes. They're all artificial demarcations. Artificially created by phony people to enjoy fake accomplishments.

Where were they when it counted? Where were they during the middle?

Pride is about as deadly as they come because of how much of a liar she is.

A house of cards built on a foundation of sand. And here comes the wind and rain.

I don't need a plaque with my name on it. I just want people to help me make my job easier. Or at least not any more difficult.

But I am alone.

A sheep on a team of lone wolves. As the shepherds count their shekels.

Alone.

Trying not to judge. But how else should I react when they keep denying my outstretched hand? Only caring when it's holding something they need.

Definitely not anything they want. They've already made that clear to me.

Alone.

Haven't begun. But already finished.

June 13th

Always enjoy writing when I'm just a little bit horny. And looking out on a new window to the world.

They're coming and they're going. They're coming and they're going.

As the halter tops keep haltering.

Pity the man behind the rickshaw. And shame to those inside of it.

The toddler in the stroller. And the fat man on the scooter.

We. Buy. Any. Car. .Com.

Cleavage separated by the straps of a purse or handbag. One of life's little pleasures.

Pay attention to the details. They are the mustard seeds that the Kingdom of Heaven is made up of.

There are a lot of people here today.

God bless all of them.

Especially the guy on crutches with one leg. I've seen him go by before. Like déjà vu.

Don't hassle him, he's local.

Another Mark. Welcoming the latest con. In a city not worth working up a sweat in.

Nucky lights up another unfiltered Lucky.

The empire is over.

June 12th

Welcome to the Rock.

It's been one year, three months, and four days since I last got a Starbucks. I just enjoyed my first sip of a grande nitro cold brew with sweet cream.

And now my second.

I didn't realize how much I missed this until right now.

Hey now, hey now. Don't dream it's over.

I remember during the early pandemic I said to myself, and anyone who would listen, that I would know that it was all over when I could finally sit in the Rockaway Mall without a mask on, drink a Starbucks, and people watch.

That's what I'm doing right now.

I would say that it's still 50-50 between mask-wearers and non-mask wearers, though. But I'm not picking up any judgement from the mask-wearers. And trust me, I'm sensitive to that sort of thing. I think they know they lost, just not ready to fully surrender yet.

I surrendered a long time ago. That's why this wasn't much of a fight for me.

Just had to play a lot of defense.

Guard myself from those intruding on His bliss and joy.

The crabs trying to pull me back in the bucket.

But the bucket is a lie. An illusion. A simulated reality. Not real shadows. Not even a real cave.

Dave was right about that.

But they don't know that.

And it's not my job to tell them.

Unfortunately.

June 11th

The men in red are out early. Taking a break from sweeping as they talk to the cop on the beat.

The empty dumpster rolls away unattended.

A couple leans on their suitcases as they take in the sights around them. This is either their first time here or their thousandth.

It doesn't make a difference either way. It is always new.

The vehicles parade by without disruption. The pedestrians are marching in step.

Everyone knows what they are doing. Everybody will get to where they're going.

The Pride flag dances along to the slow rhythm of the wind. Never forget the prisoners of war. Never forget the missing in action.

They have not forgotten about us.

Look at the jogger as he divides the scene in two. To him this is all just one big dojo. Training for the fight of his life.

It's too late for an early knockout, so you better be prepared to go the distance. Leave it in the hands of the judges.

Judge not, lest ye be judged.

For throwing in the towel.

When you still had more to give.

Don't hold back. Give it all to us.

June 10th

I find that I do this thing where I clench my lower jaw whenever I have a mask on. I have no clue what that is about. Maybe it is my way to compensate for the feeling of it constantly slipping from my nose. But I'm doing it right now. It's hard not doing it, despite being conscious of it.

I'm tired of these masks. Definitely long overdue to ditch them.

The pandemic is over, but now many are stuck in the Peter Pan-demic.

The monster inside is always far scarier than the monster outside. So many are avoiding the former by trying desperately to keep the latter alive.

They won't succeed in the end, but they will continue to make life difficult for the rest of us in the meantime.

Wake up. Grow up. Show up.

That's what Ken Wilber would tell them.

If the past year didn't wake you up, nothing will.

It's now time to grow up.

Break out of your cages if you must. The world already has enough children to take care of. Try not to be one more.

In the meantime, I'll wait. It's what I'm best at. My hedgehog concept.

I know I'm early, but I thought there'd be other people showing up by now.

I'm starting to get lonely. And a little worried.

Am I the only one who remembered?

June 9th

My attention to detail is what enables the people around me to be so sloppy and negligent.

It's like when a toddler charges around a house like a bull in a China shop. Not realizing there is an always attentive parent clearing the path forward and cleaning the mess left behind.

That's where I find myself. Among the small group of parents in a world of toddlers.

Toddlers that are materially sloppy. Toddlers that are mentally sloppy. Toddlers that are emotionally sloppy. Toddlers that are spiritually sloppy.

Toddlers that are charging into danger as they leave behind a world of mess.

And the parents are getting tired. The parents are getting frustrated. The parents are getting angry.

Too many toddlers. Too much mess.

Makes me think of Atlas Shrugged. When all the scientists, engineers, artists, musicians, intellectuals, all of them. They all just upped and left. Created their own world somewhere in Colorado. No toddlers, just parents.

Doesn't sound like much fun if you ask me.

What is a good man but a bad man's teacher? What is a bad man but a good man's job?

If you don't understand this, you will get lost.

I am not John Galt.

June 8th

I voted. Democracy in action.

Checked in by an old lady who didn't know the alphabet. Processed by an old man who didn't speak my language.

The corruption of incompetence.

It's all over the place. Schools, businesses, homes, churches, town halls. Everywhere.

The avarice of apathy.

Lack of faith is sad. Lack of care is tragic.

This world is one big chicken just waiting to get plucked. But instead we just keep hoarding all the eggs.

Wiping the yolk off my face.

I voted. Democracy in action.

Two of the people I voted for were the two who visited me. That's my rule. You take the time to talk to me and I will be on your side. I don't care what your views are. I'm just appreciative of the effort.

Especially when so many don't take the effort with me.

I also voted for the ex-mayor with the sad face. A very sympathetic character in the tales I spin in my head. Plus I know where he lives. I saw him today driving to work.

Other than that, it was a lot of random guess work. Mainly just avoided the ones who sent me too much mail.

I hate that.

Democracy in action.

I voted.

June 7th

It's like when you're driving and you're not really focused and your mind is wandering because you're a little tired, and then you get this moment of clarity and you're like, "How did I get here?"

A lot of people are waking up to that feeling right now.

How did I get here?

Today.
This moment in history.
This stage of the game.
This world.
This reality.
This life.
Today.
June 7th, 2021.

How did I get here? Or as Noelie used to say, "How did my karma lead me to this?"

I'm not one of those people. I know how I got here. I know exactly how my karma led me to this. I can retrace every twist and turn. When I was stalled, when I was smooth sailing. All my victories. All my defeats. Good decisions. Bad decisions. I remember it all.

I know how I got here. I've been here a long time.

But now I have company. And they weren't expecting to find me.

And now like any native, I am being dismissed as a nuisance at best, and actively pushed away and rejected at worst.

Infected by their sickness as they remove me from their world. A world that used to be mine. But no more.

There are no reservations on this trail.

Only tears.

June 6th

I know I shouldn't be writing when I'm in a mood like this. It's such a burden on the reader. But sometimes it's all I can do.

It's just so boring and repetitive. The same complaints and misperceived transgressions over and over again. We get the point, Doug.

If you truly believe you can't move forward without breaking away, then break away. Get it over with. Stop hemming and hawing. We always have your back.

I know. I get that. It's the time span of the breaking away that is causing the turmoil. To you, ripping off the band-aid happens in a snap. To us, it's a long-drawn-out process that may take decades. But I'll be free of it during this lifetime. You can guarantee that.

Meanwhile it's more tongue biting and stomaching get-togethers with people I don't make the cut with.

Charades and hide & go seek.

Games I'm done with played by people I'm tired of.

The stone has been rejected for the last time.

It's time to turn the corner.

Leave them behind.

Come home.

June 5th

It's morning in Vineland. And I am back from a seven-mile victory run.

There and back.

Looking out from the third-floor balcony at the intersection of Delsea and Landis.

Sipping black coffee I made in the bathroom of the Days Inn. About to light up a joint.

Meanwhile, Marcus is looking for something he can't fine. Been there, done that. Haven't we all.

It's morning in Vineland. And the feed from Shrunken Planet drops. A Bluetooth problem. Unable to hear Jeffery's farewell. But at least I got it back in time for Bob.

You are now about to begin a great adventure. The journey out of your mind.

As I sip more coffee and relight the joint.

The helicopter flies low over the Dollar Tree. The parking lot of the Mattress Factory is deserted. The broad-legged lady returns to her car.

It's morning in Vineland. And I don't know why I had to end my run at Butch's Gun World. But it just felt right. At least I got a glimpse of Gittone Stadium. Home of the Clan.

I'll have to tell Pops about that.

It's morning in Vineland. And the air feels right.

This is going to be a good day among the Immortals.

June 4th

The feeling begins. And then it fades.

The feelings begin. All of them at once.

Nothing less than feelings. And I am a long ways from the day's one l.

Barbarians at the gate. Sheep prowling around like wolves. Armed and ready to strike.

Has the shepherd lost control of his flock? Or did the flock lose sight of the shepherd?

This is what happens when you tear down a fence before remembering why you put it up in the first place.

We've grown soft. And these are hard times.

Boys are not being boys. Girls are not being girls. They are not being them.

This is something different. This is something new.

Do all the canaries have to die before we realize there is danger down the coal mine?

I hope not.

I don't want to die. I just want to sing. That's what canaries are supposed to do.

I am not your alarm, so stop snoozing.

Wake up and hear the music. It's the only message you need.

Dance. Sing. Live.

Keep the barbarians at bay.

June 3rd

Books and bats. Or maybe bats and books. Or how about books and bats, bats and books. Nah, that's a bit much. I think I'll stick with the first one.

Books and bats.

My million-dollar idea. My ticket out of here.

And by million-dollar idea, I mean I have no intention of making much profit from any of this. If people want to give me money, that's cool, but I just want to spread my art. Get my books and bats to as many people as I can. Maybe inspire people to write their own books or make their own bats. That'd be cool.

And by my ticket out of here, I mean my way of accepting where I find myself. A b-story for when the main plot line bores me. Something else to focus on. A hobby with a purpose.

Things are changing. Things are happening. But never at a rate that satisfies me. The new becomes old before it is even fully manifested. There is nothing to hold on to. Nowhere to hang my hat.

Except on books and bats.

I should be ready to go by spring of '22.

Maybe I'll start with street fairs. Flea markets would work too. I wonder how much it costs to get a spot at a flea market. So much to learn.

Art shows seem like too much of reach right now, but you never know. This could really take off. Or it could stay firmly rooted in the grass. Either way it should be fun.

Books and bats.

You heard it here first.

June 2nd

One of my earliest memories is lying awake in bed wanting to kill myself.

I was much too young to even begin to know how to act on that feeling, but the feeling was very strong and very real, nonetheless.

My bedroom was at the end of the hallway, directly across from my parents. I shared it with my brother. His bed was near the window, and mine was closest to the door. So there were mere feet between my bed and my parent's room.

I had a front row seat. To all the screaming, the yelling, the anger, the hate. Arguing and fighting. Fighting and arguing. That's all there was.

And my daytime hours were not all that better. Two older brothers that were cruelly abusive both physically and emotionally. Using me as a scapegoat to work out their own feelings.

Family dynamics.

So forgive me for not wanting to be there. It was like being forced to sit through a horrible movie. I just wanted to shut it off and go home.

And that was not my home.

Also forgive me for not getting warm and fuzzy when I think about family and for continuing to keep them at arm's length.

In a young boy's still developing mind, strong feelings have a way of being cemented in. Long after the external causes have faded, the emotional grooves remain.

And with the absence of any real affection, encouragement, acceptance, or consolation in the years since, I remain here broken. Constantly at war with my feelings. Just trying to do the best I can.

Thanks family.

June 1ˢᵗ

I'm on the right side, correct?

Correct.

Ok, it's just been feeling different lately.

Don't pay that no mind. You ain't perfect, and we may need to keep humbling you, but do not doubt the bigger path you find yourself walking. You and it are as good as golden.

Thanks. I needed to hear that.

No problem. Anytime. Just remember that resistance is not repudiation.

Got it.

So get out there and keep spreading your art.

I'm still trying to remember whether this is my art or not. I definitely wasn't the first person to tape up bats, everybody did that. But was anybody else making them look cool?

That might have been me. With the bats I made in the Bronx. Not to mention my broom. The only thing Doc gave me credit for.

"It may look weird, but it does the job."

I should open my resume with that quote.

Rewinding the tape. Another art form from the Bronx. The cradle of creativity.

Marrying form and functionality.

Lacking only acolytes.

May 31st

Drama on the Edmund Pettus Bridge. It was a hit and run!

I knew I did it. I just didn't think there were any witnesses. Those darn good Samaritans will get you all the time.

And I understand the rebuke. I appreciate yet another wake-up call. But I'm just asking for mercy and forgiveness. Mercy and forgiveness.

Be patient with me. I'm trying the best I can. This is not easy. And I'm not making excuses. I know what I have to do. Just be patient. That's all I ask.

It will all be resolved by the next time I give blood.

The skeleton for a summer is in place. Now all I have to do is give it some flesh.

Ten weeks. An eternity when you're playing in a sandbox. And that's all I plan on doing. Making castles. Looking for princesses.

Until the tide washes it all away.

Roll tide roll.

Alabama.

Once again we're on the Edmund Pettus Bridge. The moral arc of the Universe has brought us full circle.

Doctor, mine eyes have seen the glory.

His truth is marching on.

May 30th

Have I not commanded you? Be strong and courageous. Do not be afraid. Do not be discouraged. For the Lord your God will be with you wherever you go.

Mr. Potato Head. Mr. Potato Head! Back doors are not a secret!

How about a nice game of chess?

Joshua won nine times.

But my wordplay is undefeated.

Cheers to Billy Joe Thomas as raindrops keep fallin' on my head.

It's because I hate umbrellas. I find them obnoxious. And a sign of weakness. I know we live in an era where it is not popular to have clearly defined gender roles, but forget that, men should not be using umbrellas.

I am a dinosaur. And it's going to take a meteor to take me out. And then you can have all the genders you want.

It doesn't feel like Memorial Day weekend. Too cold, dark, and gloomy. When I remember all the young men who were hurled into the furnaces of history so the ship of America could keep chugging forward, I want things to be more warm, bright, and festive.

It's a holiday, right?

Kneeling maskless in church this morning.

Thanking God that it's finally ending.

May 29th

Be careful. You didn't quite make it to June yet.

Smoking a cigarette early in the morning after brushing your teeth. One of the greatest flavors on the planet. Like the milk after eating a bowl of Honey Nut Cheerios. Only those who know, really know.

Aquafresh. Listerine. And the smoke from the first hits off a Camel unfiltered. Satan's response to soma.

I remember smoking a cigarette early in the morning staring at the Hudson River. My whole future was ahead of me.

I was waiting for a Metro North train to take me to 125th Street. I was in Dobbs Ferry.

I regret a lot of what I left behind in Dobbs Ferry. And regret doesn't come easy for me.

But we had some good times.

Sitting at the kitchen table, passing a joint, listening to Astral Weeks on vinyl.

Lazy Sundays with white wine and muscle relaxers. Reading the New York Times while listening to Norah Jones.

They were simpler times. But we still managed to make them oh so complex and messy.

What fools we were.

But mostly me.

I love you. I'm sorry. Please forgive me. Thank you.

May 28th

If you love something, set it free. If it comes back to you, you know the deal.

That's what I did. I set it free. I left it in God's hands. I was ready to move on. Even relished, for a brief moment, the feeling of what it would be like to actually be free of it.

But it's back. Never went anywhere. Exactly where I left it. Shouting the message loud and clear.

This is my work. This is my destiny.

Not for long, though. Almost at the halfway point, but not quite. Still a lot of labor ahead of me.

Put your head down and keep chugging forward. Don't stop. Don't quit. Don't slow down.

You've been here before, but not quite. This is harder.

But it's working. You're opening up new heights and digging new depths. When all is said and done, you'll be inhabiting a space that no one has been able to experience before.

Man, won't that be cool.

It's just around the corner, but it's a long corner.

You'll have more setbacks, more opportunities to quit, and need more pep talks.

But you will go the distance. Don't worry about that.

So enjoy the journey. Enjoy today. Enjoy right now.

You'll miss it when it's gone.

May 27th

Samba lama. Samba lama.

The rhythms of world music fill my niche on this alien planet.

My brain freezes in calculation of cultural congruences necessary to bring these sounds to my ears.

Truly a miracle if you think about it. I just hope nobody was hurt in making this miracle materially manifested.

But I'm sure there were. People hurt. Probably some animals too.

Miracles have side-effects. They don't teach you that, but it's true.

Yet we keep praying for them. Miracles.

Trying to conform the world to our own liking and expectation. Paying no attention to the butterfly effect of negative consequences unleashed on the world.

Who died so Lazarus could live again?

What was destroyed to create this beauty?

These sounds in my ear. Consequence of a planet in flames.

You take the good, you take the bad.

You take them both and there you have.

Life.

Just the facts.

May 26th

The walls are crumbling around you. Family is fractured beyond repair. Friends are out of touch and out of synch. Work is just absurd. You have nothing left in this world. How does that make you feel?

Free? Liberated? Frustrated? Furious? Sad?

How about, ok?

Ok?

Yeah, ok. I feel ok about all of it. I'm fine.

Really?

Yeah. I'm fine. Sure, I wish I had a family that accepted me and valued me, but I don't. But they do love me and support me, so it could be worse.

It would also be cool to have friends who were more willing to include me in their lives and wanted to be included in my life, but I don't. But they do appreciate who I am and would do anything for me if I asked, so it could be worse.

And yes, it would be awesome to work every day in a functional environment with competent and committed professionals, but I don't. But I do love the kids and the work is meaningful, and, at times, even fun, so it could worse.

So yeah, it's the end of the world as we know it, but I feel fine.

If things are meant to crumble, let them crumble. I'll emerge on the other side unscathed and stronger than ever. That's just how I roll.

How about you? Are you ok? Who will you be when we get to the other side of this?

I hope to see you there.

May 25th

Just so you are aware, I am definitely well aware of how much I use the words "just" and "definitely" in my writing. Nobody is more self-aware than I am. Nobody.

Definitely is definitely my favorite word. Whether I am writing, texting, talking, speaking, whatever, I always use a lot of definitelys.

I am a very definitive person. I like things to be very black or very white. All the lines in my life are very clear and very distinct. And I am constantly re-drawing and re-enforcing them. I don't tolerate any smudges, smears, erasures, or fades to grey.

Projecting a high-definition picture to the world. Call me HD-DP. INFJHDDP.

Justice is very important to me. It fits in with my introverted, intuitive, feeling, judging personality type. Me and Atticus Finch. Mockingbirds of a feather. Flocking together.

But that's not the reason why "just" shows up so often in my writing. It's more of a filler word. A transition. I use it to create rhythm, maintain tempo, or fill in any obvious breaks in harmony. Sometimes you just need an extra word to make things sound just right. That's just how I roll.

So for all you literary critics, editors, or English professors, this is not the book for you. I am not the writer for you.

As for those who are looking for someone trying to make sounds with words in order to express the ineffable emotions and experiences of everyday life..

This is definitely just the book for you.

May 24th

A crossword puzzle losing streak extended by a Freudian slip. A little dab will do ya, but that's not exactly what I'm missing in my life.

Forsaken by family and friends. A broken record repeating the same chorus again and again. When will I be brave enough to put on a new song?

Loyal and loving to those who neglect and abuse you. All because you're afraid there's nothing waiting for you behind Door Number Two.

You are just an idea to them. A minor character in their self-important dramas. A projection. A sounding board. Something to be used, controlled, and robbed from.

They don't care about your feelings. They don't care about your ideas. They don't care about your work. They don't care about your play.

They do not care about you.

Alone and cold. Lying naked in the un-heated bedroom of your soul.

This is where they left you.

Not worth the time, money, or effort.

That is what they are telling you.

Change and conform.

What they demand of you.

Resist and rise above.

Your only path out.

Embrace what is behind Door Number Two. You deserve it.

May 23rd

Here I am quoting old songs from college radio days. The Origin of Satan with Jake Soffronoff. Pete and I trekking down to the basement at 6am in order to open it up. I can still remember the smell of the place. Man, I wish I could smell that again.

They're trying to steal my joy. I don't know why, but they keep trying to steal my joy. I admit I tend to make it easy for them, but still. What did I do to deserve this?

Or maybe it was something I didn't do.

The Port of Miami looks peaceful right now. But so does everything from a distance. I'm sure there are stories on the ground that would break all of our hearts. All your sea-sick sailors, they are rowing home.

And it's all over now, baby blue.

Last night was a sloppy reset, but a reset, nonetheless.

My throat is still burnt from the acid tsunami. I hurt myself again. At least I always made it to the toilet.

A moral victory. Thanks to a lapse in morals.

Your faith has never been stronger, but your Catholicism is hanging by a thread. Of all Sundays to miss. It's a birthday party. Forget the gift you sent, where was your presence?

You wanted to wait a year before going deeper, but you know you can't handle ambiguity.

Dive in or don't

The time has come to stop hugging the ladder.

May 22nd

Ok. I could definitely get used to this. It's like if they asked me where would be the perfect place to put a bench for me, this would be it.

Right outside the exterior entrance to the Rockaway Mall food court. Tucked away in the corner. Just enough in the sun, just enough in the shade. They don't always notice me, but I definitely notice them. My goldilocks zone.

I will be wearing this bench out this summer.

In the shadow of my spiritual home. There are certainly a lot of different types of humans. The big one with the muscles dropped his lunch on the way to his car. They can't protect him from his own lack of grace.

We are all over-compensating for something.

The quad at the table in front of me are prattling away in Spanish. They may be talking about me. I'm definitely writing about them. I think the girl facing me, with the ripped jeans, is on to me. Right now she is pretending to talk on her phone as the other three look on earnestly.

She can't fool me.

Official Batman Club. Looney Tunes. United States Navy. Boys of all ages certainly wear some silly t-shirts. When I was a boy, I wore some silly t-shirts. Pi-ano. Moe Knows. Welcome to New Jersey, Now Go Home. Now I am a man and all the t-shirts I wear are dead serious.

Music IS the Message.

Soon I will go in and take my thousandth victory lap in the place where I took many of my first steps.

I traveled far to get here, but it was always on my horizon.

Welcome to my kingdom.

May 21st

Every so often it is important to update your creed so you can clarify the beliefs that are driving you forward. I'm sure you have been able to intuit most of this by flipping through these pages, but so there's no doubt, here is where I currently stand:

I am in constant communion and communication with a living, conscious Universe who continually guides me and works towards assisting my continued growth and development as a human soul.

I worship a God who is all-powerful and all-loving. A God who listens to my prayers and forgives me for my sins. A God I love completely and am eternally grateful toward.

I serve a master, Jesus, who willingly took on human form, lived a sinless life while enduring every possible pain and indignity, died on the cross, and then resurrected three days later, forever granting Christ Consciousness as a potential for all human souls. A master who is allowing me to help co-create and serve in his Kingdom of Heaven, where I will be a resident through all of eternity.

So that's where I am, brothers and sisters. There is nothing lost about me. I have my story and I am sticking to it as long as I keep receiving the grace needed to do so.

Amen.

May 20th

Well this ought to be fun. And I could use that. A little fun.

Fat city. That brings me back.

Huddled around a computer in the G.T. room. It was the early '90's. Like '90 or '91. We were answering trivia questions. It was called Knowledge Master, or something like that. Every time you got a question right, they would feed you some corny, antiquated compliment.

Fat city! Auk-cellent! Cat pajamas!

We were bred to be trivia champs, but we never could match the accomplishments of our predecessors. The bar they set was too darn high.

But Mrs. Spear made sure we felt like champs. A bunch of white trash kids showing up to your school in a stretch limo. Never knew middle school Academic Bowl competitions could have an intimidation factor.

We never cared about it as much as she did, though. That was our problem. We were just boys having fun. Playing Summer Games and Oregon Trail and the one game where you made your own monsters. Feeling special because we didn't have to eat in the cafeteria with the general population. That was what we were all about.

McConnell was seen as our bad influence. He was a C.T. kid, not A.A. He was the reason we were playing silly games instead of practicing our Knowledge Master.

But it was Joe who broke her heart.

When the most gifted and talented among us leaves the program, the rest just crumbles like a house of cards.

All that remains in my record in the pole-vault.

Long live the Dougie-flop.

May 19th

Ok, let me go check. www.google.com. And..

Nope, still no Google Doodle for Malcolm. Even on his birthday. Doesn't his life matter?

It definitely matters to me. I don't think I'd be where I am right now if it wasn't for Malcolm X.

And by where I am right now, I mean standing at the helm of a history classroom.

"Of all our studies, history is best qualified to reward our research."

I don't just believe that, I live it every day. That's why that poster has been following me in the quarter century since I first hung it above my desk in my dorm room freshman year.

Know thyself. There is nothing more important in this world than to know thyself. So many problems being caused by people who don't know who they are.

And you can't know who you are unless you know history.

We don't stop at our skin. We are embedded. In all of it.

The past. The present. The micro. The macro. All of it.

Our biographies are as much of who we are as the dead skin and lost hairs that clog our shower drains.

We are so much more. We are eternity.

Know thyself. Know history. Know eternity.

From Malcolm Little to Malcolm X to El Hajj Malik Al Shabazz.

Take the pilgrimage.

May 18th

The echoes of the past have dissipated. Thank God for that.

All that remains are reflexes and muscle memory. Slowly degrading over fallow soil.

What will emerge is yet to be determined.

Butterflies hatch from cocoons, but so do moths. Phoenixes rise from the ashes, but so do demons.

Are you ready for Brood X to return from their home deep in the soil?

I am. This is what I have been preparing for.

They are coming. They are already here.

Speaking a new language. Destroying the old idols. Rewriting the rule book.

I'm beginning to feel like a mid-wife during end-times.

What world am I preparing souls for?

The illusory prison of human experience, or the bliss of manifested eternity.

Can I do both at the same time? Are they mutually exclusive?

If there is only one true master, it's folly to feel you're serving any others.

The horns are holding up my halo. The devils and angels are both leading us home.

There is no wrong path.

Or maybe that's just cap.

May 17th

Man, I like to hurt myself on weekends. It goes without fail. Crawl my way up a mountain each week and then do everything I can to jump off it during the weekend.

And now I'm left with that Monday morning feeling. Back at square one and even a little bit behind. Stale smoke in my lungs. Gas making my stomach feel full. Bile making its way down my intestines.

I have a feeling that's something I am going to have to deal with soon. And probably repeatedly during the day.

It's the over-eating that does it. The smoke doesn't help, but if it was just smoke, I'd be fine. Maybe just a little grumpier. But I'm so good during the week, and then I just invade my stomach. It's almost like punishment. Not sure what I'm punishing myself for, though.

I don't have the best relationship with food. Never did. Too much of a comfort eater.

Food is entertainment. Food passes the time.

That's where I go wrong.

Oh! And I can't forget the caffeine withdrawal. That'll be joining the mix at some point soon. Fun stuff.

Why do I feel the need to be more awake on a Sunday?

Silliness.

But alas, I'll crawl through another Monday. I'll feel fine later, or tomorrow morning at the latest. And then march triumphantly through another week.

Tuesday, Wednesday, Thursday, Friday.

It's the weekend again! Let's celebrate!

You deserve it.

May 16th

The return of hello thoughts. Do we have any other choice? The return of hello thoughts!

Breakfast in Mexico has such heavy meats. Heavy, heavy meats.

If I was a gambling man. Never would'a let you play your hand, with a broken-down Towel Boy like me.

Or I may simply be a single drop of rain.

I don't know what is happening at the Pasha Mezze Grill. I am getting worried. I just heard sirens headed in that direction. Muhammad is my Dasher. He is heading to me. Please arrive safely, Muhammad. Please arrive safely.

Someday we'll find it. The rainbow connection. Right after building the rainbow coalition. Keep hope alive.

Uncle Toilet Brush Salesman. Lamborghini Driver. Hello Sunshine After the Rain. Little Ayaaaaa so cuteee. Live driving to Queens, New York. My afternoon drama.

As I find my way back on the couch. Actually thought I'd be productive. Although I did get my laundry done. And food shopping. And a four-mile hike. Lazy. But always taking care of business.

My brother got me that cigarette case in Nepal. Nothing is worse than seeing my reflection on the back of it. The worst kind of carnival mirror.

I see her reflection as she makes the bed. Whose bed? I don't know. Whose apartment is this? We are somewhere in Queens. Those lights are cool.

What are you doing! I fix it and you destroy it!

Mexico City. A recurring theme of my day.

But I ain't going there anytime soon.

You can count on that.

Cuarenta y cuatro.

May 15th

Happy birthday Bruce.

I can't imagine a more appropriate way to start than with that.

No, I'm serious. No ideas were allowed into my head until I first wrote the words, "Happy birthday Bruce" on the top of the page.

That's usually how it works. I'm given an opening line and not much else. So I write the opening line on the page and then the rest just flows from there.

It's my price of admission. How I ante up.

Sometimes I stick to a consistent theme. Other times I go off in about a dozen different directions and tangents. But you probably have figured that out by now.

But today is Bruce's birthday. I didn't plan on mentioning it, but my hand was forced. It's not like I mind or anything– Bruce was an amazing human being and I'm glad he gets a mention here– it just wasn't originally my idea.

If you want to learn more about Bruce, read my mom's book. My obituary and eulogy for him are both in there.

We're having a mass said for him today. It'll be my first time at St. Jude's since the pandemic. Also going out to dinner with the Schmidt's. Another pandemic first. I'm looking forward to both. Should be a good evening.

So yeah, happy birthday Bruce.

We miss you down here.

May 14th

And the stone just came tumbling down the hill right on top of me. What did I expect? Man, I am naïve. But I guess that's why you keep sticking with me. Any less naïve and I wouldn't be putting up with your nonsense.

But, whatever. We're all caught up in it, so I'm not going to worry. I'll keep taking some deep breaths, ride out the waves of anger, and then take care of business.

That's how you play the game. This stupid, silly, meaningless, game. I'm letting it occupy way too much space in my head. Haven't fully released my competitive side, yet. Still feel the need to be on top and in the right.

Wait a minute. That's not completely correct. It's not about my need to be on top and in the right. As long as I stay aligned with Christ I will always be on top and in the right because He is the very definition of being on top and in the right.

What I truly can't let go of is my need for other people to see me as on top and in the right.

That is my sin. And it is infecting every aspect of my life.

Please forgive me and help me heal. Remove this weight from me so I can walk freely toward your light.

Sartre was right. My hell is other people.

Rescue me.

May 13th

Dear Gregory & Marissa,

I hope this letter finds you well. I miss you both dearly and I yearn to return home to see you again. But unfortunately it doesn't look like I'll be home anytime soon. This place is a lot worse than we could have ever imagined, and there is a lot of work that still needs to be done. It also doesn't look like I'll be able to send for you both to join me here. Things are just way too dangerous and there are too many forces working against me. You would just be caught in the crossfire, and I couldn't forgive myself for that. As much as I want you here, you need to stay home. Don't even think of coming here to find me on your own. Trust me. You don't know what you're up against. I'm still figuring it out myself, and this is not my first rodeo.

I'd be a liar if I didn't say how much I miss your mother. She didn't want me coming here, but I came anyway. She was right. I should have listened to her. Now I am beginning to forget what her love feels like, and that is slowly killing me. I hope she didn't follow me here like she threatened. Who knows what could have happened to her if she did? If so, please keep her safe. If you can get someone there to help bring us back together, that would be great. Every moment I am without her, more and more of me gets chiseled away. I hope you will still be able to recognize me when I return.

And if your mother is still there with you, please tell her I am sorry. I am trying my best to stay true, but it is so hard down here, so very hard. I need her love. I need her wisdom. I need her guidance. But most of all, I need her forgiveness.

Please help me correct my faults so we can salvage this family.

Thank you.

Love always and keep with Christ,

Your very human father.

May 12th

I wake up on empty. Every day.

Sometimes it's a good thing.

I'll fall asleep filled with anger. Filled with anxiety. Filled with depression. Filled with despair.

I wake up on empty. A victory.

Many times, though, it is a defeat.

I'll fall asleep filled with hope. Filled with happiness. Filled with ideas. Filled with ambition.

I wake up on empty. Not a good morning.

High intensity, nocturnal, emotional chemotherapy.

Great for killing the cancer cleaved to my soul. But it's wreaking havoc on my heart and mind.

Man, I long for the day when I can finally say I am in remission. I want to ring that bell.

But this may be a lifelong battle. So I am preparing for it. This may be who I am. So I must live with it.

At least I can finally say that the ideas and ambition are coming back quicker than the anger and anxiety. But the despair and depression are still strong.

Hope and happiness are always the last two to the party. If they show at all.

I hope for happiness and would be happy with a little hope.

But until then, I'm just blessed to keep waking up.

A miracle.

May 11th

I'm always prone to romanticize how the other people are doing this.

Sitting in your villa in Key West. Beautiful view of the ocean. Sipping your bourbon as you bang away on the keyboard.

Outside a café in Paris. The steam from the coffee clouding up your glasses. Words dancing across the screen of your laptop.

Down underneath the Manhattan Bridge overpass. Brushing the crumbs from a half-eaten avocado toast off your yellow legal pad. The subway rats prick their ears up at the scratching from your pen.

That's how it's done, right? That's how the other people are doing this.

The romance of the writing life. Caught me hook, line, and sinker before realizing it was just a big lie.

Nowhere does it show me running away from over-zealous muses, desperately looking for a place to hide.

Nowhere does it show my mind being held hostage by thoughts and memories that will not grant me a moment of peace until I put them down on paper.

Nowhere does it show me now. Alone. Isolated. Used up. Methodically rowing the oars as the whip cracks open my back.

This is what I wanted. This is what I asked for.

Mama don't let your sons grow up to be writers.

Teach them how to rustle cattle instead.

May 10th

Last week's dirt is still caked upon the floor. So much for a clean slate. They exist only in your mind. The guardians at the gate never got the message.

Every morning I wake up on the bottom. Every day I crawl myself back up among the land of the living. I think they're actually beginning to accept me this time around. Every night I go to sleep hopeful.

Every morning I wake up on the bottom..

It's Sisyphus's all the way down.

Yet somehow, I still seem to be accumulating points. Like a pinball bouncing and bumping around aimlessly. Earning bonuses. Unlocking secret levels. While I flail away aimlessly at the flippers. Just trying to avoid the end and prolong the game. Nothing more.

And an extra ball is out of the question. I'm down to one, so I better make it last.

Because after that it's no more comings and goings. Just the sterile eternity of the angelic realms.

So enjoy the drums now. And the croaking wails of the out of tune horns.

Because after that is just the harmony of harps.

It will take some getting used to. But you will. Get used to it.

The austere agelessness of androgyny.

The synthesis you are anti toward. Deny it and be doomed.

Accept it and dive in.

May 9th

Once you start looking for these things, you start to find them. It's like a language that you can start to read, and others can't read it.

Not even Eliphas Levi himself.

I've heard of weird New Jersey, but Yonkers is off the map. No wonder Robin nested there. Definitely would have been seduced by the children if he was born earlier.

Hello from the gutters. Where Sam sleeps.

The prodigal John Wheaties has returned home.

The doors were shutting all around me. And it was only getting worse. The king is dead. Long live the king.

Is it ever really safe to go back in the water?

It was an old, green Impala. Dark green. Ugly car. He wore polyester pants and a Members Only jacket. He wasn't interested in those things.

I'm not interested in those things.

I used to live such a normal life. But I knew there was no going back. And then, suddenly, the answer became clear.

He was slumped over. The gun was slid away. Blood was on the ceiling. There was skull fragments and brain matter against the wall.

He was identified then as John Carr from New York.

But nothing ever was pursued. I felt that this was a little but strange. It was too much of a coincidence.

Sometimes you gotta open your eyes wide and see the whole picture.

Finally, the immovable mountain had been shaken.

Ending my descent into darkness.

May 8th

These stupid men with their stupid guns. When will it end?

Watched the movie 13 Hours this morning as per a student's recommendation. It was entertaining and all. Engaging and such. Michael Bay, fuhgeddaboudit. But seriously.

These stupid men with their stupid guns. When will it end?

That's what I was thinking all throughout. These stupid men with their stupid guns.

Is any of it necessary? Ever? I get the whole brotherhood thing and fighting for your comrades, but how did things get so far that people are shooting at you? Could any of this have been prevented?

From Benghazi back to Bunker Hill. Stupid men with their stupid guns.

And it's not their fault. They're just pawns. Stupid little pawns in an idiotic game played by morons.

Greed. Incompetence. Self-interest. Hate. Anger. Ignorance. Problems upon problems swept under the rug. Warning signs ignored. And then BOOM!

BOOM! BOOM! BOOM! BOOM! BOOM!

Stupid men with their stupid guns.

All is well that ends well. But sometimes all is well that just ends. Period.

Because with stupid men with their stupid guns, it will most definitely not end well.

So let's just end it.

May 7th

Awake to silence. Until the thoughts start singing with the birds. And then the music comes into focus.

Follow it into your future, but still keep cleaning your past.

Your least proud moment. The furthest away you were from the Kingdom. When we knew you needed saving.

It started with a chess game. And conversations that should not have been allowed across the boundary. But I was a fugitive then. A refugee looking for a new home, and something I could call a family.

On the quest for ecstasy, left with only agonies.

The agonies of unknowns.

How many people know?
Was it a set up?
What damage was caused?
Does anybody remember?
Will I ever forget?
Can I be forgiven?

Can I continue forward knowing that God used me like a broken vessel? Allowing the sin leaking out of me to water the seeds on my path.

And now I stand undeservingly in a field of flowers. Walking cautiously as I wipe the Gehenna from the bottom of my feet.

The ecstasy you were seeking is in front of you. Leave the regret, shame, and agony of the past behind.

You have our permission.

May 6th

Go west, young man!

Yeah, I know, but does it have to be so soon? I'm just asking for a little more time.

Does everything have to be a once in a lifetime opportunity? This can't be my only chance to go.

I don't like when my hand is forced. Nobody does.

Mental exhaustion from constantly weighing the pros and cons of every path. This is not fun.

In my heart of hearts, my best-case scenario would be to stick to my original plans this year and then go next year.

But dare I say no to the Universe? Or worse yet, "Not now Universe, maybe later."

The Universe is fickle. There is no guarantee this opportunity will still be around. Sometimes it is now or never. Take it or leave it.

So what's it gonna be, boy, yes or no? I don't have all day. Yes or no?

Sorry, but no. I'm leaving it. Maybe later, Universe.

Worst case scenario, the offer won't be available next year, and I'll always live with the regret of what might have been.

But there'll be other opportunities for other adventures. The west ain't going anywhere. And I'll have a nice summer relaxing, hanging in the city, and hopefully reconnecting with family and friends.

Doesn't sound too bad.

Nope. Not bad at all.

But..

May 5th

May the Firth of Fifth be with you.

It starts with the piano. Very clear. Very crisp. Both the ivories and ebonies working together. Building toward something.

And then, boom. We have arrived.

The path is clear.

But the words are not. Lyrical ambiguity. Gods. Men. Sheep. Mountains of symbolism and metaphor cutting off the town from view.

Something about Al Madrigal singing a symphony by a waterfall. Why is the rabbit crying?

Na na na, na na.

Until the keys return with some help from the drums. Rescuing us from the lure of the sirens' cry.

And then, ah yes, here comes the flute. That's why we came here, right? The flute.

While the piano becomes more desperate. Transforming itself into.. What is that? Horns? Some sort of synthesizer? Keyboard effects?

Luckily the percussion keeps us all grounded. Turning crisis into pageantry.

Setting the stage for the obligatory guitar solo. Always have to have a guitar solo. So haunting. So earnest. Wandering like the mind of a Zen novice. Bringing us to a false conclusion.

So Neptune has claimed another soul. Eroding the sands of time with the river of constant change.

Deep.

May 4th

The smell of home lingers. I hope nobody else can smell it. At least not in this place.

The masks definitely help.

But if I had one artifact to best represent my adult life so far, this would be it.

A notebook filled with ink scribblings, cover to cover, with each page infused with the musk of joint smoke.

Yep, that's me.

I remember Steen used to try to dismiss my quest for self-discovery and thirst for human experience.

He's just doing it so he can have something to write about.

How right he was.

However, what he didn't recognize was how little control I had over the whole process.

It's not like I chose to be a writer and then purposively sought out a non-traditional path in order to have interesting things to write about.

Who would do that?

God made me a writer and then the Universe said, buckle up, you're about to go on a ride. We're gonna show you some things.

And man, what a ride it's been. To quote Russell Sprague, I have done and seen.

It's why I'm trying to write myself an exit. I'm starting to get queasy.

We'll see if they allow it.

May 3rd

Little Boy Blue. But I don't need your money and I'm tired of your jokes.

The Diceman cameth and the Diceman lefteth. Nobody won the game except he who deserves it least.

But deserve it or not, he still earned it and he still won. The rules are the rules if you can actually believe that and keep a straight face at the same time.

So don't look a gift horse in the mouth. It may not be from who should have given it to you, but you still got it. The Universe cares not about the petty details.

Instead of wasting time and energy trying to win hearts and minds, empower the souls of those who are willing.

Where there's a will, there's a way. But there's often no will among those who don't know the true Way.

It's awfully dark on the path to the light.

Blind guides, stumbling along.

I try my best to follow the laughter without following the laughers. Fools mocking the Tao, pointing me in the right direction.

A wise man once told me that wisdom is doing everything the crowd does not do. Just reverse the totality of their learning and I will have the heaven they're looking for.

I've got two tickets. Who's coming with me?

Red or blue. It doesn't matter.

May 2nd

I have never before been given the freedom to indulge to the level and duration that I have been lately. I wonder where all this is heading.

The scary thing is that I have been moderating. Taking the strictest definition of the word. This could get a lot worse if I wasn't. But I think my moderation may have hit a plateau.

Yeah, I went to church. Took a nice hike. Even got a little schoolwork done. But it's before noon, the reggae is playing, and the condo reeks from the incense of the day's first fatty.

A plateau, indeed.

I wonder where all this is heading.

A détente? A gradual dissolution? Or all out civil war?

If you are serving two masters, they will fight each other to the death. And you are the Colosseum.

Make one subservient to the other, it's the only way to survive. And make sure you know what subservient means. No grey areas.

Like a rolling stone.

I will remain firm in my suppleness and supple in my firmness.

Upon further magnification, the straight black line is crooked and porous.

The heart of the universe has a steady beat.

Life magnified is skips and palpitations.

May 1st

The feast of St. Joseph the Worker. May Day.

Workers of the world unite!

As the bourgeoisie wear fancy hats and sip their mint juleps.

It's Derby Day!

While I celebrate the birth of the coolest older brother I never had. The man who gave me a place to live when I realized that nowhere was home.

Dave!

He had to move his G.I. Joe aircraft carrier from one side of his living room to the other in order to make room for me. I snuck a twin bed and a dresser behind a couch there and he charged me two-fifty a month.

Never been poorer, never been happier. You know the cliché. I once had to cash in all my spare change in order to buy a case of Hot Pockets and a jug of wine that I had to make last as long as possible. If things got really bad, Dave would give me some of his Hamburger Helper if I did all the dishes.

And there were always a lot of dishes.

Brothers of the road. Enlightened rouges. We've been through it again and again and again.

We've done lap you fools.

Again and again and again.

Pour some whiskey from the jar and raise a glass.

Dave!

April 30th

All along the watchtower. 232 has been showing up again and again. It could be just a coincidence, but the alarms are ringing.

It shows up a lot on the way out of work. I do leave the same time every day, however, so it probably doesn't mean anything. But I'm telling you man, it definitely feels like it means something.

Like it is reminding me every day of the cycle I am continually repeating school year after school year. A cycle that began way back when.

232 will always be a reflection of you.

Bullshit!

I broke that spell. I slew that giant. And the cycle ended. Right then. Right there. All that remains are false echoes and the distorted reflection from a mirror that shattered a lot more than seven years ago.

Then what's with the 232's?

They're reminders.

Of what?

Of that victory. May 18th, 2004. Never forget.

I already won, there's nothing left to show or prove. You've done lap your demons many times already. They can't catch their breath.

It's been gravy for a long time now and so is all the rest.

Start living like it.

April 29th

A conquering hero returning to the scene of many crimes.

There's no part of me that feels the former, and I'm tired of running away from the latter.

A laurel wreath or shackles? Deserving of neither and both at the same time.

Good or bad, I am just doing my job. Don't hate the player, hate the game.

And I do. Hate the game. It's rigged. Nobody plays by the rules anymore. It's pointless.

I hate the game so much that it is becoming hard not to hold the players in contempt. Myself included.

But I already know that horse is dead. I don't understand why I can't stop beating it. It took you where you needed to go. Walk away.

Between two worlds. Two phases. Two levels. Two stages. Two lifetimes. Two eternities.

Trapped. Trying to write your way free.

The echoes are becoming deafening.

Stuck in your chamber. Only music to comfort you.

This is the modern world and there is nothing but trouble to guide you.

Backed into a corner. Surrounded. The only way out is through.

The blind leading the blind.

Shady business.

April 28th

Sub-routines running constantly in my brain.

Worry. Hope. Want. Need. Hunger. Thirst. Work. Play. Friendship. Family. Love. Future. Past. Present. Safety. Fear.

Sub-routines on top of sub-routines. Spinning, spinning, and spinning. Draining the battery. Creating a lot of noise.

I need to hit control-alt-delete. Pull up the task manager. Shut down what's slowing me down.

But that never works. Usually ends up requiring a hard reset and a lot of wasted time in recovery.

A system restore could be good too. Go back to a time when my mind was a lot quieter and running so much smoother.

But who knows when that was? I don't remember when all this started. And I don't want to lose anything I may have gained in the interim.

I miss the old days when you could defrag a hard drive. You probably still can, but you know what I'm talking about. Those old Windows P.C.s from the '90's. You could choose to defrag the hard drive and they'd show you this cool visual with all these colorful blocks, and all the colorful blocks would be mixed up. But then they would slowly rearrange them block by block. Sometimes it would take hours. But at the end everything would be nicely arranged with all the blocks of the same color side by side each other.

And it may have been psychological, but the computer always seemed to run great after a good defrag.

That's what I need. A good defrag.

My colored blocks are too mixed up. Need to fix that.

April 27th

Would you rather..

Gain the whole world or keep your soul?

There are no grey areas. There's no hedging your bets. The whole world or your soul? Pick one.

Instead of debating the parts of The Book that are vague and ambiguous, focus on the parts that are clear and direct.

You cannot serve two masters.

God or money? The world or your soul?

Would you rather..

Invite in the despair and disappointment that comes with the climb or revel in the peace that comes in surrendering to your imperfections?

There are no grey areas. There's no hedging your bets. The climb or surrender? Pick one.

Surrender is death. The climb is eternal.

Would you rather..

Have the free will to decide on your own or be effortlessly guided on a leash?

There are no grey areas. There's no hedging your bets. Freedom or bondage? Pick one.

With freedom comes discipline. With bondage comes innocence.

Would you rather..

If you choose not to decide, you still have made a choice.

No rush.

April 26th

I have not been cultivating my public persona a whole lot lately. It's not like I had much of one to begin with, but what was there has grown fallow.

It has left me as a parody of myself, socially speaking. A mere caricature. I used to refer to people like me as Bogosians.

Eric Bogosian used to do these short character pieces for his one-man shows. He would perform monologues of these larger than life, personality-driven people, teeming with exterior flaws and affectations, but with no evidence of an inner life or functional self-awareness.

Sketches of strangers we know all too well. An exponential expansion of archetypes in the collective.

That's what I see when I take a step back and watch myself interact with the others. Just another Bogosian.

Awkward. Crude. Inarticulate. Just hand me my script and get out of my way.

Predictable. Repetitive. Dull. I'll keep going until the tape runs out.

No connection. No understanding. No substance.

They've rejected the rest, so all that's left to give them is a fraud.

We all see through it and we're all getting tired of it. But I don't know how else to be.

I'm at my best when people try to get to know me instead of struggling and failing to do it on my own.

Ain't nobody has done that in a while, though. Not worth the effort. Can't say I blame them. But, man, if they just knew what's all in here.

If they just knew.

April 25th

It's a town full of losers and I'm pulling out of here to win.

I sang that line during my last karaoke before leaving for the Bronx. I didn't mean anything by it, though, and I immediately apologized. I just wanted to go out singing the song I came in with.

In reality, it wasn't more than a couple years and I was back in town, at the same bar, singing the same old songs.

Soy un perdedor.

Cruel to Be Kind was the first song I ever sang at karaoke. Back during the turn of the century.. and millennium.

I don't agree with Nick Lowe anymore, though. That whole cruel to be kind, tough love act is getting old. Life is rough enough. Just be nice.

I started singing karaoke to prove to myself I could be a teacher.

I used to be painfully shy. I'm still kinda am, but I'm better at hiding the pain. There are many people who knew me way back when who'd be surprised that I have a job that involves me having to talk so much. Some days I'm still surprised myself.

If I can sing off key and out of tune in front of a bunch of strangers, then I can stand in front of a room of kids and talk to them about history.

That's what I set out to prove to myself when I was first handed the mic, and I haven't shied away since.

But man, if they knew how much it drains me.

I am but a husk.

April 24th

My friend Dave texted us about a weed convention they were having in New Jersey. It was called CannaCon. He said we should go.

It could be fun. But if it's a convention, it's probably more about the industry. Just a bunch of vendors, demos, and seminars. You know the deal. But I don't want to learn about the thing, I want to do the thing.

I can't wait until they have weed-themed weekend packages at spas. Like they fill you up with gourmet edibles and cannabis-infused cuisine and you spend the rest of the time in the whirlpool or sauna and getting massages and stuff.

And when they have week-long weed retreats at the Omega Institute. Forget about it. Sign me up. I'll happily put on twenty pounds of fresh farm to table cuisine as I read by the lake in my hammock.

But now that recreational weed is becoming more open and accepted- they even legalized it in a Confederate state- you're going to have a real cultural divide among adults.

Pretty soon there's going to be Team Weed and Team Alcohol. And all the people who prefer getting high will hang out together in one place and all the people who want to get drunk will hang out in another.

And it will divide friends and family members. A civil war of the self-medicators. What side will you be on?

Who knows what the straight-edgers will do? And who cares?

Life's a bitch and then you die. That's why we get high.

So smoke 'em if you got 'em.

April 23rd

This is my final run. One more lap around the track. Could last another five, ten, fifteen years. Maybe more. Maybe less. Would like to at least make it past the two-decade mark.

So if you want to see the kid in action one more time, start making your appointments.

Like an old pro ball player in his final season. Each stadium giving the proper send-off during his last visit. Rolling out the rocking chair.

Each year is now a new stadium. One after another until I reach the home finale. Today I consider myself the luckiest man..

Then take it easy for a bit. Figure out what I want to do with my next slice of eternity.

This is my final run. One more trudge up the hill. It's not that I don't got it anymore, it's that I don't want it anymore. It's time. It got me where I needed to get.

So enjoy reading my walk-off. This is when I get rid of whatever is left in the basement. Rocky Balboa style.

Then maybe I'll take up painting like Paulie. Just don't give me any watches. I don't want a stinking watch.

It's not the labor I'm leaving. It's the lack of separation between the labor and the life.

Bind the service. Loose the sacrifice.

Thank you.

April 22nd

Sometimes the best part of writing is feeling the physical sensation of the pen on the paper. The words you choose are incidental.

Early in my teaching career I would tell students that the most beautiful sound in the world is when everybody is quietly working and all you hear is the sound of pens writing on paper.

Another joy lost to the laptop.

I wish reading had more of a tactile component. Holding the book and turning the pages is cool and all, but it could use a little more. I wonder how hard it is to learn braille.

Typewriters are cool. I get why Tom Hanks is obsessed with them. It's like playing a percussion instrument. Unfortunately they were just before my time. I did my first real writing on a Smith Corona word processor. Not the same feeling, though.

If I was a Brooklyn hipster with a long beard living in Williamsburg, or whatever the 'it' neighborhood is nowadays, I would probably open my own printing press. Like one of those old Ben Franklin ones where you have to hand set each tile and ink it all with a big brush before turning the crank. I bet people would be into that sort of thing.

I'm sure the main source of all the truth I've been lucky enough to remember this time around comes from multiple incarnations of lives spent copying illuminated manuscripts.

Bartleby never got what a cool gig he had. Very few of us ever do.

Ah humanity!

April 21st

A sigh of relief. A powder keg diffused. But there will be others.

The hazards are multiplying and intensifying as we skate the tightrope through the multiplicity of timelines and dimensions, trying to realign ourselves.

As a planet. As a species. As the children of God.

Where have you gone Goldilocks? I don't want to go back to Ft. Sumter just to find you.

I sought. Now it's my turn to hide.

Warned of false prophets, but it's the false narratives that make me weary.

Progress is an illusion.

Ebb. Flow. Ebb. Flow. Ebb. Flow.

The Universe is breathing as its moral arc continues to eat its own tail. The end result of bending.

Justice is relative. It all is. So turn the other cheek. Bend the other way.

Render unto Caesar the things that are Caesar's. And in this place, it pretty much all belongs to Caesar.

Et tu?

April 20th

In honor of the feast day for the Blessed Maria, Matriarch of the Immortals, here's a fully toasted seven-minute free write:

And the hourglass is turned again as the sand continues and the drum beats something squeaks in the back this is getting pretty intense like a crescendo is coming and build build and left hanging and teased will it build up again or what is happening and what do you think you're doing Dave open the pod bay doors Hal. I can't do that Dave. Daisy Daisy Daisy you'll look sweet upon the seat of a bicycle built for two. Is that what the NOS did? Was it a reset resent resent the reset Sal 900 always wondered what happened. Human error human error human error wow this is not where it would go but all kinds of minds all kinds of minds keeping an eye out too connected living in eternity where I am eternity is not a scent or meme or idea it's existence itself.

And time is up.

That was fun. I wasn't ready for it to end, though. It went quick. And I hand write these, so that definitely reduces the word count. But I'll have to try that again at some point. Maybe increase the time.

Fun stuff.

April 19th

Conversations about the universe always excite me. I guess I never lost my wonder. I hope they don't.

So many people have, though. Lost their wonder. It's very sad.

I wonder what happened to them.

I'm sure there are those that never wondered to being with. Which is even sadder. But there's nothing you can do for them.

It's the ones who did wonder at some point, and then stopped without realizing it. Like when a mother puts down her child for the last time.

Maybe that's what happened. Their wonder became too large to handle anymore, so they just put it down.

And that was it. No more wonder.

(Sigh)

Who will dare to save a world that is destined to die?

I wonder.

How much more abuse from man can she stand?

I wonder.

Seriously, what is going on?

I wonder.

It's been fifty years, Marvin, and we're still waiting on that mercy.

(Sigh)

April 18th

This doesn't seem to be vibrating as much as it has in the past. Probably for the healthier. Also becoming a little dialogue-y. And self-referential. But the journey is long and will take on a myriad of forms.

So I digress..

I saw a priest cry today. On the altar during mass. I saw a priest cry. It was beautiful. I don't think I ever saw a priest cry before. Have you?

WFMU is the cure for Sunday night dread. Thank you for that Therese, Gaylord, and the genius behind Radio Row.

Feels like I'm knockin' on heaven's door.

Nobody is answering. I should just go around to the back. That's what family would do.

That cold black cloud is comin' down.

That could be a good metaphor for the glass of coffee I'm drinking right now. A Starbucks Nitro in a can that I got at 7-11. I'm sure it's what Bob had in mind.

This has been the most unpredictable week of weather ever. Even today. It was supposed to be nice, but now it's cloudy. April is crazy.

And I'm cold. I need to put my socks back on. But they're dirty and a little bloody from the blister. So now I have to get new socks. And maybe clean the blister. And all that is upstairs. A whole other trip.

Let me just finish my coffee first.

I bet this is the first page my brother Mike turns to because today's his birthday.

What a punk.

April 17th

So you went the distance.

Yes. In all ways imaginable.

I bet you feel proud of yourself, don't cha?

Well, all credit and praise go to God the Father, Son, and Holy Spirit. Everything was done in spite of myself. But yes, I do feel a little accomplished, if you forgive me for saying so.

No need. You are maintaining the vehicle in all the ways necessary for them to continue working through you. That is an accomplishment.

Thank you.

So what's next? There are untold more distances for you to go.

Just chopping wood and carrying water. Chop wood. Carry water.

Until the gods decide to use you again.

I'm always being used. We all are. That's what chopping wood and carrying water is to me.

Such a heavy burden.

It can be. But it's such a blessing to be of service. Definitely worth the weight.

Yeah, that's cool and all. But let's not kid ourselves. You're still the same a-hole you've always been.

I know! That's what's so awesome. I can be the same a-hole I've always been, and God still has a part for me to play. No one else can reach the places I reach.

I believe that.

Keep believing.

Keep maintaining.

April 16th

When you walk around here you better keep it together. Because they will test you.

Look at that big ass moth!

Nobody plays the piano for the passengers in Port Authority as they come to and fro. They're bowling instead. I would, but I don't know how. And ain't that the story of all our lives?

Oh, the horrors that Ralph Kramden did see as he kept watch over 8th Avenue. But his smirk may be the true horror. The evil of indifference it must hide.

I guess I'm starting to feel normal again. But normal ain't exactly rainbows and unicorns. More like big toes and candy corn. Overrated. An acquired taste. But necessary to maintain balance.

And that's my normal.

My week of sloth and gluttony included over 200 chin-ups and planned-out sensible meal portions. I can't even sin correctly. My death wish isn't as strong as I thought it was.

That's a big takeaway.

My ottoman will be the big give back.

I will miss it. But all empires must fall. A sacrifice is a sacrifice.

An end of an era. Not a long era, but an era, nonetheless.

From marbles to lava to live streamers.

To ottoman, with love.

April 15th

The table is set for another feast of decadence. As you prepare to wake and fake it through the day.

A group gathers at the center of the world. I do not know what they are up to. Nobody is in charge.

A lonely traveler rushes to where the action is. But the action keeps moving and the miles become harder. Maybe you are the action.

The debts collected today have been deferred. Yours have been paid long ago. So get your hand out of my pocket. Stop knocking on my door.

The insight is as fleeting as the high. So enjoy the trip.

Arrive when you precisely mean to.

As if there is any other choice.

You've managed to make it this far in spite of yourself. With a myriad of storylines about to play out right from where you sit. Most of which you have no control over. But enough that you do to make things interesting, or at least manageable as you finish the second half of your sentence on this prison planet.

Things can't get any lower than they are right now.

But they got this low. That's what scary.

It's not how many times you fall, it's..

Whatever. After having to keep getting back up again and again, you don't stand up as tall and straight as you once did.

Atlas shrugged.

Who is John Galt?

April 14th

Ah, but I was so much older then, I'm younger than that now.

Watching the birds in the park with Bob. As I listen to the sacrificial pigeon.

But we have this treasure in jars of Clay..

A high pollen alert has been issued.

Your worth does not come from other people.

Duh. Yeah, I know. But..

No buts. Your worth does not come from other people.

Ha ha.

Stop laughing and say it. My worth does not come from other people.

My worth does not come from other people.

Good. Now go live it.

When you're out of luck. When you're down to your last buck.

Tukata-tuk!

That's the spirit!

It's never too early for the dogs to get friendly in the park. That's why they're dogs. And we all got some dog in us.

That's what worries me. I see the dog in us all.

Yes, my guard stood hard when abstract threats too noble to neglect.

Hey Bob, you got my back pages?

April 13th

Seriously, what more do you want? With all your plans and goals and ideas. Where does it always leave you? You're a fraud. An addict for disappointment.

I don't understand it either, but I assure you that it is very real.

What are you looking for?

Someone to share this all with. It is not good for man to be alone.

Then go out and find her.

If only it was that easy.

What's making it hard?

Broken. Me. Them. It. All broken.

So carry the cross of being alone.

I'm trying. But I sense a large part of me being shut off the longer I am alone. Like a pain sensor that is being way overworked, but by shutting off that pain sensor I am also preventing myself from experiencing greater levels of joy and pleasure and love. Does growing old have to be growing numb?

It doesn't have to be.

But the pain is too great. I have no choice.

Well, don't worry then. It will all be turned back on when this is finally over.

You promise?

Absolutely.

April 12th

This world should be more wonderful. Like lobster ravioli in pink sauce. Or the pink railings of the Williamsburg Bridge. Or the bridge in your favorite Pink song.

Run just fast as you can. To the middle of nowhere.

Wasn't even able to get that done today. Maybe tomorrow.

Did the bare minimum to feel functional. Said my prayers. Took my vitamins. Read the Bible. Put in a little work. Exercised. And now I'm writing.

But in between was the disjointed improvisation of laziness and cannabis. Live streams and live radio. Food and the phone.

And now I watch women's soccer. Monmouth at Quinnipiac. Semifinals of the MAAC Championship. Monmouth is poised to pull off the upset. This makes me happy because I am from New Jersey. Never cared too much about Connecticut.

Coconuts and raisins. A good combination. The fountain is on at Washington Square Park. Despite the cold rain. And my hand still hurts from punching the wall yesterday. That was a new one. Who knows what I'll be capable of next?

I'm feeling less and less in control every day. Of everything. That's scary. Depression hampers. Anxiety cripples. And that's where the pendulum is swinging back to.

There is more than a glitch in the Matrix. Something fundamentally is broken.

Yet here we are. We keep going on.

I know. I can't explain it, either.

It defies the laws of aerodynamics. Like bees flying.

April 11th

I'm not sick, but I ain't exactly well, either. It's been one trauma after another, going back years. And there's no sign it's stopping anytime soon. I can't remember the last time I was able to stick my head out without being afraid that it'd be blown off. I don't believe I ever will again. It hurts. They're hurting me. And I know that all the pain really comes from within, but still.. It hurts. They're hurting me. And I keep lashing back. Because it's the only way I know how to defend myself. To stop them from hurting me. But then I feel guilty. Guilty for lashing back. And guilty is more painful than hurt. So forgive me for wanting to run away. I'm just so tired of fighting, and things are heating up too much for me to stay frozen. I want to disappear. I want to be invisible. I want a fresh start. Nobody in my life now will give me a fresh start. Pulling me down. A weight. The fat around the middle. The only way out is to hit reset. Start over. Somewhere new. A fresh start.

Wherever you go, there you are. The fresh start will feel great for a while. Not to mention the high of leaving. But it is only a matter of time. Only a matter of time before everything you left shows up again in new forms. And you realize- in horror- that you didn't hit escape or reset, you only hit pause. The cycle is always ready to repeat. Anywhere you take it.

So what do I do?

The only thing you know how to do. Stick your head down and push forward. Day by day. Week by week. Month by month. Year by year.

You are who you need to be. You are where you need to be. You are doing what you need to do.

Have faith in God. Trust in the process. Can you do that?

Yes. Yes, I can.

April 10th

Tomorrow I shall face off with the advocate for the devil. Today I prepare by showering in combat.

Sasha believes he can weaponize his cardio. Don't we all. The victor is often the last to tire. But none of that matters if you can't protect your neck.

I bet the Korean knows how to battle Knightmares. It's in their culture. Ancestral trauma. Jung's collective unconscious. Archetypes Freudian slipping on all the blood on the mat. As the judges score the fall.

A fighting German man-mountain. Some lines write themselves. Trying not to drown in the Fall River Blues. And in a stunning upset.. rock beats paper.

A spectacle for the senses. The pride of Sussex County. Sparta vs. Solecki. A contest to stay on top. In the race to the bottom. In the fight of two Jersey boys. North can't get out from under the South. Wisdom weighs down the warrior within.

The mothers enter the octagon. The lesbian baby-mama of the GOAT. And the calendar girl with serious beauty and brawn. The marketing team earns the submission. Sex will always sell.

Some hunts require a little more silence. So says Sam the smiling slugger. Stalking the subduer of coconut bombs. One man's agony is another man's thrill. Cuban missiles brought higher up the hill.

And now for the main event. The up and comer versus the upstart. Everybody is kung-fu fighting. From Italy to Holland by way of Ft. Worth, Texas. No love lost and no gloves touched. As early blows fall low. A dominant round to the mighty from Mezzocorona.

Cue the triangle. Time to come in from the fields. It's dinner time.

You will be sated.

April 9th

Don't tear down a fence before you remember why you put it up in the first place.

So why did I put this fence up?

It's definitely beginning to fall apart. So do I finish the job, or do I put in the work needed to mend it?

It was not my plan to be here in the first place. I just wanted to be a mailman. But it's not about what I want. It's about what they need me to do.

Well, that's easy. All they need me to do is to fully be me. And fully being me means fully using my God-given gifts to help those that would benefit the most from them.

So am I still doing that? Am I using all the gifts God gave me? Am I helping the people I need to be helping?

That answer used to emphatically be yes. But I'm not so sure anymore.

My talents don't seem as welcome anymore and my help is not sought after or being fully received.

So it seems like a no-brainer.

Yes. But it's still a tough decision to make. I'm too far in the game to make a wrong move.

If you consulted the I-Ching, what would you want it to say?

I would want it to give me permission to tear down the fence.

Then start tearing down the fence.

Sigh. Ok.

Don't worry. There are no wrong moves. And we got your back.

April 8th

This is a dead end.

I don't mean this, that you are holding in your hand. This is certainly not a dead end. One of the few things that is not. Everything else, though..

Dead end.

And it's one of those dead ends that gets narrower the deeper you unknowingly drive into it. So now you have to pull off a 15-point k-turn just to navigate yourself out of it.

That's where I am now. Point two or three of this 15-point k-turn. Trying to get back in the right direction without giving or receiving too many dents or scratches. This is going to be tricky.

Hindsight is 20/20, but I guess I missed all the signs. I thought I was reading them correctly. Maybe someone was playing a trick on me. It wouldn't surprise me.

This is a broken world full of sinners, and it took me too long to realize it. I was naïve. Living as if everything was peachy when the apple cart was already fully spoiled.

So now I have to turn back.

Remove my treasures from this world. They don't belong here. They are being wasted.

I made a mistake. Help me get out of this place.

Dot. Dot. Dot. Dash. Dash. Dash. Dot. Dot. Dot.

Dot. Dot. Dot. Dash. Dash. Dash. Dot. Dot. Dot.

../---/..

April 7th

Iridescent navy blue.

One of the many colors I am blind to. An obscured palette. The invisible rainbow with the unclaimed pot of gold.

I wanted to be an artist when I was a little kid. It was one of the first things I remember telling people when they asked what I wanted to do when I was older.

I want to be an artist. I still do.

I was even practical about my dream. If I couldn't make a living selling paintings and stuff, I would work painting billboards.

Five years old and already had plans to sell out.

But then in first grade I drew and colored a landscape. Green grass, yellow sun, white clouds, and what I thought was a beautiful blue sky.

I proudly showed my drawing to my teacher, expecting the same hit of positive reinforcement I always got when I showed an adult something I drew. I loved that feeling. So much so that I planned on forging a career around always getting that feeling.

I didn't get that feeling when the teacher saw my landscape, though. Instead I got a concerned look and a note to go down to the nurse's office.

After a confusing half hour looking at dots that were supposed to be numbers or shapes, I was told I was color blind. Reds and oranges, and blues and purples. My purple sky gave me away.

I knew there was a deaf composer, but I never heard of a color-blind artist.

I guess I'll have to join the army. Or become a priest. Or play centerfield for the Angels.

April 6th

Aww. Are you trying to establish a new routine? How cute.

A nice escape for your lunch break. Get as far away mentally from the chaos and turmoil of this place. Some pleasant music. A little nourishment. Daubing the canvas with your words and thoughts. Perfect.

You know it won't last, though, right?

See, I told you so.

And now you have no choice but to pull out the shoehorn.

Squeezing and struggling. Trying to make it all fit.

Spoiler Alert: It won't. You have all the pieces you need, but they're for a dozen different puzzles. Good luck with that.

There is a reason that yours is a voice that is rarely heard and seldom listened too. Repeating yourself so often that you're drowning in déjà vu.

But you definitely have not been here before.

Quarantined in a middle of a quarantine. Both doses of the cure administered. Hopefully it won't be worse than the disease.

But in many ways we're already too late for that.

In running away from the virus we have all revealed just how sick we truly are.

Ironic. Don't you think?

And now watch everybody slowly return to normal like nothing ever happened. Hoping we all forget how we acted when the plane was going down.

Not me, though.

I will remember.

April 5th

It all boils down to my stomach. What my stomach feels like and how much I feel like stomaching.

An alien living inside me. Calling nearly all the shots. And requiring constant attention.

Travelling great distances across space and time from the bloated, gas giant they call home.

Twenty-seven lightyears away.

Twenty-seven years ago I was back on my home planet with my crew mates. It was the opening day of the junior varsity tennis season. We were hosting Lenape Valley.

Joe and Steve stopped by and broke the news to us. I don't remember if it was before or after the match. Of course Joe made the first joke about it.

"Well, I guess he really did have a gun."

He was only twenty-seven. Like the rest of them.

I seem to remember that he had stomach problems. It's what fueled the addiction, depression, and self-destruction.

Not everyone is able to get along with their alien.

It took me a long time.

If only they had kombucha and kimchi more available in the '90's. Definitely better for you than penny royal tea.

Or heroin.

Or a shotgun blast.

Oh well. At least Eddie Vedder is still alive.

April 4ᵗʰ

A return to the scene of the crime. And I still haven't figured out if I committed the crime or if the crime was committed against me.

Am I being pursued because of something I did, or because of something I witnessed?

Regardless. I rather be left alone. But I don't think that's going to happen. They're always lurking right around the corner. Making their presence known at the very moment I begin to get comfortable.

If I am guilty, forgive me. If you're afraid I will expose your guilt, worry not. That's not why I came back here.

Always on the run. I'm beginning to feel it in my heels.

A rough rider clings to life. It's dark, and hell is hot.

Bird in the sky, you know how I feel.

I've got pain for my dogs. Do they have pain for me?

Today is a day of resurrection. Will we see another? Or do all debts have to be paid back eventually. Dollar for dollar. Life for life.

Dead.

In the middle of Little Italy. Enjoying my first taste of pesto.

Little did we know what was in store for us. Or I probably would have started running earlier.

The hell with my heels.

April 3rd

A jazz quartet is playing in the park. They have an upright bass and everything. The electric guitar seems out of place, though.

Along the pond a man is making beauty with his bows and strings.

The day blossoms with colors and sounds.

I don't know where my place is in any of it, though.

I'm worse than that electric guitar.

Some guy passed me running up Vreeland today. He couldn't have been more than 20. But it still got to me. Not a lot. But enough to notice.

I had to take some stranger's clothes out of the dryer earlier so I could put mine in. All the other dryers were filled, and they were done for over 15 minutes. Who knows when someone would be back for them? I had to make an executive decision.

They were mainly men's clothes, but some black lace bras and a thong mixed in. I hate having to do that sort of thing. Always afraid they're gonna come back, get pissed, and do something to my clothes for revenge.

They didn't, though. My clothes were fine. Just finished folding them. They were probably embarrassed. That's how I would have reacted. More embarrassed than mad.

Of course I would never leave my clothes unattended in a shared laundry room that long after they finished.

If only everybody could live their lives with such precision and constant consideration of others.

The nerve of some people.

April 2nd

Moving the Earth. One load at a time!

Ain't that the truth.

My flock is without a shepherd. Thus, has been plundered and made food for wild animals.

The word of God spat me out like a moldy piece of bread.

Your dearest wish will come true. But your quest for certitude yields only new delusions.

Absolute truth is achieved by the skillful use of denial.

I think I missed the joke. Couldn't read the subtitles.

My secret heart yearns for the romantic unity of souls.

Am I hopelessly lost in translation?

I got my rice. In more ways than one. Just not what I expected, or thought I ordered.

Your transcendent vision is too esoteric for the intellectual and too remote for the layman.

It's why most creative efforts are divinely mediocre.

Except this one. And yet..

The exuberant laughter of an innocent child's delight.

Vero. The truth.

April 1st

Look at him go. Sprinting past the quarter pole. Will he be able to keep up this pace?

Little do they know that I'm still holding a lot back. Wait 'til they see Secretariat galloping down the stretch.

Measure twice, cut once. And my brother always preached the importance of triple redundancy. Engineers are like that. Form follows function and what not.

I follow no one. That's my function. Forging a path forward. I can't go back. It's already overgrown.

I wonder who's shorter, Wayne or Alan?

I've known Wayne longer. Just met Alan today. Fabio introduced him to me. Not the horse-looking guy from all the books, though. The voice on my radio.

Radio. It truly is a sound salvation.

The pulse of those who have not given themselves up to the zeitgeist yet. Those who never stopped digging.

Not an easy pulse to find, but it is getting stronger.

When it goes, there really won't be a whole lot worth sticking around for.

Just a bunch of fools with dirty feet.

Long overdue for a cleaning.

March 31ˢᵗ

Staring at this page is what allows me to be somewhere else and be someone else.

A weird feeling to have when I'm at the place where I need to be the most present and carry my most clearly defined persona.

While I lose myself in the rhythms of the music and dream of dissolving into the patter of the rain.

You can have it all. My empire of filth.

A wise man once said that Holy Wednesday is underrated.

There would not have been a resurrection if there wasn't first a betrayal.

Judas was just playing his part. We all were.

So how 'bout we cut each other a break? Nobody leaves here with clean hands.

The world is a ghetto.

Isolated by fear and ignorance. Segregated from true divinity.

Looking out through broken windows at the shining city sitting far atop the hill.

We are the rocky soil the sower stopped throwing seeds upon.

For whoever has will be given more. God bless that child.

But pity on whoever does not have. How much more will they take from us?

You'd be surprised.

March 30th

Trapped by the tyranny of orange post-it notes.

The executive functioning of my pre-frontal cortex has been vomited all over my standing desk. While I try not to choke on the expectations and demands of the future.

A modern-day Jimi Hendrix.

Instead of guitar riffs and soaring solos, it's deadlines and unanswered e-mails. And I've been at it long after hitting 27.

I wouldn't want to be part of a club that would accept me as a member, anyway.

Always been more of a solo act. The guy on a stool, strumming away, singing his feelings. Filling the dead air as the crowd filters in. But nobody came to see me.

I don't care, though. Ain't why I do it. I've rocked a lot of empty arenas in my day. Not the worst experience. Just have to avoid getting caught in an echo chamber.

Echo chamber.
Echo chamber.
Echo chamber..

Uh. Oh. Got lost again like Mr. Eko.

Stuck on my own island.

Cleansed by the healing fires of purgatory.

You needed them, and they needed you.

March 29th

The system is broken and it's folly to try to fix it.

The only hope is to temper the sharp edges of the shards and keep caring for those who will continue to get cut.

We're managing symptoms at this point. Forget about a cure.

Just trying to keep human civilization as comfortable as possible before its death throes.

Adjust the temperature. Fix the pillows. Pull up the blanket. Here's the morphine button. The TV seems kinda loud. How 'bout some nice music instead?

Dogs will miss us. So will cats, but they'd never admit it. Horses won't miss us, though. And definitely not trees.

And let's start from scratch next time.

No preserving ancient knowledge. No learning from the ascended masters. No DNA manipulation. No outside interference whatsoever.

Melchizedeks need not apply.

There's no rush. Let's see what happens when nature truly does run its course.

Could it be any worse?

(Laughs)

Famous last words.

March 28th

How'd I end up back here? It's certainly been a while. Things look completely different, yet exactly the same. I'm not going in, though. Not worth it, and no need.

I just wanted to go somewhere and not feel lost for a while.

But it's not working. I feel completely lost.

I don't know where I am or who anybody is anymore.

I only know me. And living out that truth has left me abandoned.

Alone. Amid the rain and fog. In between two places. And neither of them quite feel like home.

Eventually I'll get tired of constantly cycling back to the same place over and over again, but I'm not sure what I'll do when that happens.

I've always fantasized about escaping. Maybe someday I'll be brave enough to actually do it.

People will miss the role they've created for me to play in their lives. But I'm not known enough to be truly missed for who I am.

If I did escape, people would be more offended that they didn't have as much control over me than they thought they did. And that would fuel any attempts to bring me back in.

Control. Not concern, grief, or love. Control.

Don't worry, though. I'm not going anywhere, yet. Your resistance and rejection are still useful for my growth. Thank you for that.

But I can't stay here forever.

March 27th

You are going to take some time to appreciate the scenery, right? After you do all the things you think you need to do first.

Stuck in the middle of an endless to-do list. Camping out in the eternal now of the empty spaces between tasks.

You feel that, right?

I'm totally exposed, yet completely isolated. Just me and the turtles. All the way down. Painting these word portraits.

Just a tad too cold and windy for total comfort, though. But I bet the turtles don't mind.

It was a long journey out of the swamps to the magnificence of the White City. But I enjoyed all of it. Resting in impermanence.

And now what remains is the anticipation of endless possibilities. Where will I be taken?

Somewhere downtown. Near Canal Street. With my Filipina guide. The people are out, but masks are on. And hoods are up.

A three joint day. And you've been hitting the gum pretty hard. That coconut smoothie was the realized dreams of all who attended Chicago's Columbian Exhibition of 1893. Not exactly what I would call a harmless harvest.

Will I be awake to see the fights? Will any of us?

Don't pass me over.

Lead me to safety.

March 26th

A harvest festival. So reap.

Stipe Miocic would not approve of me eating a chicken sandwich on a Friday during Lent. But it was a really good chicken sandwich. So forgive me.

I follow the spirit, not the letter. And find repentance in the Word.

But talking of chicken sandwiches..

Every day in college for lunch I would get a chicken patty sandwich and French fries. Then I would get a cereal bowl and go to the condiments bar and fill it with everything. Ketchup, mayo, mustard, honey mustard, honey, barbeque sauce.. everything. Then I would mix it all up and slather it all over my chicken patty sandwich and use the rest to dip my fries in.

And these were prison-grade chicken patties.

But talking of college..

I heard that today was the anniversary of the Heaven's Gate mass suicide. That was second semester of my freshman year. I remember going down to the computer lab to check out their website. They had to be the first suicide cult to have a website. It was also weird seeing comet Hale-Bopp clear as day in the evening sky around campus for about a month.

Man, I loved the 90's.

But talking of comets..

I remember when my grandfather took me to Riker Hill Art Park in Livingston to see the comets crash into Jupiter. Shoemaker-Levy or something like that.

A tough t-shirt to let go of.

But aren't they all?

March 25th

Breathe in. Breathe out. Breathe in. Breathe out.

Deep breath in. Extend your stomach all the way out.. and hold it.

Now slowly release through your nose.

Nice. Now let's do it one more time.

In. Hold........ and release.

Yes! It's gone. It's over. Just that easy.

What beautiful noise. What comforting wind.

Magic happens where you fix your attention. Be magical.

Soften the sound. Focus outside.

A confabulation of birds. How fabulous.

Foreground. Background. Foreground. Different tones, pitches, and patterns.

And just like that I lost it.

Just when I think I'm out, they pull me right back in.

What is it that has its claws in me?

Why do I give it so much power?

Still learning. Still got far to go.

Rest.

March 24ᵗʰ

What did you expect? I've been the king of the Whack since the 90's.

Don't act surprised.

Been in too many rodeos. I'm dressed like a clown for a reason. Just let me stay in my barrel.

I'm not trying to provoke any bulls.

Somebody called me a non-playable character today. Yes, that's me. A non-playable character.

So don't play me.

Dolores Cannon used to write a lot about "extras". These are the people you see all around in the background of your life that are not involved in the grand universal mission of soul ascension. They're just here to fill out the scenery. They're extras. Non-playable characters.

Whenever I people watch I always keep an eye out for extras. I haven't found any yet.

The moment you take the time to see someone, they no longer are extra. Just ask Hagar.

The God who sees.

The eye in the triangle.

I've tried angles

None of them were right.

I did a 180.

Here I am again.

March 23ʳᵈ

You can't sing to a forest with an algorithm.

But it doesn't take too many steps back for that forest to become an algorithm. It's true for all of us.

Numbers, patterns, and equations. That's what we are from a distance. And how does the song go?

God is watching us.. from a distance.

It explains the indifference. We all play around with numbers, patterns, and equations without worrying about how they feel.

Imagine you're a fraction and you're just carrying a little extra weight in your numerator. You're trying your best. You exercise. You work out. But you're eating a little too many of those keto cookies and keep skipping denominator day.

So what happens? Do they just let you be? No! They call you improper and turn you into a mixed number.

Who's to say that being turned into a mixed number isn't the most painful thing that a fraction can experience?

And we call them improper. We're the real monsters.

From a distance.

Wasn't that song from the Gulf War?

Operation Desert Storm. When the Iraqi's were acting like a bunch of improper fractions.

We sure showed them.

March 22nd

Somebody once said that a large part of life is just showing up. I agree. Just show up each day and take care of the business you need to. Nothing more and certainly nothing less. Do that for a lifetime and see what kind of legacy you leave behind.

However, the same guy who said a large part of life is just showing up, ended up marrying his stepdaughter. So maybe there are some times when you're better off not showing up. It's an art, not a science. Moon, not the finger.

Ken Wilber was all about wake up, grow up, and show up. I've been awake, and I'm still showing, but there's been no signs of me growing. It's why I'm so comfortable in my body. All of them.

But Wilber was a spiritual cross-fitter. He wanted a soul that was stronger, faster, and could go further. That's not for everybody, though. Some of us are content just holding the pads for those training for the big fight. And holding pads still takes some serious skill and practice.

When your main focus is reaching new heights, your foundation becomes shaky, and you lose touch with everything going on around you.

Unchecked growth is a big problem.

Poor man wants to be rich. Rich man wants to be king. King ain't satisfied until he rules everything.

It's scary for the little guy in this battlefield of giants.

Let's start thinking about scaling down.

March 21st

The ideals of the pirate republic are falling apart.

No honor among thieves.

You have to pick up after your dog.

But the only thing worse than pirates are those that hunt the pirates.

Articulated buses. Squeeze me like an accordion. You bookish, horse girl.

Is anything connecting at this point? Or am I just throwing dots out there?

Seriously, there's a roller skate shortage? Who's out there roller-skating nowadays? David Goggins's dad has been dead for some time now.

You're not the biggest catfish in this here sea.

Neither was David Goggins's dad.

Let the lesson be to anyone who seeks to follow in his footsteps, that the same fate would await them.

You and me have a thing. We have matching t-shirts. It's bigger than us. It's a community.

So how deep do you want to go?

The staring contest was a quick immersion. Watching the docs added some color. Playing in the chat made it real.

But I'm cool on the fringe. I don't need to be known. Just like to meet some of the others, though.

Crossing the finish line.

The marathon is over.

March 20th

The robin's eggs are bigger this Paschal season.

This is when they're trying to mentally break you.

She never uses words like sorry. I'd like to hear that. She doesn't know what that word means.

Picasso sure was a horny artist. At every stage of his career.

The cars are being put back on the Wonder Wheel. In preparation for a summer return to normalcy. In the land of freaks.

It's a glorious day for so many reasons.

The mermaid parade is like a Fellini movie. It's not describable in words. You have to see it.

Freddie Hubbard seems to show up everywhere. Calypso Fred? That's shameless. And they call me self-indulgent.

How do you like dem Fiona Apples? A lot. If I'm going to be completely honest. I like them a lot. I came to age watching the Criminal video. Again and again.

Behind the scenes of the flamingo carousel.

With Castle Grayskull sitting high atop its perch. Defending the high-ground among the lowly sideshow cats.

And it's business as usual south of the panhandle. With thongs, thighs, and thirst. The spirit is willing, but the flesh is weak.

I began the day looking at art. I end the day looking at art.

Just another horny artist.

March 19ᵗʰ

My old stomping grounds.

The room above the gun shop. My window looked out to the parking lot of the liquor store. Lying on the futon. Listening to the sounds of the body shop by day, and the biker bar by night.

My dinner would either be a sandwich and a bag of chips from Quik Check, or curry shrimp from #1.

Always loved sitting on the bench by the river. Just like Peter Dinklage in The Station Agent. And that cute little library.

Speaking of books. Ray & Judy's is still the only bookstore to have one of my books in stock. They were good people. Remembered me from Dave's wedding.

Of course Park Lake. What an escape that place was. And so close. Found my own isolated spot and everything. Reached some epiphanies there.

I was a regular at Maggie's in those days. Stopped by often to eat a meal or watch a game. Frank would be behind the bar and there'd always be somebody nearby worth talking to. Sad the night we closed it for good. But my glass was never empty.

Allan Carpet ended up landing at the Thirsty Moose. Herb and Mary followed him there. So did most of the New Class. I guess it was their karaoke now. But I still maintained my spot. Even got Hewitt out there once. Can't remember if he sang, though.

My old stomping grounds.

An interesting chapter of my life.

And that's not even the half of it.

March 18th

Is that a De La Soul t-shirt?!

Yeah, but I have no idea who they are.

That's awesome!

Just me, myself, and I. Working something out. Entering a new stage of the game.

Preparing for take-off. Enjoying the witty repartee. An ayahuasca enema for the soul.

Clear skies ahead. Zero turbulence. No blockages. All engines at full power.

Man, it's going to be fun seeing what this puppy can do.

Just a smidge for the Pidge and a blob for the Fab. Loving the chemistry! It didn't make the airwaves, so here it is for eternity.

They had all these hits and they tried to get all cerebral. They tried to get all cute. And then the hits dried up.

Before the deluge.

Sweetened with honey.

Like my Simone. A classic love story for the ages, ready for a revival. The battlefield nurse tending to the wounds of a lonely soldier. Destinies entangled in a world fighting to make it through.

The audience will love it. The crowds will flock to it. The show of the century. I know the perfect guy for the role.

In my world, I'm the RZA.

Saving the best beats for myself.

March 17th

I've been turning so many corners lately it feels like I'm living in an octagon. It's the only thing that keeps me from tapping out.

Just as long as I'm not running around in circles. Although I do enjoy running around in circles. They just have to be big circles. So big that I don't even realize it's a circle until I somehow return to where I started from.

And at the end of your journeys you will return to where you started and think, "How neat! This is awfully convenient."

And it is pretty convenient. Otherwise you'd have to turn around and go back the way you came and get stuck seeing all the things you've already seen before. That doesn't sound fun.

You know what does sound fun? Two chords on an organ. It never gets old.

Organs are the soundtrack to fun. Carnivals, ball games, church services. Two out of those three things are fun to somebody, and the organ is the common denominator for all of them. Think about it.

Just don't think too hard.

As I retrieve the ball I just hit into the net.

Love-forty.

Second-serve.

March 16ᵗʰ

One down. One to go. Halfway there. Living on a prayer?

I guess. I've certainly been praying a lot lately. One of the few times when I generally feel like myself these days. I should do more of it. And stop asking for things. Just sit in His presence and be.

Be thankful.
Be humbled.
Be in awe.
Be loved.

Yep. That's the good stuff.

And safe. I can't forget being safe. Praying is one of the rare times when I am completely safe. I'm not even safe doing this, so definitely nothing is sacred.. except praying.

But man, have I been under attack. From all directions. From people I never could have expected it from. And a lot of people I'd be foolish not to expect it from.

All for being me. That, and wearing a big cross-shaped target on my chest.

It's not like I wasn't warned this would happen. We all were. I guess I was just hoping for more protection.

Oh well. All you have to do is look above any altar in any church and realize that it could get a whole lot worse. Even He was hoping for a little more protection.

So I keep praying. It's all I truly know how to do anymore.

Eternity awaits. This is just a dream.

March 15th

None of this is fun. It's just work.

Meaningless words in tiny boxes that will quickly be forgotten when filled. Gossip, flattery, and innuendo above the loud clacking of a keyboard.

Dogs running in the background. Bored faces looking on in horror. Inside jokes and insecurities. Ancient dynamics.

I get why Jenn yearned to be Amish, even though it was the furthest from her truth.

Simple. Authentic. No wasted actions. No wasted words.

Not me. I'm still sloppy with my actions and get no credit for my words.

Power struggles I didn't ask to be part of. I just want to work hard and do my job well.

It's not about me. I'm not your scapegoat or your projection screen. Just a finger pointing at the moon. When the sun is out, and the lunar cycle begins anew.

No choice but to stare at the finger. In all of its ugliness.

Look up! Look up!

I did. There's nothing there.

Look up! Look up!

Crazy finger.

The moon!

You're wasting your time.

The moon?

I see nothing.

March 14th

This is how I chill
From '77 till
Never been to Ibiza
Didn't take a pill
Never heard of Avicii
In my cocoon with Don Ameche
Put down the apple
Eat a peachy
All-men brothers of the road
Star comma eight, comma one, load
Sixty-four, parts of the I-Ching
America, of thee I sing
Lord be merciless, like Ming
Bishop pinned, by the king
Checkmate
Inspectah Deck hate
Protected your neck late
Got your funeral date
Grape, nuts
Set, hut
One Mississippi
Two dead hippies
Freedom riders
Dude abiders
White Russians
Robo-tussin
Sundays past
My sins were vast
Judgement's last
Mercy's face
Left no trace
Amazing grace!

March 13ᵗʰ

The better part of the universe.

Looking forward to the ides of March.

Prepared. Poised. In position.

And the day is still a blank page.

On a rain-slicked intersection across the world. Umbrellas parade all the colors of the rainbow. As opposite paths converge.

Am I really seeing this? Can I keep this weight up for this long when it's this early? What else is going on?

Empty bleachers. A flag no longer at half-mast. Sounds of a city about to reawaken. Conducting the rabble. Who never went to sleep. Forever. 21. Is going to be a good year. They say.

Am I really hearing this? Can I stretch things this far without something going pop? Who else is out there?

A vigilante hunting for crime. Staking out in the shadows of the Empire State. As the wind shakes the window. And the leaves dance in a swirl. The mechanical sound. Pulsating. Haunting me.

Am I really feeling this? Can I fall back asleep and pretend none of this happened, even though it did? Where else can I go?

There's no escape.

The prisoner in the village of the mind.

I am not a number! I am a free man!

Number Two: (Laughs)

March 12th

An appointment to get the alien DNA. The inevitable leap we all have to make.

A carousel of streamers. In the shadow of Cinderella's castle. Who's sleeping with who?

Turn it up world. You're going to have to face it. You're addicted to spuds.

But in all seriousness. If you notice me losing my connection to the Tao, I expect you to lock me in a room and force feed me mushrooms.

That's what friends are for.

I found what they like. And it's a bag of potatoes!

Blessings and love from the lotus plateau.

I've been looking for chocolate covered espresso beans for some time now. Another case closed.

The malt balls were disappointing, though. It's Whoppers or it's nothing.

God bless Valley Health System.

I am essential.

We all are.

Especially you.

How's that for some Mr. Rogers mojo?

I stand for the greatness of America.. Mt. Rushmore, Miss Liberty, and freedom for all!

Childhood lost. Childhood recovered.

There will be no encore.

March 11th

I remember when I first walked into Vivienne's, or Viv's as it was called.

It was October of 2002, and the Angels were playing the Yankees in the playoffs. I've been an Angel fan my whole life. Reggie Jackson hit three home runs two days after I was born, and I grew up hearing stories about it. By the time I was old enough to pay attention to games and collect cards, Reggie was an Angel. So that's my team.

But understandably I was a little reluctant to root against the Yankees in a Bronx bar, so I quietly watched while sipping my whiskey and cider.

Down the bar, though, this guy had no problem cheering for the Angels, which empowered me to get a little more vocal as they pulled away from the Bombers.

Little by little, the guy inched closer and closer to me and by the time the Angels won, we were high fiving and clinking glasses.

Then he became very interested in me.

Where you from? How long you've been in the neighborhood? What do you do? Where does your family come from? What do they do? What does your grandmother put in her meatballs?

VERY interested in me.

But whatever. I made a new friend. A fellow Angel fan.

A week later I'm back in Viv's to watch the Series and I see the same guy pulling for the Giants.

"What's up," I said. "I thought you were an Angels fan."

He gave me a dirty look and scoffed, "I root for who they're betting against. I just had to make sure you weren't doing the same."

I read today that Viv's closed permanently recently due to Covid. It's a shame. I learned a lot there.

March 10th

They're beheading teachers now.

As I sit here unconcerned on the crapper.

France is pretty far away. There's enough I have to deal with right here in front of me.

But they're beheading teachers now.

Yeah, I get it. But the dude was being pretty irresponsible. There are so many ways to meet an instructional objective without putting yourself in danger. Sloppy teaching.

Did you not hear me? They're beheading teachers now.

Teachers have always been persecuted. It wasn't uncommon during the early days of public education in America for mobs of townspeople to run the local teacher out of town, often beating and killing him at times. All because they didn't like what their children were being taught. A very thankless profession.

Yeah, but they're beheading teachers. NOW.

This is beginning to sound like that Phil Ochs song. Small Circle of Friends or something. He'd always forget the lyrics when he sang it live. Or that Holocaust poem. First, they came for the teachers..

They are beheading teachers now.

I know! What do you want from me? Am I supposed to get angry? Or outraged? Or afraid? Should I join a protest or donate to a cause? What should I do? I'm only one person just trying the best he can.

They're beheading teachers now.

(Sigh)

They're beheading teachers now.

Good. All the more reason to keep on teaching.

March 9th

This is nobody's fault but my own. I will try my best not to project blame outward, but this is going to be very difficult.

When you rip a band-aid off a wound that has been festering for over a decade and a half, it is going to take some time and it is going to hurt.

My number one goal is to minimize damage. To myself. And especially to others.

But it's time to move on. Instead of teetering back and forth and interpreting everything as either a sign to stay or a sign to go, I need to commit. It's time to go. The sooner you quietly start the process, the better. Begin now.

I don't fit in.

I'm constantly swimming upstream.

I'm kept at arm's length.

I'm no longer liked, respected, or listened to.

I'm alone, not happy, and rarely having any fun.

It's time to move on.

I don't know what is next. I don't work that way. I must fully leave before I fully commit to something else.

No wavering. No waffling.

Fully leave.

Man, this won't be easy.

Have mercy on me.

March 8th

I think the times where I get into the most trouble are the times when I have to be Doug for too long.

He's such a heavy character to be dragging around day in and day out. I'm so much lighter without him.

Work's tough. There's no avoiding him there. He's the gaseous pit I carry around in my stomach all day. I try my best to find small avenues of escape and release, but it's hard. The foxes have dens and the birds have nests, but Mr. Palermo has nowhere to lay his head.

Family's tough. They hold on to Doug the tightest. No desire to see who I am behind it all. Makes sense, though. If they did, the whole thing would crumble. Dynamics thrive on maintaining stasis. I throw the whole equation out of balance.

Friends could be tricky. If they're more friends with me, then it's usually not a problem. If they're more friends with Doug, then problems could arise. But it seems the "friends with Doug" people are abandoning me more and more these days, so I guess that's a good thing.

Relationships are damn near impossible. Either they love me, but don't want to deal with Doug. Or they want Doug, but didn't count on me being there. Nobody ever wants their cake and to eat it too.

But oh well. At least I have running, and this, and reading, and crossword puzzles, and music, and praying, and all the things I don't need Doug around to do.

He just gets in the way.

I've taken him just about as far as he can go. I'd like to see someone else give it a try.

March 7th

Hello thoughts. Sunday, workday edition.

Live from Father Duffy Square: An udderly delicious creamy and crunchy combination.

Fully exposed. But definitely nothing to be ashamed of. Those who look will always have something to see.

Scaffolding. I'm good at that. That's my hedgehog, or whatever Jim Collins calls it.

Lost Children of Eden. Painted on a wall. The dog and lady walk. Fit for her age. A part of the country I wouldn't normally see. Fuel for the sound machine.

We'll create and sustain a protocol. Do those words even belong so close together? It's like legalese for the lazy. Producing organic giggles.

Hire men in kilts to clean your gutters. You hire them and they show up wearing kilts. That's their gimmick. And they still clean your gutters. Pretty good gimmick.

Everybody hates a tourist. Especially one who thinks it's all a laugh. Out of touch with the common people. Who are essentially forgettable. Working their post.

I was a V.I.P. up in that bitch. Now they won't return my calls. I fell off. Boogie Bob's video was broadcasted with Prism Live Studio.

Numbers just keep getting higher. But the pleasure remains the same. For now. Preparing your white trash toast. Irish butter. Cinnamon. And a brioche roll. Who are you? What have you become?

A church on Wall St. A cemetery older than the times. Searching for a lost pen since 1982. You better double check. A hollow cube resting on its corner.

Down goes the sun. Down goes the sun. Down goes the sun.

Yet the stream still flows.

No end to the decadence of the day.

March 6th

The state of the mall. In a state known for its malls.

No ATM's anywhere, but a Bitcoin exchange right before hitting the food court.

More tables were added to the food court. Still not as many as before, but at least you don't have to stand.

Wendy's was closed. That surprised me. It's pretty much just Popeyes, Nathans, and the bubble tea place keeping everybody fed and nourished.

I gave Gio's a try, but they were all out of braciole. The Sicilian tuna was even scratched off the menu. That was always Pop's favorite.

No benches anywhere, and ropes and barriers out front of the more trafficked stores. Apple. Aeropostale. American Eagle. I think Yankee Candle had the longest line, though.

The anchors are pretty much gutted. J.C. Penney's was open, and maybe Macy's, but I didn't go down that wing. Lord and Taylors is closed. And Sears is a vaccine distribution site now.

Starbucks still gets a lot of foot traffic, but I'm not going there until this is all over. That was the deal.

No more Modell's, but they were struggling before any of this happened anyway. Yet, I guess you could say that about most of the stores here.

I just did a lap and a half. Ending up looking at some books. Like I really need more books. But as soon as I got there I didn't want to be here.

The mall no longer feels like home. Kinda weird that is actually did at one point.

Simon definitely did not say.

March 5th

Turning a corner. As the DJ lobs some balls for her guests to hit.

Give me a book, a movie, and an album that got you through the pandemic.

Jerusalem by Alan Moore.

Epic in scope. Perfectly executed. I never felt more at home inhabiting the mind of a genius. I've never been to England but feel like I've lived in Northampton. He already proved himself as a master story crafter with Watchmen, this solidified him as the greatest writer still walking among us. Once people begin to understand him, Alan Moore will be added to the canon.

Once Upon a Time in America by Sergio Leone.

Epic in scope. Perfectly executed. Just hit play and enjoy the escape. Four hours later you'll be left wanting more. Grieving over characters no longer in your life. Replaying scene after scene in your head as if they were your own memories. Lying in a self-made mental opium den, wondering if it all was just a dream. Unable to walk through DUMBO without hearing the pan-flute playing hauntingly all around you. This will stick to your ribs.

Sigma Oasis by Phish

Concisely perfect through all its imperfections. Wisdom preserved by the masters of jam. Lying outside watching the treetops dance above me. Inhaling the lyrical mastery. Comforted and challenged. The final destination before reaching my musical home.

Take off your mask.

The fear's an illusion.

Don't even ask.

The pandemic is not over.

But we've turned a corner.

March 4th

Indifference is not a character flaw. It's the greatest expression of love.

You just have to let go and let it ALL happen. It's the only way to do it.

The feeling of love will always swing back into the feeling of hate.

The expression of love can only be tempered by the need to control.

And if you understand what any of this means, please let me know. I'm just the guy pushing the pen.

I have a lot of words. I have a lot of memories. I have a lot of feelings.

But it's something else that puts it all together. Playing off my vanity and my muscle memory.

And there's not much that I believe more in than that something else.

The sun.
The moon.
The stars.
A baby's laugh.
Tears of joy.
Life at its fullest.

All of it.

It's not you. It's not me.

It's something else.

March 3rd

A mouthful of blood. That's what you get for biting your tongue so much. But who doesn't like the taste of blood?

Definitely better than the vomit that usually comes out of your mouth.

Better out than in, right? Unless you're the one cleaning up after what comes out splatters all over the walls and floor. And I've certainly kept some cleaning crews in business.

So now I hold it in. Digest it. Turn it into something else. Turn it into something else.

Forming diamonds. Staying gold.

Behind enemy lines, in a place you used to consider home. A freedom fighter who's getting tired of both freedom and fighting.

I've been waving the white flag for a long time now. Desperately looking for someone who'll let me surrender to them. I don't care what the cause is. I just want to be a good soldier.

This sheep was born in the year of the snake. So I know how to outsmart all the wolves among me.

But my heart is a dove. Waiting to be let out of its cage.

I'm just a soul whose intentions are good.

Please try to understand me.

March 2nd

Everybody roots for David. Poor Goliath.

Underdogs are overrated. I rather see greatness validated.

Imagine how good the Philistines could have been if they had God on their side.

I've been watching this docuseries about Japan during the time of samurais. It's pretty much the story of how Japan became unified. I think it's called the Battle for Japan. Man, is it bloody. But that's history. Very bloody. And unsympathetic.

History has a job to do. Either get out of its way or suffer the consequences. Woe to those who find themselves on the wrong side of history.

You can try to work with History. Be an agent of change and all that good stuff. But good luck with that.

Eventually history will no longer need you. It's very fickle like that.

Hegel was right. About a lot of things. He was just never good at explaining himself. At least to those who could have really used his message.

Other philosophers don't need Hegel. It's like preaching to the choir. And an off-key choir at that.

Politicians and world leaders need him. But they're too dumb to understand him. Just a bunch of Philistines.

At least there are still teachers carrying his torch. Not many, but they're out there.

Too bad nobody ever listens to them.

March 1st

I remember when Drazen Petrovic died. It was towards the end of freshman year of high school. I was devastated.

Kenny Anderson. Derrick Coleman. Sam Bowie. Chris Morris. Chris Dudley! You remember Chris Dudley? Couldn't hit a foul shot to save his life, but always grabbed the board in the clutch.

Coach Daly was brought in by Willis Reed to class up the joint. Players tend to listen more when they see the shine coming off a couple championship rings, not to mention a gold medal. Even Derrick Coleman had to be impressed.

Drazen probably wasn't, though.

He had his own silver. And he got it without a Dream Team behind him. Playing for a country that was barely a year old that had half the population of New Jersey. Even led all scorers in the gold medal game.

Jordan won the game, but never got the best of Drazen. No respecter of persons. He played with an iron will.

And he was on MY team. The Nets. The first team I ever remember rooting for. The last team I allowed myself to care about. The New Jersey Nets.

His girlfriend was driving the car. They were on the Autobahn. The infamous German highway where there are no limits. Those are the only details I know or want to know.

The Nets were not the same after that. Daly only hung around for one more year before jumping ship. Kenny Anderson never reached his potential, and Derrick Coleman got really fat. By the time I got to college I was trying to root un-ironically for Yinka Dare.

Sports can really break your heart. We need to warn more kids about that.

Pucaj Tricu.

February 28th

Mr. Jones and me. Enjoying another Sunday afternoon together. He plays the music. I tap away on the keys. I guess you could call it working.

Enjoyed a nice bowl of butternut squash soup. It's got to be autumn somewhere, if not only in my mind. Probably was more bread than soup, though. Semolina. Hard on the outside, but soft and airy inside. Just like all of us. And the way the powder goes everywhere when you break it up into pieces. That's the good stuff. Just don't get it in the keyboard.

In my head I've always pronounced it salmonella bread. Ha ha ha. I'm funny like that with pronunciations. It's the inside jokes I have with the people hitching a ride in my mind.

I certainly have a full bus of passengers. And not all of them have been invited. And those are the ones that sit closer to the front. Trying to distract me from keeping my eyes on the road.

But I guess it's my fault for letting them in. I left the door open too long and didn't collect any fares. And now it's like having a bee flying around your car. You roll down the window and wait for it to fly out, hoping that the new bees don't fly in.

An endless cycle of buzzing.

The sky is still grey. The chill in the air lingers. What snow survived the rain is covered in dirt.

Yet I think we turned a corner. I really think so.

But that could just be the salmonella talking.

February 27th

When you sweep problems under the rug, always remember that there are people under that rug that have no other choice.

I am underneath that rug. Stuck with all the problems you keep sweeping at me. Cowering in the fetal position because my nerves are too shot to handle even the slightest sound or light.

And now I got to deal with your dirt?

That doesn't seem fair, but life certainly is not.

It's always sad when a baby cries and you have no clue what to do to make her feel better. When your soul does the same thing, it's downright tragic.

I had a tragic run this morning. A fitting end to a week filled with even more tragedy.

Even old friends are no balm.

Been hoisting a lot of people up at the bottom of their pyramids. Allowing them to see the glory and touch the sky. Always ready to catch them if they fall.

But now my shoulders are sore, and my legs are shot. Finally realizing I can't keep this up too much longer. Quietly wondering when it will finally be my turn. And will there be anyone left to pick me up when it is.

And I know these are selfish thoughts and I'm not proud for having them. But I'm not as strong as you think I am.

All I know is that today is certainly not my day.

So I just have to pull it together again so I can celebrate those whose day it is.

Hooray!

February 26th

The birds!

Enjoying a nice evening meal. I hope to be doing the same pretty soon.

This far into the game and I still don't think I've figured out the whole feeding myself thing. Surprised I'm even still standing at this point. Betty never showed up to teach me how to take care of myself. No choice now but to wing it. Just like the birds.

The Byrds!

I'm usually eight miles high by now. Staking out my claim in the fifth dimension. Some days it's all I really want to do. But I chose the Christian life and there's no goin' back. I'll feel a whole lot better when Easter comes, though.

To everything there is a season.

But I've had enough of this one. We all have. Meaningless. All meaningless.

Tempted by my desire to resist temptation. The only time you really give the devil a foothold. You found your oasis, why build a desert in the middle of it?

You have to get down off your cross before you can worship at the foot of His.

Bind that.

On Earth as it is in Heaven.

Amen.

February 25th

Here comes the thaw. Breaking through the layers upon layers of ice.

Are these just growing pains? Or a sign of what is about to emerge?

Either way, this is going to be very interesting. Potentially career defining. And I've got nothing to lose. It's already been taken away from me or denied to me. To be honest, it's a very liberating place to be.

As the birds continue to fly around confused.

Does anyone know what direction is safe?

New patterns emerge. A tartan for a clan yet to be established. But it was not a clean cut. My path continues to be littered with the trash of excess. Much too sloppy for someone in my position.

Carpet bombing your way through life. Musashi would not approve.

Grabbing all the rings like Sonic, but there are only five that you need.

The Green Hill Zone has been completed. But everybody knows that's only level one.

Maybe it's time for a new game. But deep down you know it is not your decision to make.

An altered beast, yet still a beast. Always to be mistrusted and reviled.

Can you really blame them?

No.

February 24th

Oom. Pah. Oom. Pah. Oom. Pah.

Tubby the Tuba. Or was it Toby the Tuba? Probably was Toby. I don't think a movie geared toward elementary kids would use a fat-shaming name like Tubby, but the 1980's were savage times.

Oom. Pah. Oom. Pah. Oom. Pah.

You sure it wasn't Tommy or Timmy the Tuba? I don't know. It was definitely some form of alliteration. Not Tony, though. Tubas aren't Italian. Maybe I'll look it up online. Let's see what happens.

Oom. Pah. Oom. Pah. Oom. Pah.

Whoa! It was Tubby! I'll be damned. And Dick Van Dyke was the voice of Tubby. It was made in 1975 and it was a remake. The original Tubby the Tuba was from 1947. It all makes sense now.

Oom. Pah. Oom. Pah. Oom. Pah.

But anyway, they showed us Tubby the Tuba in first or second grade. It was about a Tuba who is tired of being lost in the background of the orchestra, so he leaves to try and start his own show.

Oom. Pah. Oom. Pah. Oom. Pah.

I don't remember all the details, but Tubby is not successful, and he returns to the orchestra. The other orchestra instruments joyously welcome him back, and Tubby learns to embrace his role by understanding the importance of his contribution to the symphony.

Oom. Pah. Oom. Pah. Oom. Pah.

My take-away from Tubby the Tuba as a seven-year-old? You ain't a trumpet, kid, so don't get any big ideas. Just sit in the back and do your job. They came to hear the other instruments, not you.

Oom. Pah. Oom. Pah. Oom. Pah.

(Cue sad trombone sound)

February 23rd

Everybody's talking about the good old days. The good old days. Well let's talk about them. The good old days.

Lying in bed. Screaming. Yelling. Hiding under the covers. It only gets louder. Being in the only house I've ever known. Wishing desperately to go home.

Is that when the balance of chemicals started to tip? During the good old days?

Shame. Guilt. Anger. Frustration. Disappointment. Soaking through my sheets.

I'm sorry. It wasn't my fault. It just happened.

In the good old days.

Fat. Nerd. Geek. Fat. Dork. Four-eyes. Fat. Idiot. Loser. Fat. Fat. Fat.

And that's just what the people who loved me said. In the good old days.

Rejection. Rejection. Rejection. Rejection. Rejection. Rejection. Rejection.

Never afraid of it, but definitely tired of it.

I can't remember if I ever belonged anywhere or if anybody even wanted me around. During the good old days.

They warned me to protect it. But I can feel the rope pressed against it. Getting tighter. Not trying to leave right now. Only want to escape.

The good old days.

When the laughter ended, and I ran out of Tearz.

Semi-colon.

February 22nd

I did not think we'd be getting as much as we are getting. But here it is. Another blanket. Sans the security.

Everyday things will continue to be harder. Not enough to stop you. Just enough to annoy you. Everyday. Again and again. Pick. Pick. Pick. Pick.

Laboring. Just to return to baseline. This is what makes us tough. I guess.

And what's so good about being tough, anyway?

Tough Actin Tinactin, as Michael D'Ambrose once advised me. As did that random guy on Fulton Street, now that I think of it.

I was headed to the Seaport. Where the Ambrose actually is, coincidentally. (And any form of the word coincidence I use is facetious, if you know what I mean.) I might have stopped in the Strand Annex, depending on the vintage. But that's based on pattern recognition, not memory.

All I really remember is the dude walking toward me, leaning his face in so it was directly in front of mine, and saying, "Yo, Tough Actin Tinactin," before walking by.

The Michael D'Ambrose episode was different. It was a week or so before, early in the morning, and we were hanging in the kitchen. Mike came down- or maybe up- wearing boxers and a wife beater while he was scratching his nuts. Again, pattern recognition, not memory.

He was in his own head until he saw me and looked very concerned. "Yo bro, I got a message for you."

I looked at him puzzled, waiting for the next clue he was about to give me for this spiritual scavenger hunt we're all on.

"Tough Actin Tinactin."

I still use it today. It's important to take care of your feet. Especially in the snow.

February 21ˢᵗ

I don't think I have my head in the game right now. And it kind of seems like that's a good thing. My head tends to just get in the way. No need for the extra baggage.

It felt like that for a lot of people this morning. Everything just felt two clicks off. A glitch in the Matrix that we all recognized and responded to in our own way.

The monsignor seemed especially off. But still nailed the homily. Man, I am so blessed to be able to experience him.

Speaking of men of God, Malcolm X got assassinated today. Like, not actually today, but 56 years ago. You get the point. Still no Google Doodle, though. They always diss him on his birthday too. One year they even put his friend Yuri up there instead of him. On his own birthday. Sad. But whatever, I bet they make half those people up anyway. Should just stick to having kids design them.

Speaking of Children of God, I rather not do that. Too depraved for me. If I'm gonna talk about Brazil, I rather talk about City of God. Great movie. And I loved the follow-up series, City of Men. Got me really into favela culture. Blasting my booty-shaking baile funk. As they say, shake what the good lord gave ya.

Speaking of God, when speaking to God, always start with 'thank you'. It's the polite thing to do. We all got our needs, but gratitude comes first.

I wonder if God will ever get a Google Doodle. Probably not before Zeus, though.

Get your hand out of my pocket!

February 20th

"The Sim Truck was excellent with the chopped cheese."

Did he just say that? Yep, he did. Just repeated himself for emphasis. No mistaking it.

"The Sim Truck was excellent with the chopped cheese."

Human language is fascinating. Of course this is coming from someone who wastes his time writing books that nobody reads. And when I'm not doing that, I'm writing letters in little boxes to solve crosswords. All before I lie in bed and play on my phone, unscrambling letters to form words.

So yeah, I like language. Words are my Legos.

If I was smarter, I would study linguistics. Unfortunately I'm only smart enough to understand Chomsky's books on media and foreign affairs. His other stuff is beyond me.

"The Sim Truck was excellent with the chopped cheese."

I wonder what good old Noam would think of that sentence. Or what about Wittgenstein? Semiotics is my jam! But I could care less about what Derrida says. He's not invited to the party. He destroys everything. (Ha ha! Get it? They're laughing at that joke on Europa.)

"The Sim Truck was excellent with the chopped cheese."

I'm sure it was Dutch, I'm sure it was. But I guess I had to be there.

Good night, Mrs. Calabash, wherever you are.

February 19th

Seriously, what is this noise? Where did it come from? Is this what happens when one soul contains just too much beauty? It has no choice but to push the ugliness out in a symphonic purge of chaos.

Give the Drummer Radio. Ain't no Half-Mantis.

Free will. Probability curves. Alternate realities. What do you think about when you shovel?

Was down at the crossroads. Right in front of the laundromat. Dude smoking. Kinda looked like Dave. Haven't seen him in forever. But I didn't want to come off racist, like all Asian guys look alike. So I walked by. Yet the body language. You cannot mistake body language. I turned back. What the heck, might as well try. It wouldn't be the first time I embarrassed myself. Remember Jesse Williams? Survived that. So, like, whatever. Go for it.

"Yo, Dave!?"

Just like that, all the doors swung open, and lives were changed. Two sounds I reluctantly decided to make. It doesn't take much.

Free will. Probability curves. Alternate realities.

What would have happened if I just kept walking? I didn't have to turn back.

"Hmmm. That guy kinda looks like Dave. Wonder how he's doing. Oh well, got to get back home."

Other doors open? Different lives change?

Too many butterfly wings flapping to even begin to sort it out.

Free will. Probability curves. Alternate realities.

Still doesn't get the snow off my truck.

February 18th

To be honest, Abe Lincoln was not the greatest human being. He was just the right man for the job.

No fan of slavery, but he kinda resented the fact that African-Americans were here and he had to fight a war because of them. And zero belief in racial equality. Had some Liberia-type plan to ship them to Central America after the war.

Not convinced Reconstruction would have gone any better with him instead of A.J.

To quote myself, "There are no heroes in history."

There are only very flawed human beings used as pawns to keep our history progressing from the grimiest mud of nature to the highest glories of the heavens.

God is the end; we are the means. Like it or not, we're all playing a part. What do you think you're being used for?

I guess we'll all find out in due time.

To be honest, I care less and less about this whole play as we move into the later acts.

I need a new scene. It was fun playing in the mud for a while, but now it feels like they're spraying us all with fire hoses to force us clean. And everything is just way too broken.

Yeah, took me long enough, but this is definitely the end of my circuit here.

I'll just keep scribbling in my notepads and teach whoever's willing until my shift is over.

Time to be a pawn somewhere else.

February 17th

I didn't realize how much momentum I was working off of until it just ended. I haven't been willing any of this. It was all just built-up energy working itself out. I was only along for the ride. And now the ride is over. So what now?

Sifting through the vanity and insecurity to see what remains.

I just don't want to have to buy new pants.

I've been trying to figure out what created this momentum to begin with. But you know how it is. We didn't start the fire and what not.

But I'm guessing it all really ended back in September on Rt. 202 in Montville. After that, to evoke my favorite Baudrillard analogy, was only the hair and nails continuing to grow on the dead body. And now even that has ceased.

Well, at least it got me this far.

No need to hurry. The rush is over.

Ashes to ashes. Dust to dust. Repent and believe in the Gospel. Even now.

Especially now.

This is going to be interesting. It feels different this time. Scrolls are unravelling. Ancient ones.

Please..

Do read the instructions.
Do not leave children unattended.
Do enjoy yourself.

SEBCO thanks you!

February 16th

So this is empty. I've been flirting with empty for a while, but this is no doubt the real thing. It'll be interesting to see what emerges on the other side of the next forty. A true desert-like experience.

My first trip to the desert was a disappointment. I was expecting more sand. The media ruins everything.

I'm sure I'll have my messes to clean up. Nothing too big or bad since I've become so functional and organized amid my dysfunctional excesses. But there will be messes. I already started the process. Dust gets everywhere. And hair. Forget about it.

Maybe I'll learn and grow this time. Even though I never do, yet always seem to. Yeah, I don't really get it either. Everything is always in spite of myself.

I'd like to be more connected. Be part of something. But I can't wash the outsider stench off of me no matter where I go. Some people are in the middle of it all. I'm on the fringe of everything.

I like watching too much. Consuming experiences. Excavating stories. Connecting invisible dots.

It's going to take a special person to pull me in. Make me fully part of it all. Allow all my colors to reach the surface.

Waiting on her as I continue skirting through the earth tones. Thinking this may be all there is of this life. A palate cleanser before eternity. As I skate away unnoticed.

What ever happened to that guy?

Yeah, you don't see him around no more.

February 15ᵗʰ

6:47am- The deed is done. Never easy, but I guess anything that's worth it is going to have a buy-in. The yoghurt helped a lot. I was out early yesterday, and up even earlier this morning.. listening to Bedtime Stories. Hiroshima Mon Amour.

9:15am- Nearly two and a half in and we are definitely in. At least for this. Everything else is just a distant hum. Yet another drum ensemble from a far-off land. I'll tell you one thing. I am definitely not going outside.

11:27am- Yep. Still here. Definitely more integrated at this point, but still here. Still stuck on that crossword puzzle, upper right quadrant. Still debating myself on whether to go outside or not. Man I'm weak. Can't even get Chinese food because they're closed on Mondays. What now?

1:39pm- Aware of it. But past it. Accepted that I'm out of options. No need to put a letter on it. This is the plan. A new puzzle of countless opportunities. A conversation you should not be privy to. But I don't understand a word of it, anyhow.

3:21pm- How did I end up here? If you always do what you've always done, you'll always get what you always got. Yep. Thank you for that humbling answer to what was a very rhetorical question. Oh well. At least the music is better this time around.

5:33pm- I wanted to make it to the 12-hour mark, but I am spent. A walk-off victory with cuter cactus crafted by Gail Grabowski. And now I don't know where I'll be at the other end of my next nap. So if this is it. Farewell. It has certainly been a trip.

February 14th

We're running out of opportunities to sing out Hallelujah. Trying not to horde what little supply we have left. It always seems to end up like this.

Someday I will focus on what I have in abundance. Love. Faith. Creativity. Curiosity. Beauty. And stop defining myself by what is fleeting and illusory.

I hate the ending, but I keep reading the book over and over and over again.

Time to rip out all the pages. Toss them all in the air. And see what new stories settle to the ground.

A million monkeys typing blindly away on all those typewriters. Producing reams and reams of chaos. Trying desperately to find something, anything, that makes sense.

And then you find it. Not a word is misplaced. A heartbreaking tragedy. Everybody dies. No sunsets. No horses to ride off on.

Stupid monkeys. What do they know about writing stories, anyhow?

The greatest story ever told is not in a book, but a library.

A yurt for the trans-genred.

All of the universe under one tent.

And in the beginning was the Word.

Of Mics and Men. Of words and libraries.

Even the Ol' Dirty Bastard has a father in eternity.

No need to protect your neck. Wu Tang is forever.

February 13th

I have a lot of freedom ahead of me. And most of the discipline needed to balance the equation is behind me.

My pantry is full, and my fridge is stocked.

A good place to be. I am being provided for.

The wall between reality and fantasy is sometimes so small and not so tall.

The forty-fourth day. The curtain of the temple has been torn in two from top to bottom. The Red Sea has been parted. The slaves have escaped.

I'm now waiting on my manna.

Boy am I proud of Dr. Manny.

What are your thoughts about tomorrow? The forecast is iffy, and you may or may not have the Rona.

Shah-la, la-la-la-la live for today!

I wonder how LaLa is doing. I always liked her. She was just a really cool chick. Very real. And of course I'm always thinking of Big Scott. I hope he cashed in a little on Game Stop. Debbie. Nate. Cathy. Monkey Boy. Frank the Bartender. Alan Carpet. Sigh. Those were the days.

Shah-la, la-la-la-la live for today!

My pantry is full, and my fridge is stocked.

A good place to be.

I am being provided for.

Thank you.

February 12th

I have all my chips on eternity. Which can hardly be called an underdog. So it's not going to pay back much more than you put in. That's why it's got to be all or nothing.

This life is but a blink in eternity. You can bet on that.

Running like clockwork. A Shinjuku intersection. Anonymous humans on a crosswalk. All perfectly placed. All perfectly timed. Two in the afternoon.

I was once among them. And never felt more lost.

Now I'm as far away from there as I can get. Up at 1 AM. And my alarm is set for a quarter to five. A stolen slice of waking life. Not quite yet the witching hour, but still just me alone with the ghosts.

Tonight there's going to be a jailbreak. Escape from the vibrational prison of this world.

Now I finish my breakfast as I watch the anonymous hurry home from work. Their weekend has begun. Mine is still to be earned.

Dear Mr. Fantasy. Wake me up from this reality. Send me home with the pigeons.

Now it's 4:30 PM and I just finished my chicken salad sandwich. Is this even the same day?

Talking about Alan Watts with a guy in Coney Island. I remember driving home in the snow with Erin, white knuckles on the steering wheel. She had FMU on and Alan Watts just started laughing. Over and over, just laughing. So we did the same. It was awesome. Laughter yoga.

We got home safe. We all will.

This day was but a turn of the page.

February 11th

I don't want to be old Babe Ruth, drinking beer, eating hot dogs, hitting home runs, waddling around the bases. Even though I can so pull it off.

I rather be like Lou or Joe. Consistent. Disciplined. Reliable. But I can't seem to kick the Mick.

I guess it's just me being me.

Meet me at Herald Square. Where the horns are blaring, and the perfume is heavy. Living alone in the New Jerusalem. Becky I ain't comin' back no more.

Not blocked. Just stuck.

Great seeing Danny again. He's been driving since back when we were in Boonton, so I've known him for close to 15 years. I remember back in the glory days when he would be sitting in a lawn chair, reading the Daily News, waiting to talk my ear off. Sheila hated that. All the parishioners kept complaining.

Things are different now. A lot harder to keep up a conversation about sports. But I can pull it off. I know the vocabulary well enough and I'm good at matching frequencies. Small talk can be tedious, but I'll make an exception for an old friend.

Just like these two old friends right now hanging out in Times Square. Discussing the coming year of the Ox. As the moon is silent above them. And you walk to the microphone.

Today I consider myself.

February 10th

Seriously the highlight of my day.

Nothing beats a good bowl of cereal. Even this new age keto stuff that I got at Whole Foods. I don't know what a monk fruit is, but it is suddenly in a large portion of my diet.

Wow! What a moment of clarity. Thank you for that Maxayn, whoever you are. It doesn't get much better than this. Art upon art upon art. At least I've figured this much out.

Sometimes you can't appreciate someone's art until you stop listening to them. It's their eye, not their mouth. Personality is overrated.

But seriously, going back to the highlight of my day.

Coming back from a fresh trim, pulling into the complex, and BAM, my path is blocked. Obstacles that Ganesh, himself, could not remove.

White van. Black doors swung open. Boxes everywhere. I would love to know how all this happened.

Two guys trying to fix it all. Really one. I don't think the guy in the front was doing anything. And nobody was in any sort of hurry. One box at a time. Back in the van. And there were a lot of boxes outside the van. Still don't know how they got there.

Some lady was blocked on the other end. She got out and confronted the men. It didn't increase the pace of things.

I was just watching. Listening to K-Love.

Eventually the boxes got back in the van. I drove by. And the guy gave me a big thumbs up. Highlight of my day.

And the cereal was pretty good too.

February 9th

The wheels are coming off, but the car is fully in motion.

The object of apprehension and dread has passed. But the feelings remain.

A period of transition.

The scaffolding has been removed. Will the building still stand?

This is my least favorite part.

I once tossed three pennies about my object of inquiry. It said that it would start as a great gathering or coming together, but then it would lead to great excess. 45 to 28 for those keeping score at home.

Man was it ever right about that. The gathering was amazing. Everybody made an appearance. We didn't want the party to end. But it did. As all parties do.

Some of us succumbed to the excess. I survived, but it has been debilitating. And I don't know what comes next.

Where have all my oracles gone?

This definitely is my least favorite part.

How many more weeds are there? Will these seeds actually work? Have I chosen good soil?

I control nothing.

That should free me. As my hands shake in fright.

February 8th

The early one arrives later than usual today.

Now I just wait upon the rest.

I feel like I am in multiple worlds right now. I don't know which one I owe my full allegiance to. I'm just trying to not get caught.

Inhabiting many rooms, but still living in just one mansion.

Waiting to see what comes next.

I'm feeling accomplished. Even though I know that there is still so much left undone. The waves are no longer knocking me down, but no one leaves the ocean completely dry.

Student and teacher. Alone. Not realizing that they are inhabiting the same space. Just don't bother me so I can get done what I need to. If you're not going to follow the rules, at least learn how to play the game.

Their objections are my objections, but I'm more trapped than they are. Jealous that they're close enough to freedom that they still think they can just compel it to happen.

Good luck with that. Hopefully you don't make the same mistakes we did.

But you will. We all do.

Either you learn from me, or you'll learn from life. And I'm nicer than life. At least for now.

Things are definitely getting softer. No need to keep it hard.

Flow.

Make a splash.

February 7th

The snow melts as it pelts Medusa's nude body.

Frightenly erotic.

Another round? Yep. Another round.

My weekends have become weak ends. Johnny Stumbling instead of Johnny Striding. Spending too much time on Monday picking up the hurdles I knocked over.

At least I made it to church on time. And I got my taxes done.

Frightenly functional.

My pen has no seven second delay. To prevent me from going beyond the limits of morality and good taste.

I walk the tight rope with no net below. Only Habermas standing guard. And I never really got that guy, anyway.

Beating out our swords into plowshares. Not because the war is over. But because Mother Nature is the greater threat. It's elemental.

The moments before the Big Game.

The old guard versus the new.

And is this really the side I want to be on?

I never thought I had a choice.

Blinded by the snow on this Black Sabbath.

Not a day to rest. Not a day to rest.

February 6th

Eleven miles. Nothing. One hour conversation. Nothing. Responsibilities and expectations. Nothing!

The Fugs have influenced and inspired me greatly.

The poetry of absurdity and chaos. Destroying sacred cows and idols at the same time.

Eating peanut butter and jelly sandwiches. Russ and I racing neck and neck to be the winner of the slow bicycle race. He won. Russ always was The Realist.

Cut me some slack. I'm not a genius.

Bob. Bobbing up and down. What is Meg Ryan doing? I was way too young to see the Doors. Messed up my perception. I blame King Ralph.

Taking another trip over Roosevelt Island. I'm going to have to do this for real someday. Maybe in a couple weeks if we get a warm day.

Still waiting on some confirmation. So I know what the future holds.

But right now I feel good. I earned this.

Way out West.

Not Sonny Rollins, but Bill. Graham.

Giving a stage to Jerry.

I will always be grateful.

For filling more of my heart.

February 5th

Black coffee. Straight whiskey. Unfiltered cigarettes.

Mostly Camels. But the occasional Lucky if I wanted a different flavor. Back in the Bronx I would bum a cigarette from a girl outside a bar. First thing I would do is rip the filter off and then light it.

"A lot of chemicals in those filters."

Jameson Whiskey. Loan and I would collect the empties. Stack them on the windowsill above the sink. We had to have over a dozen up there before we were even there a month. Haven't touched the stuff since I left that place. Don't get me wrong, I still drink straight whiskey, just not Jameson.

Bustelo Coffee. Whoever got there first would put the pot on. Either Mr. Ortiz or myself. I would flip through my New York Post as he told me story after story as we drank that coffee. Man the Bronx was crazy back in the day.

But I knew I had to get out. I didn't want to be who I needed to be to stay. I could have orchestrated a better exit, but I was pretty green back then. Youthful folly.

I especially regret how I left Loan. But I ain't about to turn into a pillar of salt over it.

No less than ten years of experience in under two.

I love it when a plan comes together.

Goodnight Mr. Ortiz, wherever you are.

February 4th

Civilization does not run on its own. There's a lot of work going on behind the scenes. Dirty jobs. Streets to be plowed. Garbage to be collected. Pipes to keep flowing. Wires to keep hanging.

God bless the men who do those jobs. Put your toxic masculinity to good use. We won't throw you away with the bathwater of the patriarchy.

But we may replace you with robots. Just saying.

I will never be replaced by any machine, though. There's no code to what I do. Perfectly planned random chaos. Scientific artistry. No imposter. The real thing.

Filling my niche in the Universe. Starting to begin to stretch my legs out. Meditating on the subtleties of redundancy. The wordplay version of solitaire.

Man, I would do anything to have a Klondike bar with my grandfather again. Someday.

Until then I keep doing crossword puzzles left-handed. In his honor.

42-Down. D.C. Subway. Five letters. Last letter an O. The O is courtesy of 61-Across. S.O.S. rival.

The metro has me seeing stars.

Definitely speeding up.

Yep, this is actually happening.

Thank you, Joan Weimer. I found my voice.

February 3rd

Horn blowing and back slapping. Yep, I'm insecure. Deal with it. Feel free to secure me if it annoys you so much. Otherwise move on.

There's definitely a good amount that I'm ashamed about this lifetime. But all told, it's really not too much and I seem to be on a better path by grace. It could be a lot worse. And I bet in other lifetimes it was a lot worse. Aspects of my personality that if left unchecked or allowed to flourish, would cause some serious havoc.

The shadow that scares me. By Dick Gregory.

I'm trying to think who would be the most historic person I got to see live. Dick Gregory may be it.

Saw Biden a few years back. Definitely a good speaker. Ditto for Colin Powell. Deepak bored me to death. Spirituality shouldn't be so technical.

But Dick Gregory has them all beat.

Kobe. Lebron. Santana. Sonny Rollins. I guess athletes and entertainers aren't exactly in the same league. And don't tell me Dick Gregory was an entertainer. He was entertaining, but so much more than an entertainer.

During my second year of college I did a writing piece where I had an imaginary conversation with Dick Gregory. It was called, "The Monster." It was pretty sophomoric. Didn't even make it into my first book.

It was always hard to find his cd's at malls in Jersey. Then I went to D.C. to the mall near the Pentagon where my brother lived. Hit the mother lode there. Frankenstein. Among others.

Remember Mrs. Gregory, when you hear that word, they're advertising your son's book.

A must read.

February 2ⁿᵈ

Can you dig it? I knew that I could. How are you all handling it?

Still agitated by my feelings, or lack thereof. So I escape into someone else's. A little jam for my toast. I think now I know what she did with the other L.

I forget if Phil saw his shadow or not, or even what it means if he did. All I know is that I can't escape mine. What started as a little necessary work has turned into a full-time job.

Trapped in the inner recesses of my psyche. Watching all my ugliness dance around the walls of the cave. I'm beginning to think that's all that's real. My waking life is the true shadow. Just a mask I wear to spare the world of my deformities.

That's my story until someone comes along and tells me otherwise.

And I'm still waiting. Wondering how I always allow it to get so dark. Heavy.

Motion is the only thing that keeps the sickness at bay.

So I keep moving.

Busy work.

Punching the clock when I really just want to punch a clock.

In due time.

February 1st

Sisyphus ain't smiling today.

The labor has always been futile, and the line separating humor and hopelessness continues to grow thin. Only absurdity is left to stand guard.

The emptying of the well is of no consequence. Wells are plentiful. Water no longer quenching your thirst is of great concern. What will you seek now to drink?

What part of the cycle are we on today? Are we binging ourselves on purges? Or purging ourselves of binges?

Ever eat at Wafels and Dinges?

Me neither.

Tomorrow will be another new beginning. I'm getting tired of those.

The next day will be back to square one. The only square on the board.

After that is a paradigm shift. If you believe there's more than one gear.

I guess we'll all know in a year.

Until then, at least there's music. I've been saying that a lot lately. At least there's music.

And this.

My only light today escaped when I opened this.

I may not always enjoy walking, but I am blessed to have a path.

January 31st

A storm is brewing. It will come. All that is left to be determined is how we will handle it.

Are you prepared?

Storms don't take me by surprise anymore. It's when they don't come. That's when I'm left helpless.

Left helplessly processing signs you may have missed. That's where I am right now. Learning about a hurricane for the first time, when I was the eye of it.

Who are these people that I am entangled with?

Do they know who I am? Do they have my best interest in mind?

Or am I just a concept to them? An idea they're holding on to.

That's what I'm beginning to feel like.

An amusing character. Interesting. Funny at times. A refreshing change of pace.

But nobody is about to give me a recurring role. Too unpredictable. Challenging at times. Not worth all the effort.

Keep him filed away. Good to know he's there if we need him, but a permanent exhibit may disturb the patrons.

Just remember, though.

Even when filed away, I still have to wake up every day and be me.

You have a choice. I don't.

January 30th

4am and I am up doing shadow work.

8am and I am out doing road work.

11am and I am back on the couch.

The circle of life. Hakuna matata or something like that.

We're all living in the future's past. With a whole lot of talking heads.

Are we really all burning down the house?

I'm prepared to go down with the ship.

Like Bill Hader spoiling the end of Titanic. I must have read it on the Chive.

Hunnies and Funnies. Co-dependent insecurities. Consider that daily afternoon randomness.

The idol of nostalgia. A tough one to smash.

We're all caught in the web. Shackled by the commodity chain. Waiting for our turn to be devoured by the spider.

Anderson Silva. Considered the best on the planet. Even he couldn't escape judgement. We will all meet our moment of truth.

Blasting in my headphones as I walk to the convention center. Like crabs in a bucket.

A lot of doors were opened that weekend.

Will they ever be closed?

January 29th

An intergalactic polka of emotions.

Anticipation. Pride. Relieved. Sedate.

Just another polka.

But not really. Give yourself a little more credit.

The Black Panthers feeding cereal to the children. Boogie Bob feeds pizza to the homeless.

A polka pizza party just for you.

I wonder if it will hurt. I mean, it says it is going to hurt. But what kind of hurt? Why do I do these things to myself?

Old men talking about the weather.

The future looking on in the background.

Great lumbering beast.

An Action Park full of memories.

Does any of this connect? Does any of this make sense?

In my head it does.

But you're not there. No one is.

I guess that's for the better. More room for adjustments.

Thanks. I needed that.

And in the end, it really didn't hurt.

January 28th

Nickelback? Seriously? George Harrison already did a song called Photograph.

What a bad way to start this.

I need to sage this notepad or something. Anything to get a fresh start.

But yeah, I am writing in a notepad. I'll eventually type it into Word, but my first draft is always handwritten. Old school. Pen in a notepad. On a computer the writing comes from your head. By hand the writing comes from your whole body.

My pen of choice is the Black Bic Cristal. Durable. Reliable. And smooth. Try to catch me without a Cristal in my pocket. Not happening.

I'm sitting on my couch as I write this. Keeping it casual. I used to write these at my table. Real formal like. But then at some point this month I switched to the couch. Try to figure out when. I can't wait until I can start to write these outside, or in different places like the city and what not.

My gum has lost its flavor, yet still I chew.

Thus is the human condition.

Why hath Kermit chirp the wrath of God?

Only Joe Hewitt knows. And he ain't telling nobody.

As Nico squeals in the background.

The moon is full. An evening of light.

HOWL.

January 27th

A Coney Island vacation. As I sit here on my couch.

I remember sitting on a bench in the covered atrium, among the homeless and fellow travelers. Reading my Bible. Taking copious notes.

On the pier to the ocean, where all the old men are fishing and playing the bongos. There was always that one guy waving the flag of Uruguay. What's up Hob?

Eating jerk chicken. Drinking sorrel. Surrounded by graffiti-covered walls.

Dancing on the boardwalk with the angels and spirits.

Sitting on a folding chair in an attic. Eating a bag of dry popcorn as Charlie Ahern plays breakdance videos from a projector. It's only just begun.

Cyclone. Wonder Wheel. Cyclones. Brooklyn.

This is the original. Mermaids and steeplechases. Can't stop from smiling. Bump your ass off. Bring on the freaks. One of us.

History layered upon history layered upon history.

Without a trace of it anywhere.

Just memories and stories.

The oral tradition.

Trying to out shout the ocean.

January 26th

If that's not redemption, I don't know what is.

Now you know, once and for all.

It wasn't you. It wasn't the drug. It wasn't the girl. It just wasn't to be. And you know that. You wear it on your wrist everyday as a reminder.

So move on. Put it behind you. Because it is. Behind you.

But man, I was good. I definitely showed I could hang. I killed it with my Authentic Leadership presentation. That Gandhi story always works. And Mambo #5! Legendary. It got the standing ovation. Of course no one could out-write me in the forums. That Madden Football post. Me at the height of my powers.

So I move on. Put it behind me. Because it is. Behind me.

Meditating at the top of the World Trade Center. You saw your whole future ahead of you. And you had the courage to say no.

Because something was missing.

And now you take a look at where you are. And are you really that disgusted?

You've come a long way, baby.

Take it easy on yourself.

January 25th

Wow. What was that? Was that even a day? I think I just kept hitting the snooze button this morning.

It was all a dream.

But those slides were real. And those slips will take some time to heal. A good time to follow the laws of diminishing returns.

Seriously, what happened Miss Simone?

Did I really blow it that bad? Did I really miss all the signs? You got to understand how clouded I was back then. A heart still covered in ashes. A soul turning to dust.

I wish I knew too, Miss Simone, I wish I knew.

But I do know what it means to be free. That's the problem. I know what it means to be free. And I've been chasing it like a dragon every day of my life.

Free your mind, and the rest will follow. I hope so. There does seem to be a lot my body is forced to do, regardless of how free my mind is. It's probably because I'm not dancing enough.

There're no more combustion engines.

And I am exhausted.

January 24th

The steady continuous hum of being slightly overwhelmed. Only just barely able to keep my head above the water.

But the air is cold, and the water is warm. So you know where the pull is.

Self-imposed deadlines and self-created obstacles.

Self-harming myself with ambition and work ethic.

But this is fun, right?

Of course it is.

New perspectives on old habits. As I detach from my old hobbies. It's just not who I am anymore. Doesn't anybody see that? Of course they don't because I'm the only one here.

Too many voices. Each trying to take me on their own journeys. I want to be free enough to wander. Let's go for a stroll.

I know I'll pull it off in the end. As I prolong the turmoil of the middle. Man, I am such a beginner at this.

Maybe I'm not as good as I think I am.
Maybe I'm just spinning my wheels.
Maybe it's just a matter of time.

Maybe I'm getting too old for all these maybes.

It's too late. If I turn back now, I'll get caught.

No choice but to keep digging.

January 23rd

Five-five-five on the Hutch. Getting thorough in the borough I used to call home.

In another life.

I wonder how close I can get to the water. That's my goal. I'm pretty close now, but I have no access. They say they'll be giving us access soon, but we'll see. Otherwise I might have to move. Closer to the water. Any water.

How did they get all the Coca Cola in those tiny little Tic Tacs?

The hill seemed tougher than usual this morning. It was pretty cold. The air was thin. But I was on top of it before I knew it. And the rest of the way was effortless. Almost matter of fact.

I've always had a decided preference toward that particular persuasion. But it's amplifying now. This could get interesting.

I did reopen my blister. That's a fact that doesn't care about my feelings. But I kinda expected it. So whatever.

Talking of home runs. The kings are dead. Long live the queens.

The Action is getting blurry, Kid.

Is it me or is it him?

Maybe it is time for me to move on.

In another life.

January 22nd

Besame Mucho.

As I spy upon two windows on the world.

The one above is down south. Making the long haul.

The one below is cruising the city. Taking fares. Searching for the sunset in the blue.

On to the next one. On to the next one.

A suburban setting. Bathed in white. Objects of art and a basketball hoop.

The order has been made. The delivery will come. In another space and time. Where we found peace of mind.

As I take another swat at the beehive. In order to taste the nectar that sustains me.

After flipping over the hourglass.

With sticky hands.

It must have been the duck sauce.

Wow! That just hit me in the heart. Not as strong as the second or third time around, but still.

And then the fourth.

I was just about to go outside. One hundred miles.

The door is closing.

If this life isn't a Sophisticated Boom Boom, I don't know what is.

January 21st

Yo, Bryan Norton- if that's even your name- please stop calling me. It's getting silly.

I took my step-dad to a Devil's game as a Christmas gift a few years back, and now this dude's been calling me ever since to try and get me to be a season ticket holder.

My stepdad took me to my first hockey game when I was a kid, and I wanted to show him my appreciation as an adult by taking him to a game. It was a good time. I believe it was Marty Brodeur's last year playing, so we got to see him in goal one more time. And my stepdad passed away two years ago, so I get goosebumps knowing that I got to take him to his last hockey game. I love how life comes full circle if you give it enough time.

But now it's literally every day since then that I get a phone call with a number from Newark, New Jersey that I quickly decline. And then it's the same voice mail from Bryan Norton telling me all about the exciting season ticket packages. After that is the follow-up email.

"Sorry we have yet to find a time to connect.."

Really? Is that the problem? It's not over three years of me deliberately ignoring you that's the problem? It's just bad timing? At what point do you finally give up and cross me off the list? Move on.

I never want a job where I have to sell anything to people. How pathetic.

PS- I wonder if Bryan Norton has a chapter in his book about me never picking up my phone or answering his emails. "I mean come on, all the dude has to do is answer his phone and politely tell me he's not interested, and I'll stop calling. How hard is that?"

January 20th

So am I obligated to talk about the elephant in the room? Or in this case, the elephant leaving the room.

Of course I'm not, but I might as well since I'm sure people would turn to this page sooner than others.

So yeah, meet the new boss, same as the old boss.

But not really this time, right? This time is different. We'll look back at this as a pivot point. This is when things really started to change for the better.

Man, I hope so, I really do hope so. But I don't think so.

Things may feel better for a while. The noise may quiet down for a bit. But at the end of the day, we are who we are.

I want to feel excited. I want to get goosebumps. But I'm afraid.

I'm afraid that part of me is dead, or at least beaten into submission. I've seen the good guys lose for too long. And those that did win, quickly turned heel.

I wish I could get fooled again. But I can't, so I won't.

I'm just going to keep digging my trenches and hope to find some sort of peace underneath all the struggle.

My treasures are no longer on this Earth. And I have no intention of bringing them back.

January 19th

I've been trying to let go of things, but it's tough. This whole process is hard. I definitely understand why pride is one of the deadly sins. I need to guard myself from it. Please Lord, help protect me from my pride. Allow me to understand that everything I do comes directly from you.

All praises are due to God, only the mistakes are mine.

And I've been making a lot of mistakes recently.

I've been trying to not be so hard on myself, but it's tough. This whole process is hard. I've never had another human being tell me that I was a good person or that I was doing a good job. I only know what it feels like to be inadequate. Please Lord, help me to understand that you made me who I am for a purpose. Allow me to understand that you will continue to use my mistakes and imperfections in order to help carry out your perfect plan for the Universe.

It's really humbling when you think about it. And I do think about it.. A lot.

Being humble is the only feeling I trust anymore. Happiness is untrustworthy, depression is a liar. It's only when I am humbled that I know that I am on the right track.

Please Lord, keep me humbled. Allow me to remain humble so you will never again have to humble me. I seek only to be your servant. Now, and through all of eternity.

Things will get better soon. It's just that the next 40-50 years may be rough.

January 18th

Good help is hard to find.

So is a good stapler. Pencil sharpeners too. Most office supplies are pretty shoddy. I'm sure I could trace it all back to the negative impact of hyper-capitalism on all of our lives, but I don't have the time or energy to parse it all out. Just know that it's an ugly game and we're all stuck in it.

Noam Chomsky could explain it to you. I'm sure every time he staples something and the stapler jams, he composes an essay about it in his head. I bet the phrase planned-obsolescence is in there somewhere. In addition to a long diatribe on the working conditions at the staple factory. And of course the anti-union polices of the office-supply chain, Staples. Noam Chomsky knows the score.

The rest of us are just stuck in it. Whole populations of people being shoveled in the furnace like coal in order to keep the machine running. The machine that allows me to live the life I want to live. And I consider myself one of the good guys.

But I'm not. Nobody is. We're all helpless sinners just stuck in it. There're no heroes in history and no pride among the anonymous.

If we didn't listen to Jesus, why would we listen to Chomsky?

A change is going to come.

You have been warned.

Repent and reform.

January 17th

A wall of sound. And I'm in need of a bath.

I could understand his need for perfection. He's an artist. And a genius. Of course nobody could hear what he heard. And he forever expanded what we thought we could hear.

I just don't get the guns. Especially in the music game. There's no place for guns.

But I watched a great documentary on the crack game. I am completely convinced that had it not been for different circumstances, I could have been a widely successful drug kingpin. I have all the right qualities: creativity, work ethic, emotional detachment, and moral ambiguity.

I don't think I could have killed anyone myself, but I definitely could have ordered people killed. I mean, it's all in the game, right? I'm just trying to perfect my art.

Thank God I was saved. Literally. There but for the grace of God go I.

It's always the artists that need the most saving. Those who can create, have the most power to destroy.

Better make sure they're on the right side.

Or look out!

January 16th

Hello thoughts.

Sex and drugs and rock & roll. Two out of three ain't bad.
That Action Kid really is maturing as an artist.
The fact that we need 'incognito mode' tells ya something.
Ah yes, I remember it well.
I've been down with Chobani since day one.
Sad that people know so little about what's up in the sky.
St. Gerard, pray for us.

Our next chapter has just begun. We're turning the page. (200 Park Avenue)
I purge and binge rather than binge and purge. Cake first, then icing.
Will it be two years, already?
Transpacific Sound Paradise.
I could go for a nice uneventful week. But I know I'm asking for a lot.
Whoa! Look at those light up roller blades.
At least there's music.

Somewhere people are fighting.
Would you still dance if you weren't taking their money?
It's ok to rest. We still have time.

And once again I'm back in Shinjuku. Doesn't seem as windy this time.
It's later than it seems.
Yet early.

Happy New Day, Times Square.

January 15th

In the thick of things. Behind enemy lines and I don't know who the enemy is. I hope it's not us. But I'm not so sure.

The smell definitely saluted me. A good smell..

Wait. I hear people coming. Got to go hide. I don't want to be discovered. I've been doing such a great job of that so far.

..But that smell. What a great smell. We all had our own interpretation of what it smelled like, but I think it just reminded us all of home. Comfort. Security. It's amazing how a good smell can elevate things. You don't get that in V.R.

I totally understand why the gods made early humans make burnt offerings. The smell. You don't get that in heaven. Explains the use of incense as well. Higher beings are attracted to the smell. They can't experience the rest of earthly life, so all they have is the smell.

Had to move again. Heard noises. This time they were way too close. I feel the walls caving in around me. It's becoming harder to breathe.

Rest and relief are coming, but there are still obstacles in the way. I must go. I need to regroup and prepare so I can live to fight another day.

Until then..

..Smell ya later!

January 14ᵗʰ

Man, all morning I had that feeling that I was forgetting something. I mean it was palpable. And my morning routine is pretty solidly regimented, so I may miss a step here or there, but it doesn't take long for me to catch it. But all this morning it was different. I did everything to a 't', but it still felt like I was forgetting something. Something BIG.

So on the way to work I was thinking about that tennis match against Sparta. Ivan and I were playing their first doubles who not only were undefeated but hadn't dropped a set all season. But now they came to our courts, and we blew through them 6-2 in the first set. Man, when Ivan was on, he was ON. We carried the momentum into a much tighter second set, and even had a match point at 5-4. I don't remember the details, but we lost the point, that game, the next two games, and then got smoked in the third like 1-6 or 2-6. I was too excited to win the first set off of them. I couldn't accept that we actually could win the match. Mental weakness.

But that was 25 years ago.

At school a kid asked me to play Heartbreaker and I typed in Zed Lepplin in the search bar instead of Led Zepplin. And at the end of the day the feeling I was forgetting something returned. Not as strong, but still there.

Maybe I have a brain cloud or something. Would explain yesterday's headache. I hope not, though. I don't want to have to jump in a volcano.

January 13th

I have a headache.

I don't really get headaches much, so it's kind of annoying. I never take aspirin or anything like that, so I'll just tough it out. I'm sure it'll be gone after a good night's sleep.

I remember reading years ago that people get headaches when their soul doesn't want to be stuck in their mind anymore. Even it needs a rest every so often.

I wonder if that is the case with my headache. My soul's trying to take a break and go hang out with its buddies. Well too bad soul, you're stuck here with me. So stop your fussing and start learning to get along with my mind. I know you wish that the two of you had a little more in common, but I'm working on it. I'll bridge the gap eventually. In the meantime, stick around. We're writing here. I need you.

I also read that headaches have different meanings based on where they are located. Mine is in my right frontal lobe. I have no clue what that means. I don't feel like looking it up.. since I have a headache.

In olden times they probably would have drilled my head open by now so the demons could escape. Man, we were crazy back then. Glad we're a bit saner now.

I think I've probably read too much. Filled my head with too much junk. It's starting to overflow and press against my skull. Time to start getting rid of things.

Welcome to the garage sale of my mind. Let the buyer beware.

January 12th

I guess you had to have been there.

Well I was there. And guess what? It really wasn't that funny. We were all just caught up in the moment. Deluding ourselves like we were special or something. Inside jokes are the worst.

There was actually a time in my life where the tag line to my online dating profile was: "In search of someone to share the inside joke of life with." How pathetic. No wonder I'm still single. Actually thought I could catch someone with that bait of cleverness. Instead I've probably been black-listed. My picture is hanging up inside the female collective unconscious with the words, 'do no admit', written underneath. Serves me right.

First, drop the idea that you're special. You're not. Only God thinks you're special, and he has to because he's God. Second, stop trying to be clever. Clever is annoying. Nobody likes clever. Third, quit thinking that everything has to come in threes. It doesn't. That's lazy writing. Move beyond that. Just blow your horn and play some jazz for the good people.

And lastly, not everything has to be tied into neat little bows. Right now since you started with the line, "I guess you had to have been there," you're trying to figure out a way to get back there so you can end with it. But you can't. And you don't need to. Closure is overrated and symmetry is boring.

Sometimes things just end, so it is time for you to STOP.

January 11th

You had me on the ropes. I'll give you that much. You had me on the ropes.

But did you actually think you could beat me?

I'm the Cool Hand Luke of this game. Keep knocking me down. Keep feeding me those eggs.

But I'm not yelling at God like Luke. I'm on my knees praying. Giving thanks. Asking and receiving. Worshipping.

Ten years ago I may not have survived a day like today, or even five. But that's not me anymore. I gave him up. I surrendered him. A sacrifice at the altar.

So do what you will. Put whatever obstacle you want in front of me. Turn everybody against me. Flood my head with all the worst thoughts. Try it. You'll still see me scream, you'll still see me cry, you'll still see me struggle. But you'll also still see me moving forward. Getting stronger. Thanks to His grace.

I'm not going back to you. I'm not going back to you. Even if you kill me, I am not going back to you.

So give it up. Move on. Leave me alone.

Consider this your spiritual restraining order. Signed by the highest judge.

January 10th

So I'm watching this documentary not so long ago and in the first twenty minutes they're talking about how the moon– our moon that we see up in the sky and dogs howl at– was once part of another planetary system before it was hijacked. That's right, hijacked, like forcibly taken. Like one group had the moon, and then another group came and took it. I'm trying to remember how it was hijacked– like stick 'em up, hand over the moon or the kid gets it in the kneecap– but I don't think they went into too much detail about that. We just have to accept that the moon was hijacked. And so the people who took the moon– and I can't remember if they were inter-dimensional or inter-planetary, or really what's the difference– they ended up flying the moon– yes apparently you can fly the moon around like it's a spaceship– they flew the moon into Earth's orbit where it is now and– get this– they have been living inside the moon ever since.

So yeah, the moon was hijacked, brought to Earth, and there's inter-planetary or inter-dimensional beings– and at the end of the day is there really a difference between 'em?– living inside the moon.

And there was still over an hour and a half left in the documentary.

If only one percent of the documentary was true, we would have to rewrite every textbook on nearly every subject out there.

If none of it was true, we would have to reconsider who our most talented actors, and creative screenwriters and filmmakers are.

Either way I was impressed and, more importantly, entertained.

Definitely recommend.

January 9th

I think this one hit people differently than what we have already endured. A definite moment of truth. You can't sit on the fence anymore.

I'm nowhere near the fence. I've been way out to pasture for a long time now. I only felt the light rumblings of this one. I actually thought it was kind of exciting. I am a teacher that grades on a novelty curve. And this was certainly novel.

But states are temporary, stages are permanent. And stages have to be earned. We've all been worked up into quite a state. Let's see if it allows us to enter a new stage. Or will we just fall back onto the same old familiar ground and start the whole cycle over again? Who knows? I've been saying that a lot lately. Who knows?

There's a lot of work that comes with a new stage, though. A lot of work. Probably why we've been putting it off for so long. Like Billy Madison, but on a species-wide level. Rather avoid growing up than going back and finishing all the work we missed.

But even Billy Madison pulled it together in the end, so maybe there is hope for us.

Who knows?

January 8th

It has certainly been a long trek up this mountain. But the higher I get, the more I'm beginning to appreciate the view.

Above the clouds that used to fog my vision. Looking down on the birds that would sully my head.

But the trip up was not without its costs.

I'm weary and in need of a rest. I miss my friends back at the base. And I think my family has counted me as lost.

But I'm not.

I'm as found as I've ever been. They'll see that when I come back down on the other side.

Until then I can only breathe. That's the most important thing to do up here. Just breathe.

Tired? Just breathe.
Lonely? Just breathe.

Feeling like it's all falling apart around you and it's taking every last bit of energy just to keep hold of your core?

You guessed it.

Just breathe.

January 7th

Every morning the alarm goes off and I say no. Luckily nobody ever listens to me. Myself included.

So I get out of bed, do my stretches, and lace up my sneakers. Then I'm out the door.

The walk to my starting point. So quiet. So still. Cold air waking up the parts of me that are still in bed. I cross the street as a guy in a car gives me a confused look. What am I doing out here so early?

I start running.

First I hit the main road. Past the fire department. See the cops at the bagel place. Lights are on at 1United. That's weird. Yusuf must be training someone. Here comes the liquor store. Are they ever going to change that sign? And then it's condos, condos, and more condos.

I turn toward the river. Hugging the shoulder, I see the headlights coming at me as the cars start racing by me. No margin of error. The cars pass and then it is quiet again.

That's when I hear the river. Too dark to see it, but I hear it roaring to my left. One false step and I'm down a ditch and swimming in it.

I don't relax until I cross the street and get on the sidewalk. The expansive farm to the right, as I see the half-moon in front of me in the cloudless sky. That's when I figure it out.

It's 6:30 in the morning. Below freezing. And I'm three miles from my bed running at a full stride.

I AM ALIVE.

January 6th

Sickness. Death. Decay. Chaos. Turmoil.

There is real beauty in the breakdown. But it definitely can be scary.

It all depends on what you are holding on to and what is holding on to you.

Are they demons ripping your ego and attachments to shreds? Or are they angels freeing your soul and granting your body deliverance?

Angels and demons. Working together. Pointing us to the road back home.

How's that for some chewing gum for the mind?

I've got nobody. Nobody I can depend on.

How sad.
How liberating.

Make somebody happy. But start with yourself.

Functional agreement in close proximity is pleasure. The by-product of unconditional love. And that's all there is..

..Somewhere in heaven.

January 5th

You ready, bud?
Yeah.
Happy New Year.
Happy New Year.
What number?
Two for the sides and back. Scissors on top. Just long enough to part it.
And cut the part.
Got it. Hard part.
Yeah.

(The television has a conversation going about the importance of golf during the pandemic: "We all really discovered golf in a new way. Before we enjoyed it, now we need it." The bells over the door jingle as a new character enters.)

"Hey George!"
"Happy New Year!"
"Yeah. Happy New Year, George."
"You busy?
"Nah, I'll be with you shortly, George."

(I can feel him begin to quicken his pace. I am no longer his sole focus. I am an obstacle. I can't blame him. George probably talks to him instead of sitting awkwardly silent. I may have been going to the guy just as long, but George probably actually knows his name. George probably asks how his wife and daughter are doing. I just assume he has a wife and daughter because of the picture next to the shaving talc. George probably talks to him about his golf game. I just assume he plays golf based on what's on the TV and a phone conversation I overheard him have a while back about securing a tee time. I also assume he likes soccer and is a good cook.. or at least likes watching cooking shows. Only George would know for sure. Man, he is so preoccupied he didn't even ask me if I wanted gel. Just glopped it on.)

Alright, all set, bud.
Great. Looks good.
That'll be 15.

Here. Keep the change.
Thanks bud! Take care!
Yeah, see ya.

(The bells jingle again as I exit.)

Alright George! Come on up!

January 4th

Shall we go on sinning so that grace can be increased?

Absolutely. It's not like we have any other choice.

Bite into that Radio Ravioli and taste its succulent center.

I got to take my third eye out for a run this morning. Man, it was a sight to see. I was beaming. And it did the trick. I didn't trip, my footing was firm, and the passersby's cleared me a path. I definitely recommend.

It didn't stop the snakes from biting my Achilles, though. Just when the wound is about to heal, it keeps opening up again and again. But it's my own fault, so I can't complain. I actually kind of like it. Gives me something to endure.

What have you been enduring lately?

Good luck with that. Let me know if you ever need some help.

Until then, we might as well go on sinning.

Who wants to say grace?

January 3rd

This here is a test. An early obstacle. Do you have the will to follow the Way?

When you're tired?
When you're grumpy?
When your brain is withdrawn and your mind just wants to shut off?
When the anger keeps bubbling up?
When you can't turn the hate or judgement into anything else?
When you're feeling bloated, broken, and beaten down by the world?

Will you still have the will to follow the Way?

Or will you give up?
Turn back?
Hide?
Crash?
Burn?
Die?

This here is a test.

Can you live your truth?
Are you who you think you are?
Do you have the will to follow the Way?

This here is a test.

Time is almost up.

Turn in your answer sheet when you are finished.

January 2nd

I actually thought I could win that polka contest. Zero musical ability or technical know-how, but I actually thought I could win that polka contest. Just through sheer will and a few clever rhymes. I actually thought I could win that polka contest.

What hubris. What delusion.

Still clinging to the belief that my treasure is so valuable, yet so hidden. That all it would take is just the slightest glimmer off one of its jewels- in the form of a polka song- for them all to finally come to excavate and rescue me.

Drowning in my dullness.

Trying to connect dots that are so far away or don't even exist. There are enough dots in front of me. So many of them that their density obscures the beauty of the portrait they are revealing. Those are the dots I should be connecting.

Of well. I still think I could have made a damn good polka song. Too bad I never entered that polka contest.

We never danced with Stanley in heaven.

Maybe next time.

January 1ˢᵗ

Just put the pen to the page and see what comes out. You do this all the time. At least you do this in your head all the time. All theory. An image of who you are and what you do. But you don't really do it much. So is it really who you are?

Absolutely.

The difference between potential and reality is an illusion. Everything I've written in my head survives. Chopping wood for the muses to use as kindling. No energy is wasted. But everything I've written on the page endures. Supplying bricks for the builders of the temple. Energy amplified.

Still, the waters remain dark and murky. Too thick for the light to radiate through. In motion, clarity surfaces. An answered prayer from the source. Keep moving through the murkiness to find it. Cut through the thickness to reveal it. Learn to start answering your own prayers.

Easy enough?

For the thousandth time you have first taken the single step.

The journey has begun.

The journey is now over.

Congratulations!

Printed in the United States
by Baker & Taylor Publisher Services